D1605681

Adoption, Race, and Identity

Adoption, Race, and Identity

From Infancy through Adolescence

Rita J. Simon
and Howard Altstein

PRAEGER

New York
Westport, Connecticut
London

Library of Congress Cataloging-in-Publication Data

Simon, Rita James.
   Adoption, race, and identity : from infancy through adolescence /
Rita J. Simon, Howard Altstein.
       p.   cm.
   Includes bibliographical references and index.
   ISBN 0-275-93748-8 (alk. paper)
   1. Interracial adoption—United States—Longitudinal studies.
2. Children, Adopted—United States—Family relationships—
Longitudinal studies.   3. Race awareness in children—United
States—Longitudinal studies.   I. Altstein, Howard.   II. Title.
HV875.64.S557   1992
362.7'34'0973—dc20   91-23869

British Library Cataloguing in Publication Data is available.

Library of Congress Catalog Card Number: 91-23869
ISBN: 0-275-93748-8

First published in 1992

Praeger Publishers, One Madison Avenue, New York, NY 10010
An imprint of Greenwood Publishing Group, Inc.

Printed in the United States of America

The paper used in this book complies with the
Permanent Paper Standard issued by the National
Information Standards Organization (Z39.48-1984).

10 9 8 7 6 5 4 3 2 1

Copyright Acknowledgments

The authors and publisher are grateful for permission to reprint from the following:

David Fanshel, *Far from the Reservation: The Transracial Adoption of American Indian Children* (Metuchen, NJ: Scarecrow Press, 1972). Used by permission of the publisher.

J. Kenneth Morland, "Race Awareness among American and Hong Kong Chinese Children" (*American Journal of Sociology*, Vol. 75, No. 3). © 1969 by The University of Chicago. Used by permission.

Judith D. R. Porter, *Black Child, White Child: The Development of Racial Attitudes* (Cambridge, MA: Harvard University Press, 1971). Used by permission of the publisher.

H. J. Greenwald and D. B. Oppenheim, "Reported Magnitude of Self-Misidentification among Negro Children—Artifact?" (*Journal of Personality and Social Psychology*, Vol. 8). © 1968 by the American Psychological Association. Reprinted by permission.

J. E. Williams and J. K. Roberson, "A Method for Assessing Racial Attitudes in Preschool Children" (*Education and Psychological Measurement*, Vol. 27). © 1967 by the American Psychological Association. Reprinted by permission.

Joseph Hraba and Geoffrey Grant, "Black Is Beautiful" (*Journal of Personality and Social Psychology*, Vol. 16, No. 30). © 1970 by the American Psychological Association. Reprinted by permission.

Morris Rosenberg and Roberta G. Simmons, *Black and White Self-Esteem: The Urban School Child* (Washington, DC: American Sociological Association, 1971). Used by permission of the publisher.

Michael Shapiro, *A Study of Adoption Practice: Adoption Agencies and the Children They Serve*, Vol. 1 (New York: Child Welfare League of America, 1956). Used by permission of the publisher.

Lucille Grow, *A New Look at Supply and Demand in Adoption* (New York: Child Welfare League of America, 1970). Used by permission of the publisher.

Lucille J. Grow and Deborah Shapiro, *Black Children, White Parents: A Study of Transracial Adoption* (New York: Child Welfare League of America, 1974). Used by permission of the publisher.

Child Welfare League of America, *Standards for Adoption Services*, revised edition (New York: Child Welfare League of America, 1988). Used by permission of the publisher.

For
David, Judith, and Daniel
and for
Sam and Rachel

Contents

Preface

This volume incorporates all three phases of the longitudinal study of transracial adoptees and their families that we began in 1972 and continued in 1979 and 1984. It traces the subjects from early childhood into adolescence.

In each phase, we collected information about the adopted children's social and racial identities, the attitudes and awareness about race and racial differences held by the birth and adopted children, and the parents' beliefs about the cohesiveness of their family and the strength of the commitments the children had to them and to each other. In all of our encounters with these families, we were impressed with their openness and with their willingness to lay their feelings on the table. When some of them were going through particularly difficult times, years, for example, when their adopted children were stealing from them or their birth and adopted children were drinking and using drugs, they talked about those events in great detail and with a lot of affect. The children also, especially when they were adolescents, shared their feelings—about their families, about their attitudes toward having been adopted by a white family, about their birth parents and cultures, and about their future—in an open manner.

Bringing together this 12-year study in one volume gives the reader a richer and deeper understanding of what the experiences have involved for the parents, for the adoptees, and for the children born into the families. We are very grateful to our subjects for their cooperation and support. Obviously, without their willingness to open up their homes to us, to give us of their time, and to share with us the pleasures, as well as the pains, of their experiences, this work could not have been done.

We also owe a great deal to our field staff, who conducted interviews that often lasted more than three hours and sometimes involved several trips to the same family to meet with all of the respondents. We thank our editor, Alison

Bricken, for the strong support and appreciation she showed for the worth-whileness of bringing together all of the materials into one volume. Finally, we are grateful to Joyce Turner for her extraordinary diligence, patience, quickness, and efficiency in processing this manuscript from draft stage to final form.

Transracial Adoption:
An Overview

The history of adoption is the history of hard-to-place children. Adoption agencies historically have attempted to equate a child's individual characteristics with those of the intended adoptive parents: "A child wants to be like his parents . . . parents can more easily identify with a child who resembles them . . . the fact of adoption should not be accentuated by placing a child with parents who are different from him."[1] Not only were similar physical, and at times intellectual, qualities seen as important components in adoptive criteria, but identical religious backgrounds were defined, at times by law, as essential.[2] Thus the battle of transreligious adoption preceded the movement toward transracial adoption, and it was not until the conceptual and pragmatic acceptance of transreligious adoption occurred that transracial adoption could, and did, develop.

As adoption moved toward becoming an acceptable means to deal with children who needed parents and couples who wanted children, so too did social work evolve into a recognized discipline. This relationship was not coincidental. Adoption agencies are a relatively new phenomenon. Historically most adoptions resulted from negotiations between attorneys for potential adoptive parents and an orphanage or a private physician whose patient wanted to surrender a child. The natural parent's rights would be waived, and the court would usually grant the adoption petition. A gap existed, however, between a couple's desire to adopt and the courts' ability to determine whether the petitioners would indeed be adequate parents. Social work, or what was to develop into social work, sought to fill this gap by being the advocate for couples who wanted to adopt and for women or institutions who wanted to surrender their children.

Transracial and intercountry adoption began in the late 1940s, following the end of World War II, which left thousands of homeless children in many parts of the world. It gained momentum in the mid-1950s, diminished during the early 1960s, rose again in the late 1960s, and began to decline in the mid-1970s. When our first volume was published in 1977, transracial adoption had almost ceased to exist. For example, of the 4,172 black children who had been adopted in 1975 by unrelated petitioners, only 831 were placed with white families.[3]

The development of transracial adoption was not a result of deliberate agency programming to serve populations in need, but rather an accommodation to reality. Social changes regarding abortion, contraception, and reproduction in general had significantly reduced the number of white children available for adoption, leaving nonwhite children as the largest available source.[4] Changes had also occurred regarding the willingness of white couples to adopt nonwhite children. Whatever the reasons, in order to remain "in business," adoption agencies were forced by a combination of social conditions to reevaluate their ideology, traditionally geared toward the "matching" concept, in order to serve the joint needs of these two groups.

THE MATCHING CONCEPT

The assumptions of matching are simple, but naive. In order to ensure against adoptive failure, adoption agencies felt that both the adopted child and his or her potential parents should be matched on as many physical, emotional, and cultural characteristics as possible. The most important were racial and religious characteristics.

Thus it was not uncommon for potential adoptive parents to be denied a child if their hair and eye color could not be duplicated in an adoptable child. The hypothesis of matching was one of equalization. If all possible physical, emotional, intellectual, racial, and religious differences between adopter and child could be reduced, hopefully to zero, the relationship stood a better chance of succeeding. So ingrained was the matching idea that its assumptions, especially those relating to religion and race, were operationalized into law under the rubric of a "child's best interests." Seventeen states, including the District of Columbia, had at one time or another statutes pertaining to the religious matching of adopted children and parents.[5]

A 1954 study requested adoption agencies to indicate whether certain factors were significant for evaluating the possibilities of placing a child with a particular family. Table 1.1 summarizes the agencies' responses.[6]

While there appears to have been wide variation in the matching factors considered important by the individual agencies, all the characteristics mentioned on the checklist were defined as important by at least two-thirds of the agencies. Only 10 agencies felt that it was not important to equate a child's race to that of his prospective parent. Shapiro, the author of the study, commented:

Table 1.1
Matching Factors Adoption Agencies Considered Important

Matching Factors	Important		Total Number of Responses
	Yes	No	
Level of intelligence and intellectual potential	253	1	254
Religious background	240	13	253
Racial background	240	10	250
Temperamental needs	235	12	247
Educational background	204	41	245
Physical resemblance to child	212	30	242
Geographic separation from natural parents	192	49	241
Cultural background	195	40	235
Nationality background	163	69	232
Physical characteristics of child's family	187	42	229

Source: Michael Shapiro, *A Study of Adoption Practice,* vol. 1: *Adoption Agencies and the Children They Serve* (New York: Child Welfare League of America, 1956), p. 84, Table 7, "Basis for Matching."

We know from practice that agencies are not placing Negro children in white homes or white children in Negro homes. Some agencies use homes for children of mixed racial background where the background of the adoptive parents is not the same as the child's. However, in most instances the characteristics of the child are primarily white, for this kind of placement occurs more frequently with children of mixed Oriental or Indian and white background, than with children in whom the non-Caucasian blood is Negro.[7]

In its *Standards for Adoption Service (SAS),* the Child Welfare League of America (CWLA) continued to make matching a responsible part of adoption practice. In 1959, under the subtitle "Matching," the CWLA recommended that

similarities of background or characteristics should not be a major consideration in the selection of a family, except where integration of the child into the family and his identification with them may be facilitated by likeness, as in the case of some older children or some children with distinctive physical traits, such as race.

When the age of the child and of the adoptive parents was considered, the *SAS* suggested that "the parents selected for a child should be within the age range usual for natural parents of a child of that age."[8]

Recognizing that social and cultural attitudes are learned rather than inherited, the *SAS* did not recommend that these factors enter into the matching equation. The educational background of both the child's biological family and the prospective adoptive parents was likewise minimized: "The home selected should be one in which the child will have the opportunity to develop his own capacities, and where he is not forced to meet unrealistic expectations of the adoptive parents."[9]

Religion was handled in the 1959 *SAS* by inclusion of a rather lengthy statement representing the positions of the three major faiths:

Opportunity for religious and spiritual development of the child is essential in an adoptive home. A child should ordinarily be placed in a home where the religion of adoptive parents is the same as that of the child, unless the parents have specified that the child should or may be placed with a family of another religion. Every effort (including interagency and interstate referrals) should be made to place the child within his own faith, or that designated by his parents. If, however, such matching means that placement might never be feasible, or involves a substantial delay in placement, or placement in a less suitable home, a child's need for a permanent family of his own requires that consideration should then be given to placing the child in a home of a different religion. For children whose religion is not known, and whose parents are not accessible, the most suitable home available should be selected.[10]

When dealing with physical characteristics, the *SAS* reiterated its overall stance toward racial matching and defined the latter as a "physical characteristic": "Physical resemblances should not be a determining factor in the selection of a home, with the possible exception of such racial characteristics as color."[11]

By 1964, the matching concept underwent a subtle but significant shift. In a CWLA publication, Viola M. Bernard made the following statement:

In the past much emphasis was placed on similarities, especially of physical appearance, as well as national, sociocultural, and ethnic backgrounds. It was thought, for example, that matching the child's hair color, physique, and complexion to that of the adoptive parents would facilitate the desired emotional identification between them. Experience has shown, however, that couples can identify with children whose appearance and background differ markedly from their own. Instead, optimal "matching" nowadays puts more stress on other kinds of correspondencies between the child's estimated potentialities and the parents' personalities, values, and modes of life. Respective temperaments, for example, are taken into account. Whether similarities or differences work out better depends on many factors, which also must be considered.

Although it has been proved repeatedly that parents can identify with children of different emotional and racial backgrounds, and with all sorts of heredities, not every couple, of course, feels equally accepting of each type of "difference." Accordingly, the child of a schizophrenic parent would not be considered for a couple who has deeply rooted fears about the inheritance of mental illness; a child of interracial background who appears predominantly white is likely to adjust best in a white family. [Emphasis added.][12]

No longer were the most ostensible characteristics to be matched between child and parent. Instead, emphasis was to be placed on a child's "estimated potentialities." In other words, the "unseen" instead of the "seen" was to be matched except with regard to race. Racial matching, however, continued to be stressed by the CWLA, as indicated by the following statement: "A child who appears predominantly white will ordinarily adjust best in a white family."[13]

In 1968, the subtitle "Matching" was deleted from the CWLA's *SAS*. In its stead appeared a category titled "Responsibility for Selection of Family." Its wording was broad and somewhat ambiguous with regard to matching but quite clear about the role of the professional social worker and the adoption agency:

The professional social work staff of the agency (including the social worker who knows the child, the social worker who knows the adoptive family and the supervisor) should carry the responsibility for the selection of a family for a particular child on the basis of their combined knowledge about both the child and the adoptive family and the findings and recommendations of all the consultants.[14]

Age as a matching criterion was expanded past the 1959 statement and, as a result, became less potent as a critical matching factor: "The parents selected for a child should be ones who are likely to retain the capacities needed to adapt to the changing needs of a child as he grows up."[15]

The social, cultural, and national background of both the child and the adoptive parents was treated in a manner similar to the 1959 *SAS* treatment. Educational background was also generally reflective of the 1959 statement.

Two important revisions appeared within the categories "Religion" and "Physical and Personality Characteristics." Absent from the "Religion" category was the lengthy statement in the 1959 description that related to the rationale for religious matching. In its place was the following: "The family selected for a child should be one in which the child will have an opportunity for religious or spiritual and ethical development but religious background alone should not be the basis for selection of a family for a child."[16]

But in 1975, a New York State court upheld the practice of placing children along religious lines. The court found no constitutional inconsistency with the provisions of the law that stated that "so far as consistent with the best interests of the child and where practicable" a child should be placed with an agency that reflected the child's religious faith.[17]

Since most blacks were Protestant and the number of homeless black children far exceeded the capability of Protestant agencies to care for them adequately, a situation developed in New York whereby such children, for lack of other alternatives, were placed in state agencies.

Absent from the category "Physical and Personality Characteristics" was any reference to color as a criterion for adoption: "Physical resemblances of the adoptive parents, the child or his natural parents should not be a determining factor in the selection of a home."[18]

By 1971, then, most of the characteristics traditionally encompassed within the matching concept had been reworded to the point of being broad guidelines rather than precise definitions. Witness the following statement from the CWLA's *Guidelines for Adoption Service* (not to be confused with the *SAS*):

When adoption has been found desirable for the child, and the couple has met the agency's requirements for adoption, an appraisal must be made of their suitability for each other. In most instances, similarity in background or characteristics need not be a factor. It should be recognized, however, that people vary in their capacity to accept differences. If the couple want a child who is like them in certain ways, this desire should be taken into consideration.[19]

Although it was significantly diluted, matching continued to be a classic principle of adoption practice.

TRANSRACIAL ADOPTION

The institutionalized beginnings of transracial adoption of American black children are traceable to the activities of the Children's Service Center and a group of parents in Montreal, Canada, who in 1960 founded an organization called the Open Door Society.[20]

In the United States, 1961 marked the founding of an organization whose original purpose was to provide placements for black children in black adoptive homes. Parents to Adopt Minority Youngsters (PAMY) was founded in Minnesota and worked in cooperation with the Minnesota Department of Public Welfare. PAMY was one of the first groups to be formed in this country along the lines of the Open Door Society in Canada and provided similar referral, recruitment, and public-relations functions. But PAMY's involvement with transracial adoption, unlike that of the Open Door Society, came as an unexpected by-product of its original intent, which was to secure black adoptive homes for black children. From 1962 through 1965, approximately 20 black children in Minnesota were adopted by white families through the efforts of PAMY. These adoptive parents seemed not to fit the traditional stereotyped model of the adoptive family. For the most part they were not infertile, and their act was not seen by them as a substitute for natural parenthood.[21]

By 1969, 47 organizations similar to the Open Door Society were in existence in the United States. Among the major ones were: Families for Interracial

Table 1.2
Approved Homes and Available Children, by Race and by Agency Auspices (240 agencies)

Auspices	Number of Agencies	Race	Approved Homes		Children Available		Difference between No. Homes and Children
			Number	Percentage	Number	Percentage	
Public	73	White	4,960	91	4,239	78	721
		Non-white	511	9	1,162	22	-651
		Total	5,471	100	5,401	100	70
Voluntary	167	White	16,456	94	14,153	83	2,303
		Non-white	1,073	6	2,883	17	-1,810
		Total	17,529	100	17,036	100	493
Total	240	White	21,416	93	18,392	82	3,024
		Non-white	1,584	7	4,045	18	-2,461
		Total	23,000	100	22,437	100	563

Source: Lucille Grow, *A New Look at Supply and Demand in Adoption* (New York: Child Welfare League of America, 1970), p. 8, Table 4.

Adoption, the Council on Adoptable Children, Opportunity, the National Council of Adoptive Parents, and Adopt-A-Child-Today.[22] Their primary function was to help secure adoptive homes for all parentless children, with particular emphasis on children with "special needs."

Historically, both private and public adoption agencies have had a bank of white adoptive families in excess of the number of available white children.[23] For example, a 1955 study indicated that at any given time there were between two and eight approved white adoptive homes for every white child, whereas there was only one approved black family for every 10 to 20 black children.[24]

As shown in Table 1.2, by 1970 the number of available nonwhite children still far exceeded the number of approved nonwhite homes. There were 21,416 approved white homes for 18,392 available white children, and 1,584 approved nonwhite homes for 4,045 available nonwhite children. This resulted in 2,461 nonwhite children being technically without (nonwhite) adopters.

The combined figures for public and private agencies show that there were 116 approved white homes for every 100 white children and only 39 approved nonwhite homes per 100 nonwhite children. The fact that transracial adoption was not considered by the agencies in this survey as a way of reducing the excess of available nonwhite children is demonstrated by the following excerpt:

Again, the reader must be cautioned that the data do not take account of the white adoptive homes that are in fact available for the placement of nonwhite children. If it

Table 1.3
Nonwhite Children Available and Nonwhite Approved Homes per 100 Nonwhite Children, by Region (185 agencies)

Region	Number	Percentage of All Children	Median Number of Approved Homes
New England	219	11	13
Middle Atlantic	1,235	31	24
East North Central	645	25	25
West North Central	159	12	10
South Atlantic	332	22	42
East South Central	92	25	40
West South Central	20	6	80
Mountain	192	23	50
Pacific	336	19	44
Canada	193	10	19
Total	3,423	19	25

Source: Lucille Grow, *A New Look at Supply and Demand in Adoption* (New York: Child Welfare League of America, 1970), p. 13, Table 8.

were *possible* to place a nonwhite child in about one out of every nine approved white homes, there would be an available adoption resource for all children reported by the 240 agencies.[25]

The implication of this 1970 statement is that it was impossible to consider the placement of nonwhite children with white families.

As shown in Table 1.3, the Middle Atlantic region, with the largest number of nonwhite children available for adoption (1,235), had 24 nonwhite homes approved for adoption (close to the median of 25 for all agencies combined), whereas in the West South Central region, with the smallest number of nonwhite children (20), 80 nonwhite homes were approved, a figure well above the combined median.

Table 1.4 reports the number of white and nonwhite homes for the years between 1967 and 1972.

The figures in Tables 1.3 and 1.4, although from different sources, suggest

Table 1.4
Approved Homes per 100 Available Children, by Race and Year

	Number of Approved Homes			
	1967	1970	1971	1972
White	114	116	133	108
Non-white	60	39	39	51

Source: 1971 and 1972 figures are from Opportunity, Division of the Boys and Girls Aid Society of Oregon, *Opportunity Reports,* August 1973, September 18, 1973, and December 2, 1974.

only general estimated ratios. It appears, however, that by 1972 a trend had been reversed in that the number of approved white homes decreased sharply from the previous year, falling below the 1967 level, whereas the number of approved nonwhite homes rose.

As shown in Table 1.5, after having experienced an approximate three-and-a-half-fold increase between 1968 and 1971, the number of transracial adoptions fell sharply thereafter, decreasing to 20 percent by 1974.

The data in Table 1.6 indicate the ebb and flow of transracial adoption in states that have compiled and released such figures. When examining these figures, note that the number in parentheses represents the reporting adoption agencies and that there are wide discrepancies (for example, 72 agencies in Pennsylvania and 2 each in Georgia and New Hampshire in 1972).

Many have argued that the ratio between adoptable black children and available black homes is deflated as a result of a conscious (that is, racist) effort by white-controlled adoption agencies not to involve the black community more fully in attempting to reach black potential adoptive parents. According to a 1972 study, there is a relationship between the number of adoptable black children on an agency's caseload and the frequency of transracial adoption.[26] An agency that has many available black children is less likely to look for white adoptive parents than an agency that has only a few black children. The implication is that adoption agencies located in black communities with large constituencies of adoptable black children have more contacts and programs within the black community and are therefore in a better position to locate black adoptive couples.

In a 1972 doctoral dissertation, Dawn Day Wachtel examined the relationship between adoption agencies' practices and the placement of black children.[27] Her findings supported the earlier results of David Fanshel and Trudy Bradley indicating that the use of mass media to attract potential adoptive black couples was not an altogether effective method of recruitment.[28] In examining

Table 1.5
Number of Black Children Placed in White and Black Homes, 1968–73

Placement	1968	1969	1970	1971	1972	1973	1974	1975
Total Black Children Placed	3,122	4,336	6,474	7,420	6,065	4,665	3813	4172
With Black Families	2,389	2,889	4,190	4,846	4,467	3,574	3066	3341
With White Families	733	1,447	2,274	2,574	1,569	1,091	747	831
Percent of black children placed in white families	23%	33%	35%	35%	26%	23%	20%	20%
Number of Reporting Agencies	194	342	427	468	461	434	458	565

Source: Opportunity, Division of the Boys and Girls Aid Society of Oregon, 1976, *Opportunity Report,* January 1977.

the dropout rate of black couples attracted to adoption agencies by the media (ethnic and nonethnic radio, television, newspapers, and so on), Wachtel noted that there was a lower rate of application completion among these individuals than among black applicants who were informally referred. The latter were defined as successful black adopters who had positive experiences with (black) friends who were themselves potential adoptive parents. She therefore concluded that the informal system (that is, word-of-mouth communication) was the best method by which to ensure eventual black inracial adoption. The difficulty lay in the ability of white-administered adoption agencies to attract enough black adopters into "the system" in order to establish credibility.

Adoption agencies that serve black children predominantly tend to have a higher proportion of black social workers on their staffs than agencies with small populations of black children. Two other studies revealed that a social worker's race appeared to be one of the strongest factors affecting attitudes toward transracial adoption, with black social workers disapproving more often

Table 1.6
Number of Nonwhite Children Adopted by White Families (numbers in parentheses represent reporting adoption agencies)

States	1968	1969	1970	1972	1974
California	70(5)	308(6)	187(19)	215(26)	62(28)
Illinois	42(7)	75(25)	174(33)	56(16)	11(12)
Massachusetts	65(10)	97(16)	149(18)	38(17)	20(13)
Michigan	35(13)	61(16)	161(18)	130(22)	37(27)
Minnesota	76(6)	170(9)	246(9)	64(8)	18(4)
New Jersey	2(4)	29(8)	131(8)	74(9)	38(8)
New York	75(16)	100(31)	168(39)	124(38)	76(52)
Ohio	15(14)	36(33)	95(33)	116(61)	83(51)
Oregon	56(5)	65(7)	81(7)	71(7)	13(4)
Pennsylvania	25(11)	51(36)	137(57)	105(72)	70(60)
Washington	81(6)	106(7)	107(8)	43(5)	9(8)
Wisconsin	45(8)	87(8)	107(8)	61(8)	29(8)
Colorado				32(6)	20(6)
District of Columbia				27(6)	6(4)
Florida				20(7)	27(7)
Indiana				36(9)	28(9)
Iowa				33(10)	17(8)
Maryland				16(19)	11(12)
Tennessee				3(7)	5(10)
Georgia				4(2)	5(2)
New Hampshire				9(2)	6(3)
Total	587	1,185	1,743	1,277	591

Source: Survey by Opportunity, Division of the Boys and Girls Aid Society of Oregon. The 1968, 1969, and 1970 surveys are reported in *National Adoptalk* (November–December 1969): 7; 6 (July–August 1970): 9; 7 (July–August 1971): 9; 1972 in September 18, 1973; 1974 in December 22, 1975.

than white social workers.[29] One study found a correlation of $-.85$ between the number of white social workers employed and the frequency of inracial adoptions (black-black).[30]

Elizabeth Herzog and Rose Bernstein hypothesized in 1965 that middle-class blacks were no less interested in, informed about, and disposed toward adoption than middle-class whites.[31] Indeed, financially able nonwhites appeared to adopt at a higher rate than whites in similar financial circumstances. Using 1967 adoption figures, the pool of potential adoptive parents was defined as married couples between the ages of 25 and 44 earning at least $5,000 per year. The ratio of prospective nonwhite adopters to available nonwhite children was then 15.3 per 1,000, whereas the ratio for inracial white adoptions was 9.2 per 1,000.[32]

Adoption agencies have historically exercised a good deal of control in establishing, maintaining, and enforcing what can be termed a "worthiness scale" against which potential adoptive couples are measured.[33] Thus couples wanting to adopt healthy white infants when the latter were in available supply would usually have to demonstrate that they had been married for a specific length of time and were of a certain age,[34] religious (attended church),[35] middle-class,[36] in good health (mental and physical),[37] and infertile.[38] Commenting on the "measuring process" whereby agencies establish the criteria by which adoptive applicants are either accepted or rejected, Clayton Hagen, director of the Adoption Unit of Lutheran Social Services in Minnesota, said:

The evaluative approach often has extremely negative effects on the adoptive parents. Several years after placement, adoptive couples often retained a distressing amount of hostility toward the agency through which they had adopted. The evaluative approach made the couple's position inherently defensive as they labored to prove that they would be suitable parents. Approaching adoptive applicants as a resource of the agency, and effectively stripping them of rights and responsibilities, did little to enhance their feelings of adequacy.[39]

So strict were the adoption agencies, especially private ones, in enforcing these regulations that one white couple known to one of us was rejected by an adoption agency because there was a gap of a few months between the time they were married in a civil service and their church marriage. The adoption agency claimed that this constituted moral indiscretion and denied their application.

In 1975, the last year of federal reporting, approximately 129,000 children were adopted, down from about 175,000 adoptions in 1970, but significantly higher than 1951, when an estimated 72,000 adoptions were reported.[40] The above figures are of limited accuracy insofar as not all 50 states reported and in some instances the data from reporting states are incomplete. In a March 1985 interview, the president of the National Committee for Adoption indicated that a low estimate of the number of inracial adoptions occurring that year was around 65,000. He cautioned, however, that in all likelihood there were "huge numbers of unreported adoptions."[41]

If it is difficult to predict with any degree of accuracy the number of inracial adoptions occurring in the United States since 1975, it is virtually impossible to place even the most general figure on the number of transracial adoptions. As in the case of overall adoption figures, there are some informed guesses, statistical projections, and demographic deductions. But they are weaker and less convincing than general adoption figures and require a greater leap of faith. Transracial adoption continues to be identified in most areas as a highly charged racial issue and a rallying point symbolic of historical grievances. Most adoption agencies would rather not draw attention to themselves by actively supporting or encouraging this type of child placement.

What data, then, are available? Again, we turn to 1975. In that year the Department of Health, Education, and Welfare reported 831 transracial adoptions, down from its recorded high of 2,574 in 1971.[42] In April 1983, the North American Council on Adoptable Children (NACAC) reported that federal authorities (presumably the Department of Health and Human Services [DHHS]) estimated the number of children in foster care to be "approximately 500,000–750,000," 60 percent of whom were racial or ethnic minorities.[43] Approximately 100,000–120,000 children in foster care were legally free for adoption; about 30 percent of these were black.[44] Thus, relying only on the rough figures suggested by the foster care system, we estimate that there should have been about 33,000–40,000 black children awaiting adoption placement.

But one year later, in 1984, the DHHS reported that in 1982 there were only 243,000 children in foster care, of whom 50,000 were free for adoption.[45]

Number of Children in Foster Care and Free for Adoption (in parentheses)

1977	*1982*
500,000	243,000
(102,000)	(50,000)

Also in 1984, the president of the National Committee for Adoption suggested that of the approximately 2 million white couples who would like to adopt, about 68,000 would do so transracially. If that were in fact to happen, all the black children available for adoption would have homes with white parents.

In short, the disparity among the figures, some of which came from the same federal agency, highlights the difficulties in establishing a credible count of adoptions since 1975. Indeed, the level of our knowledge regarding available adoptable children can be summed up by quoting a statistician employed at the Administration for Children, Youth, and Families who wrote in 1982: "There are no reliable national statistics available on virtually all . . . aspects of adoption."[46] To remedy this important gap in national statistics, Congress mandated the government to resume collecting national figures on adoption by October 1991.

In January 1990 the National Center for Health Statistics published a report titled *Adoption in the 1980's*.[47] Relying on a 1987 national sample of more than 30,000 women between the ages of 20–54, the report's investigators noted a slow but somewhat steady decline in the rate of adoption. Interestingly, although not statistically significant, never-married black women continue to adopt related children at a higher rate than their white counterparts (0.6 to 0.2). But when the relationship between race and the adoption of unrelated children was examined, whites tended to adopt at a higher rate than blacks: 1.4 to .8.

The following chart demonstrates the rate at which interracial adoption is occurring.[48]

Race of Adoptive Mother and Child

Same race	92.4
White	85.4
Black	5.9
Other	1.1
Different race	7.6
White mother, black child	1.2
White mother, child of race other than black	4.8
Mother of other race, white child	1.6

As shown above, 7.6 percent of all adoptions reported by women between 20–54 were transracial. The largest percentage of transracial adoptions (4.8 percent) consisted of the adoption by white mothers of children other than black. They were mostly Korean and Latin American children. The adoption of black children by white parents represented about 1 percent of all adoptions in 1987. This compares to 2 percent in 1975.

THE ANTI–TRANSRACIAL ADOPTION MOVEMENT

At its 1972 national conference, the National Association of Black Social Workers (NABSW) presented a position paper in which transracial adoption was attacked and repudiated. The following excerpt establishes the flavor of the attack.[49]

Black children should be placed only with black families whether in foster care or adoption. Black children belong physically, psychologically and culturally in Black families in order that they receive the total sense of themselves and develop a sound projection of their future. . . . Black children in white homes are cut off from the healthy development of themselves as Black people.

The socialization process for every child begins at birth. Included in the socialization process is the child's cultural heritage, which is an important segment of the total process. This must begin at the earliest moment; otherwise our children will not have the background and knowledge which is necessary to survive in a racist society. This is impossible if the child is placed with white parents in a white environment. . . .

We [the members of the NABSW] have committed ourselves to go back to our communities and work to end this particular form of genocide [transracial adoption].

The popular black press, especially *Ebony,* continued to feature articles in which adoption and transracial adoption were the central themes.[50] These were wide-ranging reports that attempted to present the gamut of positions and ramifications involved in black adoption. In August 1974, an entire special issue of *Ebony* was devoted to the black child, with the adoption controversy woven throughout several reports.[51]

Many of the readers' letters that were published in *Ebony* after that issue appeared contained the following sentiments: Whites are responsible for having produced a white racist society. Their act of adopting blacks is insulting and psychologically damaging and dangerous. It's ironic; once whites enslaved us because they considered themselves superior, and still do. Yet, now they want to "rear and love us." Why?[52]

In 1974, the Black Caucus of the North American Conference on Adoptable Children recommended "support [for] the consciousness development movement of all groups" and "that every possible attempt should be made to place black and other minority children in a cultural and racial setting similar to their original group." In May 1975, the dean of the Howard University School of Social Work and president of the NABSW stated that "black children who grow up in white homes end up with white psyches."[53]

In one of the more moderate attacks on transracial adoption, Leon Chestang in the May 1972 issue of *Social Work* posed a series of critical questions for white parents who had adopted or who were considering adopting a black child:

The central focus of concern in biracial adoption should be the prospective adoptive parents. Are they aware of what they are getting into? Do they view their act as purely humanitarian, divorced from its social consequences? Such a response leaves the adoptive parents open to an overwhelming shock when friends and family reject and condemn them. Are they interested in building world brotherhood without recognizing the personal consequences for the child placed in such circumstances? Such people are likely to be well meaning but unable to relate to the child's individual needs. Are the applicants attempting to solve a personal or social problem through biracial adoption? Such individuals are likely to place an undue burden on the child in resolving their problems.

And what of the implications for the adoptive family of living with a child of another race? Are negative societal traits attributed to blacks likely to be inherited by the adoptive family, thereby subjecting the family to insults, racial slurs, and ostracism?

The white family that adopts a black child is no longer a "white family." In the eyes of the community, its members become traitors, nigger-lovers, do-gooders, rebels, odd-

balls, and, most significantly, ruiners of the community. Unusual psychological arma-
ments are required to shield oneself from the behavioral and emotional onslaught of
these epithets.[54]

But Chestang concluded his piece on a more optimistic note than most critics
of transracial adoption. "Who knows what problems will confront the black
child reared by a white family and what the outcome will be?" he asked. "But
these children, if they survive, have the potential for becoming catalysts for
society in general."

Most black writers opposed to transracial adoption challenged two main hy-
potheses: (1) there are insufficient black adoptive parents willing to adopt black
children; and (2) the benefits a black child will receive in a white family sur-
pass those received in an institution.

They observed that many potential nonwhite adoptive parents are disqualified
because of adoption agencies' widespread use of white middle-class criteria for
selection. They also observed that blacks historically have adopted informally,
preferring not to rely on agencies and courts for sanction. Therefore, the figures
cited by agencies cannot reflect the actual number of black adoptions. They
also claimed that no longitudinal outcome data were available to show that
transracial adoption of black children outweighed the known disadvantages of
institutional or foster care and predicted family and personal problems as the
children grew into preadolescence and adolescence. A leading black organization pointed to transracially adopted black children who were being returned to
foster care because the adoption was not "working out" or were being placed
in residential treatment by their white adoptive parents because they could not
manage them.[55]

Amuzie Chimuzie attributed "all consciously motivating human actions [for
example, transracial adoption] (to) . . . selfish needs."[56] He argued that young
children are rarely consulted when a major decision is to be made in their lives
and that this sense of powerlessness is exacerbated for a young black child in
a white adoptive family. Chimuzie suggested:

It seems appropriate that blacks collectively as parents should speak for the black child
in matters touching transracial adoption. . . . It is up to the agent of the child—in this
instance blacks as a group—to accept or reject it [transracial adoption]. . . . [I]t has
not been determined whether a majority of the blacks are for or against transracial
adoption of black children.[57]

One of the most prevalent arguments against transracial adoption is that white
families, no matter how liberal or well intended, cannot teach a black child
how to survive in an essentially racist society. Nonwhites opposed to transracial
adoption insist that because white adoptive parents are not black and cannot
experience minority, black status, they will rear a psychologically defenseless
individual, incapable of understanding and dealing with the racism that exists

in our society. Amuzie Chimuzie articulated that position when he emphasized the fears that black social workers and other experts in the child-rearing field have that black children reared in white homes will not develop the characteristics needed to survive and flourish in a predominantly white society. After first observing that children tend to acquire most of the psychological and social characteristics of the families and communities in which they are reared, he added: ''It is therefore possible that black children reared in white families and communities will develop antiblack psychological and social characteristics.''[58]

Some black professionals argue that a major bottleneck in the placement of black children in black adoptive homes is caused by the predominantly white child welfare agencies staffed mainly by white social workers, who exercise control over adoptions. The fact that these white agencies are in the position of recruiting and approving black families for adoption causes some blacks to insinuate that there is institutional racism on the part of whites. In contrast, there have been several instances where concerted efforts by black child welfare agencies to locate and approve adoptive black families resulted in the adoption of comparatively large numbers of parentless black children.

The above position was strongly argued by Evelyn Moore, executive director of the National Black Child Development Institute. In an extensive interview on the child welfare system published by the National Association of Social Workers (NASW) in April 1984, a significant part of which dealt either directly or indirectly with transracial adoption, Moore said that 83 percent of all child welfare workers in the United States are white, while 30–40 percent of their cases deal with black families.[59] This skewed ratio, she contends, is one of the reasons that there are so few inracial black adoptions: ''The adoption system in this country was established to provide white children to white families. As a result, most people who work in the system know very little about black culture or the black community.'' Moore also argues that ''white middle-class standards'' are largely responsible for the rejection of low- and working-class black families as potential adopters, who are instead encouraged to become foster parents: ''While black children under the age of 19 represent only 14 percent of the children in America, they represent 33 percent of all children not living with their birth parents'' (for example, in foster care or institutionalized).[60]

Two National Urban League studies are cited by black professionals and organizations as further evidence of the likelihood that institutional racism is one of the primary reasons that more black children are not given to prospective black adoptive families. These studies reported that of 800 black families applying for adoptive parent status, only 2 families were approved (.25 percent), as compared to a national average of 10 percent.[61] Another study concluded that 40–50 percent of black families sampled would consider adoption.[62] An acceptance rate of .25 percent becomes somewhat more dramatic when compared to black inracial adoption rates of 18 per 10,000 families. (Figures for whites and Hispanics are 4 and 3 per 10,000 families, respectively.)[63]

How can one explain the discrepancy between the apparently widespread desire to adopt among blacks and a dearth of approved black homes for adoption? First of all, blacks have not adopted in the expected numbers because child welfare agencies have not actively recruited in black communities using community resources, the black media, and churches. Second, there is a historic suspicion of public agencies among many blacks, the consequence of which is that many restrict their involvement with them. Third, many blacks feel that no matter how close they come to fulfilling the criteria established for adoption, the fact that many reside in less affluent areas makes the likelihood of their being approved slight.

NATIVE AMERICAN OPPOSITION

The case of Native Americans is a special one. Native Americans have been subjected to a singularly tragic fate, and their children have been particularly vulnerable.

Large numbers of Native American children have been adopted transracially. In 1968, Native American minors constituted 7 percent of the population and 70 percent of all adoptions in South Dakota. In Wisconsin, the likelihood of Native American children being removed from their families was 1,600 percent greater than that for non–Native Americans. In Washington State, Native Americans constitute less than 2 percent of the population, but 19 percent of the adoptions. Only 19 of 119 Native American children were adopted by Native American families. The remaining 100 were adopted transracially. In 1969, a 16-state report indicated that about 89 percent of all Native American children in foster care were placed transracially.[64]

In 1972, one out of four Native American children under one year of age was adopted in Minnesota. These children were placed into foster care at a rate approximately five times greater than that for non–Native Americans. In 1974, up to 35 percent of all Native American children were removed from their families and placed in foster care, institutionalized, or adopted. By 1978, Minnesota reported that 90 percent of all nonrelated Native American adoptions were transracial.

In 1978, Ann W. Shyne and Anita G. Schroeder found that Native American children constituted 2 percent of all children legally free for adoption in the United States, or approximately 2,040 children.[65] Overall, the rate at which Native American children were being adopted was 20 times higher than the national rate.[66]

The Indian Child Welfare Act of 1978 (PL95-608) was designed to prevent the decimation of Indian tribes and the breakdown of Indian families by transracial placement of Native American children.[67]

Sec. 3
The Congress hereby declares that it is the policy of this Nation to protect the best

interests of Indian children and to promote the stability and security of Indian tribes and families by the establishment of minimum Federal standards for the removal of Indian children from their families and the placement of such children in foster or adoptive homes which will reflect the unique values of Indian culture, and by providing for assistance to Indian tribes in the operation of child and family service programs.

Reduction of transracial placements is supported in Title I, in which all proceedings dealing with Native American child custody are transferred to tribal jurisdiction.

Title I: Child Custody Proceedings

Sec. 101

(a) An Indian tribe shall have jurisdiction exclusive as to any State over any child custody proceedings involving an Indian child who resides or is domiciled within the reservation of such tribe. . . . Where an Indian child is a ward of a tribal court, the Indian tribe shall retain exclusive jurisdiction, notwithstanding the residence or domicile of the child.

(b) In any State court proceeding for the foster care placement of, or termination of parental rights to, an Indian child not domiciled or residing within the reservation of the Indian child's tribe, the court, in the absence of good cause to the contrary, shall transfer such proceeding to the jurisdiction of the tribe. . . .

Sec. 105

(a) In any adoptive placement of an Indian child under State law, a preference shall be given, in the absence of good cause to the contrary, to a placement with a (1) member of the child's extended family; (2) other members of the Indian child's tribe; or (3) other Indian families.

(b) In any foster care preadoptive placement, a preference shall be given, in the absence of good cause to the contrary, to a placement with

(i) a member of the Indian child's extended family;
(ii) a foster home licensed, approved, or specified by the Indian child's tribe;
(iii) an Indian foster home licensed or approved by an authorized non-Indian licensing authority; or
(iv) an institution for children approved by an Indian tribe or operated by an Indian organization which has a program suitable to meet the Indian child's needs.

Title II: Indian Child and Family Programs

Sec. 201

(a) The Secretary is authorized to make grants to Indian tribes and organizations in the establishment and operation of Indian child and family service programs on or near reservations and in the preparation and implementation of child welfare codes. The objective of every Indian child and family service program shall be to prevent the breakup of Indian families and, in particular, to insure that the permanent removal of an Indian child from the custody of his parent or Indian custodian shall be a last resort.

PL95-608 is intended to safeguard Native American culture by keeping families and tribes together and within their native environments. It resulted from almost 10 years' effort by individuals and organizations sensitive to the needs of Native American peoples. It makes tribes, states, and federal governmental agencies responsible for its implementation.

STUDIES OF TRANSRACIAL ADOPTION

In 1974, Lucille J. Grow and Deborah Shapiro of the CWLA published the results of their study of 125 families who had transracially adopted black children.[68] Its major purpose was to assess how successful the adoptions had been. The authors measured successful adoptions as follows:

How best to evaluate transracial adoption is a question we may not have answered well, but we did it to the best of our ability. The committee that reviewed our application suggested a comparison group of black children adopted by black families. Serious consideration was given to this, but it was ruled out as unnecessary, since no one had questioned the preferability of within-race adoption if feasible. The question is whether children are better off adopted by parents of a different race than they would be if they lived with neither natural nor adoptive parents. To answer that would necessitate following up black children who had been adopted by white parents and children comparable with the adoptees in all respects except that they had not been adopted. Identifying a comparable sample of nonadopted children did not seem possible.

We, therefore, confined the research to a descriptive study of adoptions of black or part-black children by white parents. We decided to focus on children who were at least six years of age so that they would have had some experience in the community, and on children who had been in their adoptive homes at least three years, long enough for initial adjustments to be worked out.[69]

Later, in discussing the specific measures of success they relied on, Grow and Shapiro discussed the techniques employed by other social work researchers who had been confronted with similar problems. They commented:

This study of black children adopted by white parents shares the common problem of adoption studies—indeed, of most studies of social programs—that of identifying a valid, operational definition of "success." In an ideal society all adopted children, like their biological peers, would have a happy childhood and develop into well-adjusted, well-functioning adults. In a much-less-than-ideal society, it is evident that many, like their biological peers, will not. Since they do not all become "successful" adults, a series of difficult, usually unanswerable, questions is raised. Is the failure necessarily related to the fact of adoption? Is the rate of failure any different from that observed in the rearing of children by their biological parents? Are the problems of rearing adopted children essentially those inherent in the child-rearing process and subject to the same risks or are they greater? In the specific type of adoption under scrutiny here, is a black child more "successful" in a white adoptive home than he would have been in a black foster home or a series of them?[70]

. . . assessment obviously requires considerable information in a variety of areas and from diverse sources. In this respect, adoption studies also share the dilemmas of child-rearing studies. It is usually not until well into adolescence that children can give valid information about themselves. Their parents, usually the persons best informed about their behavior, are also the most emotionally involved and usually the most biased in their favor. Paper-and-pencil personality tests, which require reading and writing ability on the part of the children, are often not standardized or validated. Tests administered by psychologists and psychiatric evaluations make heavy demands on the research budget, produce more resistance in respondents and also have questionable validity. Seemingly neutral sources of information—case records, social workers' reports, and teachers' evaluations—all have inherent biases and limitations.[71]

The outcome measures developed for this study exploited the possibilities created by the use of computers in which a broad array of different types of data could be used to define different forms of outcome.[72]

In the end, Grow and Shapiro decided on the following measures: (1) the child's responses to the California Test of Personality and the Missouri Children's Behavior Check List Test, (2) three scores based on physical and mental symptoms reported by the parents as present or absent in their child, (3) significant adults' evaluation of the child, that is, mothers', fathers', teachers', and parents' assessment of the child's relations with his or her siblings, and (4) the parents' assessment of the child's attitude toward race.

Note that the only measures that directly reflected the children's opinions and responses were those obtained on the California Test of Personality and the Missouri Children's Behavior Check List Test. All the other scores or outcome measures were derived from the parents' or teachers' evaluation of the children.

On the basis of the children's scores on the California Test of Personality (which purports to measure social and personal adjustment), Grow and Shapiro concluded that the children in their study made about as successful an adjustment in their adoptive homes as other nonwhite children had in prior studies. They claimed that 77 percent of their children had adjusted successfully and that this percentage is similar to that reported in other studies, some of which are described in Table 1.7.

Table 1.8, from Grow and Shapiro, compares the scores of transracially adopted children with those of adopted white children on the California Test of Personality. A score below the twentieth percentile was defined as reflecting poor adjustment, and a score above the fiftieth percentile was defined as indicating good adjustment. As shown in Table 1.8, the scores of transracially adopted children and those of white adopted children match very closely.

Grow and Shapiro questioned the parents about their expectations concerning their adoptive children's adjustments after adolescence and about the children's ties to them when they became adults. They report that by and large the parents were optimistic. One-third of the parents did not anticipate that their adoptive children would experience future difficulties. In fact, 18 percent did not believe that any trouble lay ahead.

When Grow and Shapiro asked the parents why they chose to adopt a non-white child, 54 percent had reasons and motivations that were essentially so-

Table 1.7
Comparison of Success Rate of Transracially Adopted versus White Children

	Percent
Summarized rate for 11 studies of	
white infant adoption[a]	78
Racially mixed[b]	72
Japanese[c]	89
Older white[d]	73-78
Indian children[e]	88

Source: (a) Alfred Kadushin, "A Study of Adoptive Parents of Hard-to-Place Children," *Social Casework,* 43, no. 5 (1962): 227–33; (b) Marian Mitchell, "Transracial Adoptions: Philosophy and Practice," *Child Welfare* 48, no. 10 (December 1969): 613–19; Ethel Roskies, "An Exploratory Study of the Characteristics of Adoptive Parents of Mixed Race Children in the Montreal Area," *Montreal Star,* October 19, 1963; (c) Andrew Billingsley and Jeanne Giovannoni, "Research Perspectives on Interracial Adoption," in Roger Hiller, ed., *Race, Research and Reason* (New York: National Association of Social Workers, 1969), p. 58; (d) Grace Galley, "Interracial Adoptions," *Canadian Welfare* 39, no. 6 (November–December 1963): 248–50; (e) Harriet Fricke, "Interracial Adoption: The Little Revolution," *Social Work* 10, no. 3 (July 1965): 92–97.

cial. (See Table 1.9.) Forty-two percent said they wanted to provide a home for a hard-to-place child, and 10 percent characterized transracial adoption as a "Christian act."

Forty-nine percent of the mothers and 60 percent of the fathers felt that a benefit of transracial adoption was that they were able to "give a home to a child whom nobody seemed to want." (See Table 1.10.) Seventy-one percent of the mothers and 66 percent of the fathers felt that transracial adoption enabled them "to express the deep love for children . . . [they] . . . have always had." Reinforcing the latter statement, and weighted against the idea of transracial adoption as a gesture to right society's wrongs, was the evidence supplied by the parents that "helping to compensate for the inequities in our society" was not perceived to be very much of a benefit of transracial adoption.

Eighty-three percent of the mothers and 82 percent of the fathers said they were not concerned about how their neighbors would react to their adopting a nonwhite child. But, as the data in Table 1.11 suggest, about half of the parents were concerned about how their extended families would react to a transracial adoption.

Grow and Shapiro wanted to find out more about how these parents felt about the concept of transracial adoption. They described four types of transracial adoptions and asked which type the parent would encourage or discour-

Table 1.8
Total Adjustment Scores on the California Test of Personality of Transracially Adopted Children and White Inracially Adopted Children

Percentile Rank on Test	Transracially Adopted Children (N=111) %		White Adopted Children (N=100) %	
2nd	--		1	
5th	1		2	
10th	6	21	5	22
20th	14		14	
30th	13		14	
40th	19		17	
50th	11		9	
60th	13		7	
70th	10		11	
80th	7	47	7	47
90th	4		10	
95th	2		2	
98th	--		1	
Total	100		100	

Source: Lucille J. Grow and Deborah Shapiro, *Black Children, White Parents: A Study of Transracial Adoption* (New York: Child Welfare League of America, 1974), Table 2-6.

age. An "unsure" category was also allowed. As shown in Table 1.12, 91 percent of the mothers and 87 and 83 percent of fathers would encourage transracial adoption by white and black parents of either part black or part white children, respectively. More uncertainty existed with regard to the other two types of adoption.

Fifty-five percent of the parents who felt some anxiety or had some reservation about the adoption also believed that their adopted child felt some discomfort about being adopted, in contrast to 20 percent of the parents who felt no anxiety about their decision to adopt.

Table 1.13 shows the relationship between the parents' perception of their child's racial discomfort and the child's racial appearance. The more a child

Table 1.9
Reasons for Adopting Transracially

Reason	Number of Responses	Percent
Social motivation	68	54
Provide a home for hard-to-place child	53	42
Aid to integration; Christian duty	13	10
Integration a benefit to family	2	2
Personal Motivation	40	32
Wanted a child, race unimportant	28	22
Became attached to foster child	10	8
Knew child; made parents feel special	2	2
Second Choice	14	12
No other children available	12	10
Assurance that child looks Caucasian	2	2
Unclear	3	2
Total	125	100

Source: Lucille J. Grow and Deborah Shapiro, *Black Children, White Parents: A Study of Transracial Adoption* (New York: Child Welfare League of America, 1974), p. 70, Table 3-2.

appeared to be black, the more the parents felt the child was racially uncomfortable.

In 1986 and 1987, Joan Shireman and Penny Johnson describe the results of their study involving 26 inracial (black) and 26 transracial adoptive families.[73] They reported very few differences between the two groups of eight-year-old adoptees. Using the Clark and Clark Doll Test (the same measures we used in our first study)[74] to establish racial identity, 73 percent of the transracial adoptees identified themselves as black, compared to 80 percent for the inracially adopted black children. Interestingly, although three-fourths of the families lived in white neighborhoods, 46 percent of the transracial adoptees named a black

Table 1.10
Effects of the Adoption Experience on Parents

Possible Benefit	Very Much Or Much		A Little		Not at All	
	Mother	Father	Mother	Father	Mother	Father
			(In Percent)			
Has enabled me to give a home to a child whom nobody seemed to want	49	60	26	20	25	20
Has enabled me to fulfill my duty to have a family	16	19	10	15	74	66
Has made me feel less lonely	24	20	19	19	57	61
Has made me feel that I'm doing something toward furthering the cause of an integrated society	31	38	44	41	25	21
Has enabled me to express the deep love for children I have always had	71	66	22	19	7	15
Has brought my spouse and me closer together	19	36	37	32	44	32
Has made me feel more like a "whole" person	34	38	28	30	38	32
Has prevented me from becoming too selfish, too self-centered	27	27	38	41	35	32
Has made me feel that I am helping to compensate for the inequities in our society	23	22	37	36	40	32
Has made my marriage richer	44	54	33	30	23	16
Has made me feel proud about being able to make a contribution to the community	22	24	35	36	43	40
Has given me a great deal of satisfying companionship	79	75	13	15	8	10

Source: Lucille J. Grow and Deborah Shapiro, *Black Children, White Parents: A Study of Transracial Adoption* (New York: Child Welfare League of America, 1974), p. 83, Table 3-5.

Table 1.11
Reservations about Adopting Transracially

Area of Concern	Degree of Concern: Considerable		Moderate		None	
	Mother	Father	Mother	Father	Mother	Father
	(In Percent)					
How it feels to be a parent to an adopted child	2	2	12	14	86	84
How it feels to be a parent to a child of a different race	1	3	10	13	89	84
What extended family's reaction to adoption would be	6	6	17	18	77	76
What extended family's reaction to transracial adoption would be	10	10	35	37	55	53
How black child would fit into family	-	-	23	23	77	77
What neighbors might think	1	1	16	17	83	82
How neighborhood children would treat black child	3	3	36	37	61	60
Whether black child would be happy with white parents	7	7	33	33	60	60

Source: Lucille J. Grow and Deborah Shapiro, *Black Children, White Parents: A Study of Transracial Adoption* (New York: Child Welfare League of America, 1974), p. 72, Table 3-3.

among their best friends. The authors concluded that 75 percent of the transracial adoptees and 80 percent of the inracial appeared to be doing quite well.

In 1988, Richard P. Barth, Marianne Berry, Roger Yoshikami, Regina K. Goodfield, and Mary Lou Carson reported that transracial placements were no more likely to disrupt than other types of adoptions.[75]

The fact that transracial placements were as stable as other more traditional adoptive arrangements was reinforced by data presented at a North American Council on Adoptable Children (NACAC) meeting on adoption disruption held in 1988. There it was reported that the rate of adoption disruptions averaged about 15 percent. Disruptions they reported did not appear to be influenced by the adoptees' race or gender or the fact that they were placed as a sibling

Table 1.12
Parental Convictions about Transracial Adoptions

Racial Characteristics	Mothers			Fathers		
	Encourage	Unsure	Discourage	Encourage	Unsure	Discourage
			(In Percent)			
Whites adopting all-black children	65	25	10	67	23	10
Blacks adopting all-white children	59	27	14	61	27	12
Whites adopting part-black children	91	8	1	87	12	1
Blacks adopting part-white children	91	8	1	83	14	3

Source: Lucille J. Grow and Deborah Shapiro, *Black Children, White Parents: A Study of Transracial Adoption* (New York: Child Welfare League of America, 1974), p. 87, Table 3-7.

Table 1.13
Relationship between Child's Appearance and Parent's Perception of Child's Discomfort about Appearance*

Discomfort	Fair, No Negroid features	Fair, Negroid features/ light brown no Negroid features	Light brown or dark, Negroid features
		(In Percent)	
Yes	10	27	42
No	90	73	58
Total	100	100	100

*$\chi^2 = 8.01$, 2 df, $p < .02$.

Source: Lucille J. Grow and Deborah Shapiro, *Black Children, White Parents: A Study of Transracial Adoption* (New York: Child Welfare League of America, 1974), p. 183, Table 9-1.

group. When examining adoptive parent characteristics, neither religion, race, marital status, length of time married, educational achievement, nor income seemed predictive of adoption disruption.[76]

Thus the limited recent research on transracial adoption continues to demonstrate that transracial adoptees do not seem to be losing their racial identities, they do not appear to be racially unaware of who they are, and they do not display negative or indifferent racial attitudes about themselves. To the contrary, it appears that transracially placed children and their families are doing as well as their counterparts have done in the past, living quite normal and satisfying lives.

AMERICAN INDIAN CHILDREN[77]

Until the 1960s there was little mention of any major adoption study involving American Indian children.[78] The Indian Adoption Project, a program described in David Fanshel's work *Far from the Reservation* (1972), resulted from a 1957 study that indicated the legal availability of 1,000 American Indian children for adoption, who were living either in foster care or in institutions.[79] The project, which lasted from September 1958 to December 1967, was a joint effort sponsored by the Bureau of Indian Affairs and the CWLA (neither of which is an adoption agency) initially to promote nationwide conventional and transracial adoptions of between 50 and 100 American Indian children. At its conclusion in 1968, when most of its activities were subsumed by the Adoption Resource Exchange of North America (ARENA), the project had successfully placed 395 children from 11 states. Ninety-seven of these children were adopted by white families living in 15 different states. *Far from the Reservation* is an examination of the adjustment patterns of these 97 children and their adoptive white parents.

Articles written in the 1960s, especially those by Arnold Lyslo, director of the Indian Adoption Project, describe some of the initial attempts at and success of transracial adoption of American Indian children. These articles examine a series of related adoption programs, many of which were to be incorporated into the Indian Adoption Project.[80]

In 1961, Lyslo stated that 30 Indian children had been adopted, mostly by white couples living in areas geographically distant from the reservations. By 1964, a total of 150 Indian children had been adopted transracially, mostly by families who lived in eastern states. The degree of tribal acculturation and the availability of social services appeared to be strongly associated with positive feelings toward transracial adoption on the part of tribal representatives. Most of the adoptive parents were described in the reports as being motivated by humanitarian and religious principles and appeared to be making successful adjustments to their children and their community. The children also seemed to be adjusting to their new society.

In 1967, Lyslo reported the results of a survey sent by the CWLA to 102 adoption agencies with significant Indian populations.[81] The results from the adoption agencies indicated that the majority of Indian children were being transracially adopted by white families. Of 1,128 Indian children available for adoption, 66 of the 90 reporting agencies indicated that 696 had been adopted, 584 of whom had been placed with white families. Only 14 were adopted by Indian couples. Thirty-two children had been adopted by couples with one Indian parent. The remainder had been placed with nonwhite, non-Indian families (for example, black, Mexican, Spanish-American). Several of the adoption agencies implied that were it not for state racial prejudice, more Indian children could have been transracially adopted. Four of the state agencies reported that several tribes, the Hopi, Navajo, Pueblo, and Colorado River, were reluctant to have their children adopted by non-Indian families.[82]

In *Far from the Reservation,* David Fanshel saw grounds for cautious optimism. As shown in Table 1.14, he divided his families into seven adjustment levels and distributed them according to the degree to which the parents reported that they believed their adopted child had made the adjustment described at each level.

Only 10 percent of the parents perceived their children's future adjustment as "guarded" (Level 5), and only one child was seen to have a "dim" (Level 6) future. In Fanshel's words,

More than fifty percent of the children were rated as showing relatively problem-free adjustments (Levels 1 and 2) and another twenty-five percent were rated as showing adequate adjustment with strengths outweighing weaknesses (Level 3). Another ten percent of the children were rated at Level 4—located midway between adjustments regarded as adequate and those viewed as guarded.[83]

Many of the parents acknowledged that difficulties lay ahead and that they expected that those difficulties would surface when their children reached adolescence and adulthood. Many felt that the difficulties would be proportional to the "full-bloodedness" of their children and therefore children who appeared less distinctively Indian would have less turbulent experiences. The existence of anxiety or lack of it therefore rested on the degree to which the children were of mixed blood.

In examining which social and demographic factors correlated best with the parents' perceptions of the child's adjustment, Fanshel found the strongest relationship between age and adjustment. The older the child at the time of initial placement, the more difficult the adjustment. Fanshel also discovered an association between age at placement and parental strictness, noting that the older the child, the more strict the adoptive parents tended to be.

The child's sex appeared minimally related to adjustment, boys being defined as slightly more problematic than girls. A family's social position was also related to the child's adjustment.[84] The higher the family's status, the more difficulty the child seemed to experience, and therefore the more problematic

Table 1.14
Level of Adjustment Perceived by White Parents of American Indian Children

Number	Percent	Description of Level
10	10	Level One (Child is making an excellent adjustment in all spheres--the outlook for his future adjustment is excellent.)
41	43	Level Two
24	25	Level Three (Child is making an adequate adjustment--his strengths outweigh the weaknesses he shows--the outlook for this future adjustment is hopeful.)
10	10	Level Four
10	10	Level Five (Child is making a mixed adjustment--generally the problems he faces are serious and the outlook for his future adjustment is guarded.)
1	1	Level Six
None	None	Level Seven (Child is making an extremely poor adjustment--the outlook for his future adjustment is unpromising.)

Source: David Fanshel, *Far from the Reservation: The Transracial Adoption of American Indian Children* (Metuchen, NJ: Scarecrow Press, 1972), p. 280.

his or her behavior. Fanshel explained this phenomenon by suggesting that parents of higher socioeconomic status set higher standards of behavior for their children and thus had higher expectations of adoption. There was no relationship between the parents' religious affiliation or degree of religiousness and a child's adjustment.

It is important to emphasize that all these impressions were based on the parents' responses to their children's adjustment over three different time periods. The professional evaluation of parental impressions (referred to as the Overall Child Adjustment Rating) was the yardstick by which the children's adjustments were viewed, and it served as the basis for predictions for the future. At no time did Fanshel involve the children in attempting to predict future adjustments.

In his conclusion, Fanshel addressed the issue of whether the transracial adoption of American Indian children should be encouraged.[85] He described the costs involved in transracial adoption and concluded that adoption was cheaper than foster care or institutionalization. He established that the children were secure and loved in their adoptive homes. He found that the adoptive parents were happy and satisfied with their children. Nevertheless, in the end, he predicted that the decision as to whether the practice should or should not continue would be made on political grounds and not on the basis of the quality of the adjustment that parents and children experienced.

Since the publication of *Far from the Reservation* in 1972, practically no additional information has appeared in the professional literature regarding the transracial adoption of American Indian children. Some data may be found in the periodic newsletters published by various organizations concerned with both conventional and transracial adoption.[86] These data, however, are usually presented as general categories, and details are, by and large, lacking. For example, in the 1975 annual report of ARENA, one notes that of 238 white, black, Indian, Oriental, and Spanish children who were adopted, 120 were American Indian. One cannot tell, however, whether any of these Indian children were transracially adopted.

It seems reasonable to assume that the limited momentum achieved by the transracial adoption movement as it relates to American Indian children is on the decline. American Indians, like other racial minorities, probably will continue to organize and demonstrate (as in the 1973 "occupation" of Wounded Knee, South Dakota, by members of the American Indian Movement) in order to reawaken both their own and white America's attention to their historic rights. The resurgence of Indian consciousness will undoubtedly lead toward viewing the transracial adoption of their children as yet another form of humiliation—in the explosive jargon of the 1970s, "as a final contemptuous form of robbery."

CONCLUSION

In an article titled "Should Whites Adopt Black Children?" published in *Ebony* in September 1987, the president of the NABSW was quoted as follows: "Our position is that the African-American family should be maintained and its integrity preserved. We see the lateral transfer of black children to white families as contradictory to our preservation efforts."[87]

The article also reported that many of those who opposed transracial adoption see it as "tantamount to racial and cultural genocide" and claim that "there's no way a black child can develop as a total black person if s/he lives in a white family."[88] To counterbalance these statements, it quoted several paragraphs from our 1987 book in which we stated that our data did not suggest that these children were lost to the black community and that the fears of some blacks that transracially adopted black children would develop into racially confused adolescents and adults had not been realized. The article ended on a hopeful note, stating: "[T]he challenge before us is one of extending successful black adoption programs and ultimately, creating a new society in which the racial identity of potential adoptive parents (black and white) is irrelevant."[89]

Very few, if any, responsible organizations or individuals support transracial

adoption as a placement of first choice. Were there sufficient black families for
all black children, Hispanic families for Hispanic children, Asian families for
Asian children, and so forth, there probably would be no need for transracial
adoption. An increase in efforts to locate minority families and especially black
families for these children should be welcomed and supported by all reasonable
people. Altering of "traditional" agency policies and practices based on by-
gone white middle-class assumptions to meet current realities of nonwhite communities, thereby increasing the likelihood that larger numbers of potential minority adopters will be located, also should be promoted by child welfare
advocates.[90]

Most, if not all, who see transracial adoption as a viable arrangement see it
only when a child's options are less permanent types of placements, such as
foster care or group homes. In fact, arguments are rarely, if ever, heard in
favor of transracial adoption that do not define it as "second best" to permanent inracial placement and do not also include strong support for community
agencies to vigorously recruit minority adoptive parents. Witness the following
declarations.

The CWLA in its most recent *SAS* (10) once again, as it has consistently
done in the past, reaffirms that transracial adoption should be considered only
after all efforts at inracial placement have been exhausted. Under the title "Factors
in Selection of Family: Ethnicity and Race," the *SAS* reads:

Children in need of adoption have a right to be placed into a family that reflects their
ethnicity or race. Children should not have their adoption denied or significantly de-
layed, however, when adoptive parents of other ethnic or racial groups are available.
. . . In any adoption plan, however, the best interests of the child should be paramount. If aggressive, ongoing recruitment efforts are unsuccessful in finding families of
the same ethnicity or culture, other families should be considered.[91]

Another example where transracial adoption is considered the second choice
to inracial placements is the statement made by Father George Clements, a
noted black clergyman and founder of One Church, One Child. The latter is a
national plan whereby one family from each black church would adopt a black
child. After stating that inracial adoptions were preferable to transracial adoption, Father Clements was quoted as saying, "But you cannot always have the
ideal, and in lieu of the ideal, certainly I would opt for an Anglo couple, or
whatever nationality, taking a child in . . . ."[92]

Yet a third example of advocacy of the supremacy of inracial to transracial
adoption is the recent statement made by the NACAC on August 3, 1988.
Titled "Minority Placement Position Statement," it begins by acknowledging
that

it has been demonstrated that there are numerous family resources within Black, Hispanic, and Native American communities, [and that] children are denied permanent
homes because potentially available resources of the same race are not fully utilized.

NACAC believes that education and commitment must be a priority on a local and federal level so that Black, Hispanic and Native American children are not denied the right to be placed with families of the same race and culture.

Stating that

We as the national network of parent groups must advocate at the federal, state, and local levels. . . .

it includes some of the following goals:

Partnership with the minority communities in recruitment, assessment and placement of children in appropriate, culturally relevant homes . . .
. . . Placement of children in need of foster care with foster families of the same race/culture as many of these become the child's permanent home through adoption.[93]

Thus, by the beginning of the 1990s, it appears that the major child welfare and adoption organizations remain strongly committed to the idea of recruiting minority adoptive parents for similar children. In all likelihood, these agencies would abandon support for transracial adoption were there a sufficient number of racially similar parents to accommodate waiting nonwhite children.

In some cases, however, organizations continue to cling to the policy that race should be the primary determinant of a child's placement even if the child has already been placed with and integrated into a family of another race. Support for the concept of inracial placement in these cases would seem to work to the detriment of the child's best interests.

For example, in 1988 the Connecticut Task Force on Transracial Adoptions stated that race remained an important factor in making adoption decisions. The task force was convened in reaction to a 1986 Connecticut law that banned the Department of Children and Youth Services from refusing to allow the adoption of a child "solely on the basis of a difference of race."[94]

In 1989, the plight of several middle-class white families in California's Napa Valley reached national prominence when they agreed to provide (temporary) foster homes for black infants born addicted to heroin or crack.[95] After several years, when some of the families applied to adopt these children (placement was to be for 45 days), local departments of social service began proceedings to remove the children and place them with black foster parents. The forces supporting and opposing transracial adoption were once again engaged. Considerations such as racial matching, parent-child bonding, hair and skin care, neighborhood/church/school racial balance, participation in ethnic activities, and so forth, were raised as critical issues in the evaluation of the degree to which a particular white family was able to raise a nonwhite child. At the time of writing, the battle continues; the most likely victims will be the children.

NOTES

1. Michael Shapiro, *A Study of Adoption Practice,* vol. 1: *Adoption Agencies and the Children They Serve* (New York: Child Welfare League of America, 1953), p. 84, quoted in Ruth Taft, "Adoptive Families for 'Unadoptable' Children," *Child Welfare* 32, no. 6 (June 1965):5–9.

2. Alfred Kadushin, "Child Welfare: Adoption and Foster Care," *Encyclopedia of Social Work,* Vol. 103 (New York: National Association of Social Workers, 1971), pp. 107–11.

3. Opportunity, a Division of the Boys and Girls Aid Society of Oregon, Portland, OR, mimeographed, January 1977.

4. Historically, there has always been a much larger number of potential adoptive parents than available healthy adoptable children. See Steven V. Roberts, "Supply of Adoptable White Children Shrinks," *New York Times,* July 18, 1981, p. 28, and Judith Klemsrud, "Adoption Costs Soar as Births Decline," *New York Times,* February 20, 1973, p. 40.

5. Jacqueline and Stewart Macaulay, "Adoptive Placement of Black Children: A Study of Discretion and Legal Norms," *Research in Law and Sociology* 1 (1978):265–318.

6. Shapiro, *A Study of Adoption Practice,* p. 84, Table 7.

7. Ibid., p. 85.

8. Child Welfare League of America, *Standards for Adoption Service* (New York: Child Welfare League of America, 1959), p. 24.

9. Ibid., p. 26.

10. Ibid., p. 25.

11. Ibid., p. 26.

12. Viola M. Bernard, *Adoption* (New York: Child Welfare League of America, 1964), p. 99.

13. Child Welfare League of America, *Standards for Adoption Service,* n. 16, p. 34.

14. Child Welfare League of America, *Standards for Adoption Service, Revised* (New York: Child Welfare League of America, 1968), p. 34.

15. Ibid.

16. Ibid., p. 35.

17. "Court Finds No Religious Conflict in *Wilder v. Sugarman,*" *Child Welfare League Newsletter* 5, no. 1 (Winter 1975).

18. Child Welfare League of America, *Standards for Adoption Service, Revised,* p. 35, n. 22.

19. Child Welfare League of America, *Guidelines for Adoption Service* (New York: Child Welfare League of America, 1971), p. 13.

20. In 1961, there were approximately 32,127 blacks living in all of Canada (0.01 percent of the population) (*Canadian Yearbook* [Ottawa: Canadian Government, 1966], p. 201, Table 14).

21. Elizabeth Shepherd, "Adopting Negro Children: White Families Find It Can Be Done," *New Republic,* June 20, 1964, pp. 10–12; Harriet Fricke, "Interracial Adoption: The Little Revolution," *Social Work* 10, no. 3 (July 1965):92–97.

22. Bernice Madison and Michael Shapiro, "Black Adoption—Issues and Policies," *Social Service Review* 47, no. 4 (December 1973):531–54.

23. "The Parents Who Wait," *Chicago Daily News,* August 23, 1975, p. 25.

24. Michael Shapiro, *Adoption of Children with Special Needs* (New York: Child Welfare League of America, 1957), p. 86.

25. Lucille J. Grow, *A New Look at Supply And Demand in Adoption* (New York: Child Welfare League of America, 1970), p. 9.

26. Andrew Billingsley and Jeanne M. Giovannoni, *Children of the Storm: Black Children and American Child Welfare* (New York: Harcourt Brace Jovanovich, 1972), p. 198.

27. Dawn Day Wachtel, *Adoption Agencies and the Adoption of Black Children: Social Change and Equal Opportunity in Adoption,* dissertation, University of Michigan, Ann Arbor, 1972, p. 84.

28. David Fanshel, *A Study on Negro Adoption* (New York: Child Welfare League of America, 1957); Trudy Bradley, "An Exploration of Case Workers' Perception of Adoptive Applicants," *Child Welfare* 45 (October 1966): 433–43.

29. Anne Stern Farber, "Attitudes of Social Workers toward Requests for Transracial Adoption," Research Project, University of Maryland, School of Social Work, 1972; Dawn Day Wachtel, "White Social Workers and the Adoption of Black Children," paper presented at the August 1973 meeting of the American Sociological Association, New York.

30. Wachtel, *Adoption Agencies,* n. 14, p. 29.

31. Elizabeth Herzog and Rose Bernstein, "Why So Few Negro Adoptions?" *Children* XII (1965): 14–18.

32. *Adoptions in 1967,* Supplement to Child Welfare Statistics 1967, Children's Bureau Statistical Series 92 (Washington, DC: U.S. Department of Health, Education, and Welfare, 1968); *Current Population Report,* Series P-60, no. 59 (April 1969), Bureau of Census.

33. Henry Maas, "The Successful Adoptive Parent Application," *Social Work* 5, no. 1 (January 1960):14–20; Helen Fradkin, "Adoptive Parents for Children with Special Needs," *Child Welfare* 37, no. 1 (January 1958):1–6.

34. Shapiro, *Adoption Agencies,* pp. 75, 80–83.

35. Child Welfare League of America, *Standards for Adoption Service* (New York: Child Welfare League of America, 1958), p. 25, Section 4.9; Shapiro, pp. 76–86.

36. Florence G. Brown, "What Do We Seek in Adoptive Parents?" *Social Casework* 32, no. 4 (1951):155–61.

37. Child Welfare League of America, *Standards for Adoption Service,* p. 75.

38. Ibid., pp. 75–76.

39. Clayton Hagen, quoted in David C. Anderson, *Children of Special Value: Interracial Adoption in America* (New York: St. Martin's Press, 1971), p. 169.

40. Penelope L. Maza, "Adoption Trends: 1944–1965," *Child Welfare Research Notes,* no. 9 (Washington, DC: Administration for Children, Youth and Family, 1984, p. 5).

41. Michael Gold, "The Baby Makers," *Science* (April 1985), p. 53.

42. Rita James Simon and Howard Altstein, *Transracial Adoption: A Follow-up* (Lexington, MA: Lexington Books, 1981), p. 96.

43. North American Council on Adoptable Children, *Adoptalk,* March/April 1983, p. 1.

44. Reflecting the 100,000–120,000 figure, *U.S. News and World Report* in June

1984 estimated about 100,000 children available for adoption (Harold Kennedy, ''As Adoption Gets More Difficult,'' June 25, 1984, p. 62).

45. ''A Place For Foster Children,'' *New York Times,* June 27, 1984, p. C15.

46. Christine Bachrach, ''Adoption Plans, Adopted Children, and Adoptive Mothers: United States, 1982'' (Working Paper no. 22), U.S. Department of Health and Human Services, Public Health Service, Office of Health Research, Appendix II.

47. Christine A. Bachrach, Patricia F. Adams, Soledad Sambrano, and Kathryn A. London, *Adoption in the 1980's,* advance data from *Vital and Health Statistics,* no. 181 (Hyattsville, MD: National Center for Health Statistics, 1989).

48. Ibid., p. 511.

49. In testimony before the Senate Committee on Labor and Human Resources on June 25, 1985, then president of the NABSW William L. Merritt reiterated the NABSW's position by testifying as follows:

Some experts and others believe that transracial adoption (white families adopting Black children) will alleviate the problem of the large numbers of Black children in care. However, this is a myth because:

· The majority of white families who would consider transracial adoption want healthy infants and toddlers. However, the majority of Black children in need of adoption are eight years old and older and are special needs children.

· The placement of Black children in white families does not decrease the large number of Black children in need of families.

· Black children who have grown up in white families suffer severe identity problems. On the one hand, the white community has not fully accepted them and, on the other hand they have had no significant contact with Black people.

· Black children adopted transracially often do not develop coping mechanisms necessary to function in a society that is inherently racist against African Americans.

· Transracial adoptions in the long term often disrupt and the Black children are returned to the foster care program. Children suffer a further sense of rejection as they try to understand why their adoptive as well as their biological parents gave them up.

· In addition, what about the over 50 percent hard to place white children who are not being adopted?

We are opposed to transracial adoption as a solution to permanent placement for Black children. We have an ethnic, moral and professional obligation to oppose transracial adoption. We are therefore legally justified in our efforts to protect the rights of Black children, Black families, and the Black community. We view the placement of Black children in white homes as a hostile act against our community. It is a blatant form of race and cultural genocide.

50. Helen H. King, ''It's Easier to Adopt Today,'' *Ebony,* December 1970, p. 120.

51. *Ebony,* Special Issue on the Black Child, August 1974.

52. *Ebony,* Letter to the Editor, August 1974.

53. Sandy Banisky, ''The Question: Is It Bad for Black Children to be Adopted by Whites?,'' *Baltimore Sun,* May 28, 1975, p. B1.

54. Leon Chestang, ''The Dilemma of Bi-Racial Adoption,'' *Social Work* 17 (May 1972):100–105.

55. ''Transracial Adoption Update: 1978,'' New York Chapter, National Association of Black Social Workers, mimeographed, pp. 4–5.

56. Amuzie Chimuzie, ''Transracial Adoption of Black Children,'' *Social Work* 20 (July 1975):296–301.

57. Ibid.

58. Amuzie Chimuzie, "Bold but Irrelevant: Grow and Shapiro on Transracial Adoption," *Child Welfare* 56, no. 2 (February 1977):75–86.

59. "Black Children Facing Adoption Barriers," *NASW News,* April 1984, p. 9.

60. Ibid.

61. Ibid.

62. Ibid.

63. Ibid.

64. "An Indian Perspective on Adoption," workshop, North American Council on Adoptable Children, Seattle, WA, July 27–29, 1978.

65. Ann W. Shyne and Anita G. Schroeder, *National Study of Social Services to Children and Their Families,* The National Center for Child Advocacy, U.S. Department of Health, Education and Welfare, Office of Human Development Services, Administration for Children, Youth, and Families, Children's Bureau, DHEW Publication no. (OHDS) 78-30150, Washington, DC, 1978.

66. "An Indian Perspective."

67. For an excellent discussion of historical and legal events leading to enactment of PL95-608, see "A Report Together with Dissenting Views," Report no. 1386, House of Representatives, Committee on Interior and Insular Affairs, Washington, DC, 1979 (Morris Udall, Chair).

68. Lucille J. Grow and Deborah Shapiro, *Black Children, White Parents: A Study of Transracial Adoption* (New York: Child Welfare League of America, 1974).

69. Ibid., p. ii.

70. Ibid., p. 90.

71. Ibid., p. 90.

72. Ibid., p. 94.

73. Joan Shireman and Penny Johnson, "A Longitudinal Study of Black Adoptions: Single Parents, Transracial and Traditional," *Social Work* 31, no. 3 (May/June 1986):172–176; Penny Johnson and Joan Shireman, Kenneth Watson, "Transracial Adoption and the Development of Black Identity at Age Eight," *Child Welfare* (January/February 1987).

74. Kenneth B. Clark and Mamie P. Clark, "Racial Identification and Preference in Negro Children," in E. E. Maccoby, T. M. Newcomb, and E. Hartley, eds., *Education and Psychological Measurement* (New York: Holt, Rinehart and Winston, 1958).

75. Richard P. Barth, Marianne Berry, Roger Yoshikami, Regina K. Goodfield, and Mary Lou Carson, "Predicting Adoption Disruption," *Social Work* 33, no. 3 (May/June 1988) 227–33.

76. *Face Facts,* January/February 1989, p. 35.

77. Neither the National Center for Social Statistics nor the Children's Bureau of the Department of Health, Education, and Welfare (HEW) had as separate category for Native Americans.

78. Shapiro, *Adoption Agencies,* Chapter 7; Grace Gallay, "International Adoptions," *Canadian Welfare* 39, no. 6 (November/December 1963):248–50; Donald E. Chambers, "Willingness to Adopt Atypical Children," *Child Welfare* 49, no. 5 (May 1970):275–79; Barbara P. Griffin and Marvin S. Areffa, "Recruiting Adoptive Homes for Minority Children—One Approach," *Child Welfare* 49, no. 2 (February 1970): 105–7.

79. David Fanshel, *Far from the Reservation: The Transracial Adoption of American Indian Children* (Metuchen, NJ: Scarecrow Press, 1972), p. 280.

80. Arnold Lyslo, "Adoptive Placement of Indian Children," *Catholic Charities Review* 51, no. 2 (February 1967):23–25.

81. Ibid.

82. Ibid.

83. Fanshel, *Far from the Reservation*, p. 280.

84. Ibid., pp. 326, 328.

85. Ibid., p. 339.

86. For example, *ARENA News*, Newsletter of the Adoption Resource Exchange of North America; *National Adoptalk*, National Council of Adoptive Organizations; *Opportunity Reports*, Opportunity, a Division of the Boys and Girls Aid Society of Oregon.

87. Walter Leavy, "Should Whites Adopt Black Children?" *Ebony*, September 1987, p. 78.

88. Ibid., p. 78.

89. Ibid., p. 79.

90. "Adoption Agency Rules Called Unfair to Blacks," *New York Times*, February 2, 1987, p. C11.

91. Child Welfare League of America, *Standards for Adoption Service, Revised* (New York: Child Welfare League of America, 1988).

92. Chris Mihill, "Minister Backs Adoption by Race," *International Guardian*, January 30, 1989.

93. North American Council on Adoptable Children, *Adoptalk*, Fall 1988.

94. *A Study of Transracial Adoption in the State of Connecticut*, Final Report of the Task Force on Transracial Adoption, Office of Policy and Management, Comprehensive Planning Division, June 15, 1988.

95. Kathy Dobie, "Nobody's Child: The Battle over Interracial Adoption," *Voice* 8 (1989):18.

2

Court Decisions Involving
Transracial Adoptions

Adoption is a legal process in which a child's legal rights and duties toward his natural parents are terminated and similar rights and duties are created toward the child's adoptive parents.[1] Adoption, unknown in common law, was first created in the United States through an 1851 Massachusetts statute. By 1931 every state in the union had passed adoption statutes, and by 1985 each of the states had extended these statutes to include transracial adoption as well as same-race adoptions.

Since the inception of adoptions in this country, the courts have played an important role in shaping adoption law. The criterion applied in resolving adoption cases in 41 states and the District of Columbia is "in the child's best interest." Recognizing that they lack the requisite expertise to make such a determination, the courts have historically placed heavy reliance on the recommendations of social workers as to whether potential adoptive parents are fit to serve in that capacity. But the final decision as to whether it is in the child's best interest to permit prospective adoptive parents to adopt the child remains within the exclusive discretion of the presiding judge.

Every state has its own statutes and case law concerning transactional adoption, and as is the case with many issues, the statutes and cases vary significantly from state to state. In 1967 two states, Texas and Louisiana, still had statutes in effect that prohibited transracial adoption. From the mid-1950s until the present, the courts have slowly moved away from the initial approach of considering race, that of both the parents and the child, as the determining factor in selecting the best home for the child, to the approach of the U.S. Supreme Court in the 1984 case of *Palmore v. Sidoti*,[2] in which the Court held that race is not a proper basis for deciding child custody cases.

One of the earliest and most important cases concerning transracial adoption

is *In re Adoption of a Minor,*[3] decided in 1955 by the District of Columbia
Court of Appeals. In 1949, a child was born out of wedlock to a white woman.
The putative father was also white. In 1951, the woman married a black man
who, with the mother's permission, petitioned to adopt her son. The whereabouts of the boy's father were unknown. Even though the child had been
living with his mother and her husband, the district court denied the adoption
petition, stating: "This situation gives rise to a difficult social problem. The
boy, when he grows up, might lose the social status of a white man by reason
of the fact that by his record, his father will be a Negro. We feel the court
should not fashion the child's future in this manner."[4] The court of appeals
reversed the trial court on the ground that the trial court failed to properly
address the dispositive issue: what was in the best interest of the child. Furthermore, the distinction between the "social status" of whites and Negroes
was not a proper consideration for the lower court to undertake.[5] The court of
appeals held that race was not to be the sole factor in determining a child's
future.

Seven years later, a New York State court followed the District of Columbia
court's ruling and denied the petition of a wealthy Long Island, New York,
couple to adopt a black child who was being boarded by the county Welfare
Department at a county-operated geriatric center.[6] The couple had three natural
children and two adopted children, one black and one Korean. When the com-
missioner of welfare initially refused their request, they petitioned the supreme
court of the county and were again denied relief. As grounds for the denial,
the court noted that the family already had five children (that is, they had
demonstrated fecundity), that they had only recently adopted a child, and that
the mother desired to continue her career as a teacher. The court did not address the question of race, but chose instead to defer to the Department of
Welfare's decision, citing as precedent the 1955 District of Columbia Court of
Appeals decision.

That same year, the Ohio Court of Appeals rejected the approach of the D.C.
Court of Appeals and ruled that the child's best interests, rather than race,
should be the determining factor in adoption cases.[7] In this case, the probate
court in Cleveland, Ohio, denied a petition for adoption because of the racial
background of both the intended adoptive parents and the child.[8] A white male
and his naturalized Japanese wife sought to adopt an English and Puerto Rican
child born out of wedlock who had been placed in a social agency. Because of
the child's racial background, the agency had difficulty placing her in foster
care. Eventually, the child was placed with the petitioners for adoption. The
agency reported to the court that its investigation revealed the intended adoptive
parents to be qualified to assume their roles, but the court declined to follow
the agency's recommendation.

The Ohio Court of Appeals ruled that the child's best interests should be the
decisive factor in the proceeding, especially since the social agency fully en-

dorsed the petitioners as highly capable. The court ordered the probate court to grant the adoption petition.[9]

In 1973, in *Lucas v. Kreischer*,[10] the Pennsylvania Supreme Court held that the Pennsylvania Superior Court and the Court of Common Pleas had both erred in awarding custody of three white children to their biological father because the children's mother had married a black man. Immediately after their parents' separation, the children had lived with their mother for a short period of time before going to stay with their paternal grandparents until the mother could find adequate housing. While the mother was looking for housing, the children moved from their paternal grandparents' home to their father's home. The father subsequently requested that the mother take the children to live with her, and she agreed. At that time, the mother was sharing an apartment with a black man. Shortly after their divorce, both parents remarried, the father to a white woman and the mother to the black man with whom she had been living. Within weeks of the mother's second marriage, the children's father asked for and received permission from his former wife to take the children to his home for a visit. He then refused to return them. The mother petitioned for their return. The Court of Common Pleas awarded custody to the father, stating that although the biological mother and her husband were "fit persons to have custody of the children . . . [the children would be near certain casualties of the] almost universal prejudice and intolerance of interracial marriage."[11]

On appeal, the Pennsylvania Superior Court affirmed the ruling below. The dissenting opinion[12] faulted the majority for relying on an "ancient phobia." "This bias (against racial intermarriage), however silly and unreasonable, is also exhibited toward the children (of interracial marriages); and it must be admitted the plight of these children in the past has not been a happy one and in our opinion, this ancient phobia merits consideration in this case."[13] The dissenting opinion argued that the proper basis for deciding custody cases is on the "presumption that children of tender years should remain with their natural mother"—a rule of law so ingrained and generally accepted as to be almost a given. Moreover, the dissenting opinion stated:

The "separate but equal" racial doctrine was condemned a decade ago in *Brown v. Board of Education*.[14] Subsequent decisional law has made it axiomatic that no State can directly dictate or casually promote a distinction in the treatment of persons solely on the basis of their color. To be within the condemnation, the governmental action need not effectuate segregation of facilities directly. The result of the statute or policy must not tend to separate individuals by reason of difference in race or color. No form of State discrimination, no matter how subtle, is permissible under the guarantees of the Fourteenth Amendment freedoms.[15]

The Pennsylvania Supreme Court, in reversing the superior court and granting custody to the mother, stated: "The real issue posed by this appeal is, whether a subsequent interracial marriage by the mother, in and of itself, is such a compelling reason as will warrant a court in denying her the custody of her children. We rule it is not.''[16]

But in 1977 the Fifth Circuit Court of Appeals upheld a Georgia county Department of Family and Children's Services denial of the petition of Mr. and Mrs. Drummond, a white couple, to adopt their three-year-old racially mixed foster son.[17] The child had been placed for temporary care in the Drummonds' home when he was one month old. Within a year the Drummonds requested permission to adopt him. The court upheld the agency denial based on the racial differences between the foster parents and the child. The court[18] held that in locating the most appropriate adoptive family, legitimate consideration should be given to their respective races. The U.S. Supreme Court declined to review the Fifth Circuit Court's decision. In its opinion denying certiorari, the Supreme Court stated:

It is obvious that race did enter into the decision of the Department. It appears to the Court that the consideration of race was properly directed to the best interest of the child and was not an automatic type of thing or of placement, that is, that all blacks go to black families, all whites go to white families, and all mixed children go to black families which would be prohibited.

The court cited professional literature on the subject of transracial child placement and stated that ''a couple has no right to adopt a child it is not equipped to rear.''[19]

Just one year after the Fifth Circuit Court's ruling that race was an important consideration in child custody cases, a New Mexico court[20] reversed the state's Department of Human Resources' decision to deny a request from a Mormon couple to adopt their nine-month-old racially mixed (black and white) foster son. The boy had been placed with the family when he was four days old. In opposing the adoption, the Department of Human Resources noted that the Church of Jesus Christ of Latter-Day Saints (Mormons) barred nonwhites from priesthood. The trial court disagreed with the department's decision, citing the positive characteristics of the adoptive family. Interestingly, one month prior to this decision, the Mormon church had revoked its long-standing practice of barring nonwhites from the priesthood.[21]

In 1979, a Connecticut superior court followed the Fifth Circuit Court's ruling and upheld a decision made by the Department of Children and Youth denying the petition of white foster parents to adopt the four-month-old black infant placed with them since birth. The court ruled[22] that it was appropriate for the state to consider the racial backgrounds of the child and the prospective parents in deciding whether to grant the adoption:

The court has no doubt that the plaintiffs are excellent foster parents. Unfortunately, no family in our present society can be an island. Granted that society and the community should not harbor attitudes against interracial mixture, the subject of the foster-home placement and the adoption is the child, whose life will be affected by the community values and prejudices as they exist, not as they ought to be.[23]

In addition to racial differences as one reason to oppose the adoption, the court also noted other factors, including the state's policy of discouraging foster parents' petitions for children already in their care. The policy was intended to prevent "child shopping." Another consideration was the fact that the foster mother was pregnant with her third child. The prospective parents believed that in addition to the state's policy toward transracial adoption, the court denied their petition because the parents were of the Baha'i faith.[24]

In 1980, in *Kramer v. Kramer*[25] the Iowa Supreme Court ruled that race should not be a determining factor in deciding child custody cases. In this case, a divorcing white couple were disputing the custody of their two minor children. Shortly after the couple separated, the husband returned to the family home and found a black man sleeping on the couch. The wife stated that she had had sexual relations with the man and that he had moved to the couch when the daughter had come into the bedroom. The woman also stated that she had sexual relations with the man on two or three occasions. At the time of the divorce trial, she testified that she had not seen the man for over five weeks and that she had no intentions of marrying him. The trial court stated that to allow a "biracial relationship . . . to exist in the presence of the children is not in their best interest and is going to make their lives in the future much more difficult."[26] The court awarded the father custody of the children.

On appeal, the Iowa Supreme Court reversed and held that "the trial court erred in basing its custody decision primarily on racial considerations" and that race cannot be a decisive factor in questions of custody.[27] The father retained custody, however, because the court found the mother's emotional instability a compelling reason not to reverse the original custody decree.

In deciding *Kramer,* the Iowa Supreme Court developed a set of principles to be applied in Iowa adoption cases:

1. Unsubstantiated judicial predictions concerning the effects of racial prejudices in the community are not proper considerations in child custody issues.
2. Child custody decisions should not be affected by the existence of racial tension or prejudice in the community unless it can be clearly demonstrated that this tension is specifically relevant to the decision.
3. Even when race is shown to be relevant as evidence, race should serve only as one of several considerations.

Also in 1980, the Iowa Supreme Court decided *Mikelson v. Mikelson.*[28] In this case, a white couple, who had one son born to them four years earlier, adopted two biracial infants, a boy and a girl born one year apart, each with one black parent. Ten years after the transracial adoption, the couple divorced.

They agreed that all three children should remain with the mother and that the father should pay child support and have visitation rights. Eight months after the divorce, with both parents' consent, the biological son returned to his father's home, leaving the two transracially adopted children with their mother. The father then petitioned the court for custody of his remaining two (transracially adopted) children, who continued to live with his former wife. As one of the grounds for seeking custody, the father contended that the children's mother "did not adequately assist them in developing a positive view of their racial identity."[29] As evidence that he would be more equipped to parent his transracially adopted children, he cited his role as a Unitarian minister, his friendships with black people, and his election to the vice presidency of the local chapter of the National Association for the Advancement of Colored People (NAACP). The father claimed that he would be better able to help his children "associate with black persons in order to establish a sense of their own black identity and to appreciate black values."[30]

The Iowa Supreme Court acknowledged that even though the children's mother did not herself have any black friends, the children did, and that, "on balance, she had done well for the children and has been a good parent."[31] In citing their previous decision in *Kramer v. Kramer*,[32] in which the court held that race "is not a controlling factor in child custody adjudication," the Iowa Supreme Court denied the father's appeal for custody of his transracially adopted children.[33] It could not, however, resist commenting on its reluctance regarding this type of permanent child placement:

Impressive evidence was received concerning special problems in transracial adoptions. Black children adopted by white parents risk a loss of identity which affects their self-esteem, their ability to cope with community prejudice, and their relationship as adults with black peers. In addition, they risk being deprived of the enriching influence of black culture.[34]

Finding in a third 1980 case, the Michigan Court of Appeals went even further than the Iowa Supreme Court in limiting the role of race in child custody cases. In *Edel v. Edel*[35] a white couple were each suing for custody of their minor daughter. The court, citing the mother's plans to marry a black man[36] and the continuous adjustment difficulties the child was certain to experience if she were to live with parents of different races, awarded custody to the father.

The mother appealed and the Michigan Court of Appeals determined that race should not be a consideration in establishing the best interests of the child. The court stated:

There has been a marked increase in the United States in recent years of interracial marriages and transracial adoptions, and sociological studies establishing that children raised in a home consisting of a father and a mother who are of different races do not suffer from this circumstance.[37]

This statement, acknowledging that transracial adoptions cause no detrimental effects to a child's welfare, supported the court of appeal's position that it is unreasonable to consider race a factor in deciding adoption cases and that such consideration should be prohibited.

In the New York case of *Farmer v. Farmer*,[38] race was once again held to be but one of several factors to be considered in adoption cases. A divorcing interracial couple (black husband, white wife) each sued for custody of their six-year-old daughter. The father's petition asserted that his daughter would be identified by American society as black—an undisputed claim—and that therefore she should be reared in a black environment, which he, a black man, could provide. In arguing that his daughter would experience identity problems if awarded to her mother, he claimed that "social and psychological problems can result from the unresolved internal conflicts which are the product of confused identity."[39] One of the father's expert witnesses offered the following opinion:

What I'm trying to say, a black youngster who is raised in a black home, of course a possibility exists that the youngster will still grow up with problems. I [am] trying to put things into perspective. If I'm a black youngster raised in a black home, if I clearly know who I am, if I have all sorts of role models around me, even though there may be a number of slings and arrows thrown at me from without, at least I can sustain myself within the groups.[40]

Witnesses for the child's mother argued:

Nuturing is the relationship between parent and child that accords the child a sense of security, stability, warmth, love, and affection. . . . Economic stability is valuable; emotional stability is crucial. . . . How the parent relates to the child, the parents' communication with the child, which includes the sharing of emotions, is crucial. . . . [R]ace has low priority on the scale of values determining best interests. The color of the custodial parent is immaterial to the child. . . . [T]his child is white as well as black and what will be important to her is how her parents' sensitivity to her will affect her.[41]

The court concluded that:

Race is of little or no significance where the issue is custody. . . . It is simply one of the many factors which may be considered in a contest between biological parents for custody of an interracial child . . . that the best interests of this child . . . compel the award of custody to him [the father] because society will perceive her to be black must be rejected.[42]

In a similar case in Georgia, a white mother was given custody of her son after her divorce from the child's (white) father. Two years later, in 1981, after she had given birth to an interracial daughter whose father was black, the boy was ordered removed from his mother's custody and awarded to his paternal grandmother upon the latter's petition. The mother argued, and the Georgia Supreme Court agreed, that the boy was removed on racial grounds. The high court ordered the boy sent back to the mother. Before the child was returned to his mother, his biological father petitioned for custody and the trial court found in favor of the father. The lower court concluded that the mother was "sexually irresponsible" and had an "unstable life-style." Not only, the court added, was her conduct with her black paramour "immoral and a bad influence on the child," but she had "failed to set an appropriate moral example." The biological father, on the other hand, had remarried a woman with two daughters; presumably the woman is white. The father had, according to the court, "given the appearance of being a hard-working man . . . part of a wholesome family unit."[43] The boy's mother's cries that she was "rejected by a good majority of the community. . . . [I was] rejected by the white people" were to no avail.[44]

In 1982, in *In re Custody of Temos*,[45] the Pennsylvania Superior Court followed the rule established by the Pennsylvania Supreme Court in the 1973 case *Lucas v. Kreischer*.[46] This case involved a dispute between a white couple over the custody of their two minor children. In awarding custody to the father, the trial court placed considerable weight on the fact that the mother "maintained a close relationship with a married man" who was black and whom she planned to marry.[47] Referring to race, the court stated: "As far as we're concerned, it's relevant. . . . [I]t [race] is a factor. There are many factors to consider in a child custody matter and . . . this is a factor. It certainly may not be a determinative factor."[48]

The Superior Court of Pennsylvania overturned the lower court's decision.

This was an error, of the most serious dimension. In a child custody case, race is not a "consideration," or "concern," or "factor." Questions about race are in no respect "appropriate." In stating that race "ought to be" a consideration, the lower court was fundamentally mistaken.

A court may not assume that because children will encounter prejudice in one parent's custody, their best interests will be served by giving them to the other parent. If the children are taunted and hurt because they live with a black man, with love and help they may surmount their hurt and grow up strong and decent—the sort of children any parent would be proud of.

We know that may not happen. No feature of our society, neither religious intolerance nor economic greed, is more damaging than racial prejudice. Perhaps the children will not surmount their hurt. But a court must never yield to prejudice because it cannot prevent prejudice. Let the court know that prejudice will condemn its award; it must not trim its sails. Coke said it best: God send me never to live under the law of Convenience or Discretion.

A court should declare the law. If the court frames its decree in consideration of convenience or discretion, it betrays the law, for it yields to the anticipated reaction of those who object to the law and would object to the decree if the decree declared the law. A court that yielded to considerations of convenience and discretion would not have declared that a black child may attend any public school; play at any public park; live in any neighborhood. The fundamental principle of our law is that all persons are created equal. A court's decree should always exemplify that principle.[49]

Citing the authors' previous work, the District of Columbia Court of Appeals in January 1983 followed its 1955 decision in *In re Adoption of a Minor*[50] and reversed a 1979 superior court decision that denied the petition of white foster parents to adopt their two-year-old black foster daughter.

The trial court had ordered the child placed with her paternal grandparents, who, upon learning of the foster parents' petition, filed their own petition for adoption. Social workers interviewed the two sets of petitioners and recommended that "based on the premise that the best place for a child is . . . with blood relatives," the child be placed with the grandparents. A psychiatrist testifying at trial stated, "Cross-racial adoption always will be harmful to a child and—at the very least—should be discouraged."

The court of appeals disagreed with the social workers, the psychiatrist, and the lower court's assessment, stating: "[A] presumption based solely upon the race of competing sets of would-be parents has no place in adoption proceedings. . . . [Race is] an impermissible intellectual shortcut." The court further noted that the concept of "identity" had at least three dimensions: a sense of "belonging" in a stable family and community, a feeling of self-esteem and confidence, and "survival skills" that enable the child to cope with the world outside the family. In a dissenting opinion, one judge wrote: "[B]lack children in interracial families may be even more exposed to racist attitudes than other blacks . . . their need for survival skills is more acute. White parents, however, tend to be less equipped to pass on those skills. . . . [It is] unrealistic to blind ourselves to color in such instances."[51]

In *Miller v. Berks County Children and Youth Services*,[52] the Pennsylvania Supreme Court clearly considered race an important factor in determining the child's best interest. Pennsylvania law states that the

paramount concern in all custody cases is best interest and permanent welfare of the child; all other considerations are deemed subordinate to the child's physical, intellectual, moral and spiritual well-being . . . the . . . racial . . . background of the child shall decide its desirability on the basis of the physical, mental and emotional need and welfare of the child.[53]

In *Miller*, an 83-year-old farmer and his 75-year-old wife parented a biracial boy (black mother, white father) from the time he was three days old until he was 4 years old, when he returned to his natural mother, a young black woman who had also been parented by the elderly white couple. She was living with a Caucasian man who was the father of a set of twins also born to this woman. The twins, the boy in question, his mother, and her paramour were all living together. The elderly couple asked for and received visitation and intermittent custody rights. After the murder of the child's mother by the twins' father, an act witnessed by all three children, the elderly couple obtained temporary custody of the child. The trial court then awarded custody of the boy to the county Department of Children and Youth Services, after deciding that the couple were not legal guardians. All three children were subsequently placed in a black foster home (the foster mother's age was 39, the foster father's age younger than 50), with summer and weekend visitation rights given to the white couple. Both the trial and the appellate courts rejected the couple's petition to have the boy returned.

In 1984, the U.S. Supreme Court, despite its tradition of refusing to hear domestic dispute cases, decided *Palmore v. Sidoti.*[54] In *Palmore v. Sidoti,* a divorced white mother who had custody of her child entered into a relationship with a black man whom she subsequently married. Because the mother had entered into a mixed race marriage, the child's father petitioned for custody of his daughter. Even though the court found "there is no issue as to either party's devotion to the child, adequacy of housing facilities, or respectability of the new spouse of either parent,"[55] the court went on:

This court feels that despite the strides that have been made in bettering relations between the races . . . it is inevitable that [the child] will, if allowed to remain in her present situation and attains school age and thus more vulnerable to peer pressures, suffer from the social stigmatization that is sure to come.[56]

The court awarded custody to the father, and the child's mother appealed to the Supreme Court, which reversed the trial court, stating:

A core purpose of the Fourteenth Amendment was to do away with all governmentally-imposed discrimination based on race. Classifying persons according to their race is more likely to reflect racial prejudice than legitimate public concern; the race, not the person, dictates the category. . . .

Whatever problems racially mixed households may pose for children in 1984 can no more support a denial of constitutional rights than could the stresses that residential integration was thought to entail in 1917. The effects of racial prejudice, however real, cannot justify a racial classification removing an infant child from the custody of its natural mother found to be an appropriate person to have such custody.[57]

Despite the Supreme Court's admonition in *Palmore* that "reality of private biases and possible injury they might inflict are not permissible considerations under the equal protection clause,"[58] controversies surrounding transracial adoption continue.

Writing in the *Notre Dame Law Review,* Margaret Howard argued against placing nonwhite children into white adoptive homes.[59] Admitting that the number of parentless nonwhite children exceeds the availability of nonwhite families willing to accept them, Howard urged: "The alternative to transracial adoption

. . . is not in racial adoption, but non-adoption, i.e., continued institution or foster care.''[60] She stated:

If the goal is to maximize the possibility of healthy emotional growth, then our best information tells us that a stable family is of paramount importance, and the transracial placement should be made. If, however, cultural identity is more important, then transracial adoption should not be permitted.[61]

In conclusion, Howard posited: ''There is very little to recommend transracial adoption—except that the alternatives are so often worse.''[62]

Race continues to have a powerful influence in child custody cases today. For example, in 1985 in Detroit, Michigan, the county Department of Social Services dissuaded white foster parents from petitioning to adopt their 17-month-old biracial (black-white) foster daughter afflicted with Down's syndrome, who had been placed in their home at the age of one month, on the grounds that racial matching of children and adoptive parents is important to foster the child's development. The foster parents were also told that the child ''had the racial identity of her 'non-Caucasian' parent.''[63] After seeing the child's picture in the newspaper, a black couple filed a petition for adoption. The foster parents subsequently filed a petition as well. The Wayne County Circuit Court ordered that the adoption be postponed until the Department of Social Services could complete an investigation as to which couple would be most suitable and awarded temporary custody of the child to the foster parents pending the Department of Social Services' recommendation.

One year later, in a second Michigan case, white foster parents sued the state Department of Social Services for ''invidious discrimination''[64] when social workers abruptly removed a two-and-a-half-year-old black child from their care solely because they were white. The child had been with them since the age of 14 months, having been in seven prior foster homes.[65] The American Civil Liberties Union (ACLU) joined the suit on the grounds that the department's policy of racial matching was unconstitutional. The court ordered the child returned to the foster parents. The judge described the department's policies as ''absolutely and utterly absurd.''[66]

Several more cases decided after 1986 demonstrate that race continued to be a factor in child custody decisions. After a Chinese boy had lived for seven years with a foster family consisting of an Italian father and a Puerto Rican mother, the court ordered him returned to his natural mother.[67]

The same court also dismissed the abandonment and neglect charges against the mother that led to the boy's original placement into foster care. The judge criticized the child welfare agency for initially placing the child in the foster home, stating:

The young and inexperienced Caucasian social worker apparently had no frame of reference within which to understand this highly educated and sensitive woman attempting to adjust to an alien world. The problems were exacerbated when the Chinese child was placed so inappropriately.[68]

After seven years in foster care, there was no indication, behavioral or otherwise, that the child's placement had been "inappropriate."

That same year, in divorce proceedings involving two white parents,[69] a Maryland trial court awarded custody of their son to the mother. The husband appealed, arguing that the trial court based the award on its finding that the husband's relationship with a black woman was "irregular." The father argued that the court's consideration of his "irregular" relationship was, according to the Supreme Court's decision in *Palmore v. Sidoti,* improper. The Maryland Court of Appeals stated that the court's characterization of the father's relationship as "irregular" was not because of the parties' respective races, but because the parties were living together but were not married. The court of appeals found, nevertheless, that the trial court had placed undue emphasis on the husband's "irregular" relationship with another female. The court of appeals remanded with instructions to determine the child's best interest without placing such emphasis on the father's relationship.

In 1989, in *McLaughlin v. Pernsley,*[70] white foster parents challenged the city of Philadelphia's sudden removal, on racial grounds, of their black foster son, who had been living with them for two years, from the time he was four and one-half months old, to a black foster family. Pennsylvania law required that if a child has been with a foster family for a period of six months or longer, the foster parents must be notified and given the right of appeal if the child is to be removed from their care. The family in question, a black foster family, was given no such notice. They therefore sought and obtained an injunction against the child's removal. The Third Circuit Court of Appeals reversed the grant of the injunction on the grounds that close bonds had been established between the original (white) foster parents and the child, closer in fact than subsequent bonds between the child and the black foster family with whom he was living for the three years since his removal.

Finally, in *J. H. H. v. O'Hara,*[71] white foster parents sued a state family service agency for damages because the agency had removed two black foster children from their care. The foster parents claimed that the agency's policy of placing children into ethnically, racially, religiously, and culturally similar environments violated the foster parents' equal protection rights. The foster parents lost both the trial and the appeal. In affirming the trial court, the Eighth Circuit Court held that race may be taken into consideration in determining the child's best interest, if long-term plans called for reunification with the birth parent(s). The court distinguished the Supreme Court's holding in *Palmore* by noting that the case presented to the Eighth Circuit Court involved *temporary* rather than permanent placement. Moreover, *Palmore* held only that race may not be the determining factor but did not prohibit courts from considering race as one of several considerations. Finally, the Eight Circuit Court stated that

Palmore should not be interpreted as "a broad proscription against the consideration of race in matters of child custody and child care placement."

The history described above of state and federal courts' decisions in child custody cases where either the child was of a different race from the parents or one of the parents was of a different race from the other demonstrates significant progress toward an approach where the primary focus is on the child's best interests *aside* from any considerations of race. Many courts began with the principle that race should be the decisive factor in child custody cases and progressed to embracing the principle that race should be but one of several factors considered, finally adopting the principle that considerations of race had no place in child custody cases. Clearly, not all courts have adopted the latter principle, and some courts have adopted it for only certain classes of child custody cases. Nevertheless, it is clear that nationwide progress has been made toward an approach in child custody cases that reflects a greater concern with adhering to the Fourteenth Amendment's proscription against denying a person equal protection under the laws.

All of the cases discussed above considered child custody disputes between parents of different races, parents of a different race from the children, or one parent and another who, after divorce, entered into a mixed race relationship. Decisions in such cases are complicated by the communities' and the courts' prejudices and biases regarding racial mixing. The courts have been faced with a second type of child custody case that raises different concerns and causes different problems: petitions by white parents seeking to adopt Native American children.

The following cases are ones in which the child involved was a member of an Indian tribe. In 1975, the Maryland Court of Appeals ruled that the Montana Crow Indian Tribe could regain custody of a seven-year-old child born to a tribal member despite an order issued by the tribal court three years prior granting a white family permanent custody of the child. The court of appeals held that as a state court, it had no jurisdiction in the case: "There can be no greater threat to essential tribal relations, and no greater infringement on the right of the Crow tribe to govern themselves, than to interfere with tribal control over the custody of their children."[72]

In contrast, in 1979, a Texas appeals court upheld a lower-court decision to award permanent custody of a half–Native American child (Sioux) to her non-Indian grandparents,[73] but reversed the lower court's decision to terminate the mother's parental rights. The lower court found that it would be "detrimental" and "unnatural" for the child to be returned to her biological mother on a South Dakota Rosebud Sioux reservation.[74]

In 1989, the U.S. Supreme Court reversed the Supreme Court of Mississippi and held that the adoption petition for a Native American baby was governed by the Indian Child Welfare Act (ICWA) even though the baby had been surrendered voluntarily.[75] The case involved twin Native American babies, known for our purposes as B. B. and G. B., who were born out of wedlock on December 29, 1985, to J. B., the mother, and W. J., their father. Both parents were members of the Mississippi Band of Choctaw Indians (Tribe) and were residents and domicilaries of the Choctaw reservation in Neshoba County, Mississippi. J. B. gave birth to the twins in Gulfport, Harrison County, Mississippi, some 200 miles from the reservation. On January 10, 1986, J. B. executed a consent-to-adoption form before the Chancery Court of Harrison County, record 8–10.[76] W. J. signed a similar form.[77] On January 16, appellees Orrey and Vivian Holyfield filed a petition for adoption in the same court, and the chancellor issued a Final Decree of Adoption on January 28. Despite the court's presumed awareness of the ICWA, the adoption decree contained no reference to it, nor to the infants' Indian background.

Two months later, the tribe moved in the chancery court to vacate the adoption decree on the ground that under the ICWA, exclusive jurisdiction over this (and all cases involving Indian babies) was vested in the tribal court.[78] On July 14, 1986, the court overruled the motion, holding that the tribe "never obtained exclusive jurisdiction over the children involved herein. . . ." The court's one-page opinion relied on two facts in reaching its conclusion: first, that the twins' mother "went to some efforts to see that they were born outside the confines of the Choctaw Indian Reservation" and the parents had promptly arranged for the adoption by the Holyfields; and second, "At no time from the birth of these children to the present date have either of them resided on or physically been on the Choctaw Indian Reservation."[79]

The Supreme Court of Mississippi affirmed the decision below.[80] It rejected the tribe's arguments that the trial court lacked jurisdiction and that the trial court had not applied the standards laid out in the ICWA. The court recognized that the jurisdictional question turned on whether the twins were domiciled on the Choctaw reservation.

The court distinguished Mississippi cases that appeared to establish the principle that "the domicile of minor children follows that of the parents."[81] It noted that "the Indian twins . . . were voluntarily surrendered and legally abandoned by the natural parents to the adoptive parents, and it is undisputed that the parents went to some efforts to prevent the children from being placed on the reservation as the mother arranged for their birth and adoption in Gulfport Memorial Hospital, Harrison County, Mississippi."[82] Therefore, the court said, the twins' domicile was in Harrison County and the state court properly exercised jurisdiction over the adoption proceedings. The court further concluded that *none* of the provisions of the ICWA were applicable. Third, the Court rejected the tribe's contention that the trial court had erred in not conforming to the applicable procedural requirements of the court: "[T]he judge did conform and strictly adhere to the minimum federal standards governing adoption of Indian children with respect to parental consent, notice, service of process, etc."[83]

The U.S. Supreme Court, in an opinion written by Justice Brennan, reversed the Mississippi Supreme Court and held that the Native American babies were

domiciled on the reservation and the trial court was, accordingly, without jurisdiction to enter the adoption decree. The Supreme Court did not find the fact
that the children were "voluntarily surrendered" for adoption a relevant consideration in light of the court's stated purpose to address the "finding that the
removal of Indian children from their cultural setting seriously impacts on long-
term survival and has a damaging social and psychological impact on many
individual Indian children.[84]

The Supreme Court's decision in *Mississippi Board of Choctaw Indians v.
Holyfield* indicates the degree to which the courts are constricted in their approach to adoption cases involving Native American children. Pursuant to the
ICWA and the superior court's determination thereof, courts are required to
consider what Congress has identified as the best interests of the particular
Indian tribe into which the child was born, as well as the best interests of the
child. Moreover, parents seeking to adopt Native American babies are frequently forced to proceed in the Indian tribal courts, with little recourse to
challenge the tribal court's rulings in state or federal court.

NOTES

1. *Black's Law Dictionary,* 4th ed. (St. Paul, MN: West Publishing, 1979).

2. *Palmore v. Sidoti,* 466 U.S. 429, 104 S.Ct. 1897 (1984).

3. *In re Adoption of a Minor,* 228 F. 2d 446 (D.C. Cir. 1955).

4. Id. at 447.

5. Id. at 448.

6. *Rockefeller v. Nickerson,* 36 Misc. 2d 869, 233 N.Y.S. 2d 314 (N.Y. Sup. Ct.
1962).

7. It is implicit in the court's ruling that the child's best interests and the respective
race of parents and child are *not* inextricably linked to one another.

8. Unrecorded decision in Cleveland, Ohio, probate court, 1962.

9. *Matter of the Adoption of Baker,* 117 Ohio App. 26, 185 N.E. 2d 51 (Ohio Ct.
App. 1962).

10. *Lucas v. Kreischer,* 450 Pa. 352, 299 A.2d 243 (Pa. 1973).

11. Id. at 245.

12. *Lucas v. Kreischer,* 221 Pa. Super. Ct. 196 (1972) (Dissenting Opinion).

13. Id. at 199.

14. *Brown v. Board of Education,* 347 U.S. 483 (1954).

15. Id. at 201.

16. Ibid.

17. *Drummond v. Fulton County Department of Family and Children's Services,* 547
F.2d 835 (5th Cir. 1977).

18. Id. at 837.

19. *New York Times,* November 29, 1977, p. 18.

20. *State of New Mexico v. Jones,* 107 N.M. 503, 760 P.2d 796 (N.M. Ct. App. 1988).

21. "Mormon Couple Wins on Adoption," *New York Times,* June 19, 1978, p. 12.

22. *Lusa v. State of Connecticut,* 2817, 2780. *Family Law Reporter,* no. 40 (August
1979):5.

23. "Court Bars Adoption of a Black by Whites," *New York Times*, August 2, 1979, p. 6.

24. "Whites Find Black Baby Adoptions Harder," *New York Times*, August 21, 1979, p. 3.

25. *Kramer v. Kramer*, 297 N.W. 2d 359 (Iowa 1980).

26. Id. at 360.

27. Id. at 360.

28. *Mikelson v. Mikelson*, 299 N.W. 2d 670 (Iowa 1980).

29. Id. at 672.

30. Id. at 673.

31. Id. at 674.

32. *Kramer v. Kramer*, 297 N.W. 2d 359 (Iowa 1980).

33. Id. at 674.

34. Id. at 675.

35. *Edel v. Edel*, 97 Michigan App. 266, 293 N.W. 2d 792 (Mich. Ct. App. 1980).

36. Id. at 272.

37. Id. at 273.

38. *Farmer v. Farmer*, 109 Misc. 2d 137, 439 N.Y.S. 2d 584 (N.Y. Sup. Ct. 1981).

39. Id. at 586.

40. Id. at 586–87.

41. Id. at 588.

42. Id. at 589.

43. 168 Ga. App. 66, 308 S.E. 2d 193 (Ga. Ct. App. 1983).

44. "White Who Had Mixed Race Child Again Loses Custody of Her Son," *Baltimore Sun*, March 15, 1983, p. 3.

45. *In re Custody of Temos*, 304 Pa. Super. Ct. 82, 450 A.2d 111 (Pa. Super. Ct. 1982).

46. Ibid.

47. Ibid., at 83.

48. Id. at 98–99

49. Id. at 99–101.

50. 454 A.2d 266 (D.C. 1983).

51. Id. at 267.

52. *Miller v. Berks County Children and Youth Services*, 502 Pa. 110, 465 A.2d 618 (Pa. 1983).

53. *In re David*, 465 A.2d 614 (Pa. 1983).

54. *Palmore v. Sidoti*, 466 U.S. 429, 104 S.Ct. 1897 (1984).

55. Id. at 1880.

56. Id. at 1881.

57. Id. at 1882.

58. Id. at 1897.

59. Margaret Howard, "TRA: Analysis of the Best Interests Standard," *Notre Dame Law Review* 59 (1984):503.

60. Id. at 535.

61. Id. at 584.

62. Id. at 586.

63. "Couples Fight to Adopt Down Syndrome Girl," *New York Times*, February 28, 1985, p. C11.

64. Suit filed by James and Margaret Quinn against the Michigan Department of Social Services.

65. Jan Daugherty, "State Agrees to Interracial Adoptions," *Detroit Free Press,* May 4, 1986, p. A1.

66. Sheila Gruber, "Agreement Seeks an End to Foster Bias," *Detroit Free Press,* May 4, 1986, p. A1.

67. *Matter of "Male" Chiang, New York Law Journal,* June 30, 1987, p. 13.

68. Ibid.

69. *Queen v. Queen,* 521 A.2d 320 (Md. 1987).

70. *McLaughlin v. Pernsley,* 876 F.2d 308 (3rd Cir. 1989).

71. *J. H. H. v. O'Hara,* 878 F.2d 240 (8th Cir. 1989).

72. Edward Colton, "Vista Pair Loses Child to Indians," *Baltimore Sun,* November 14, 1974, p. C1.

73. *Brokenleg v. Butts,* 559 S.W.2d 853 (Tex. Cir. App. 1977).

74. "Indian Custody," *New York Times,* June 19, 1979, p. 12.

75. *Mississippi Board of Choctaw Indians v. Holyfield, et ux,* 490 U.S. 30 (1989).

76. Section 1913(a) of the ICWA requires that any voluntary consent to termination of parental rights be executed in writing and recorded before a judge of a "court of competent jurisdiction," who must certify that the terms and consequences of the consent were fully explained and understood. Section 1913(a) also provides that any consent given prior to birth or within 10 days thereafter is valid. In this case, the mother's consent was given 12 days after the birth.

77. W. J.'s consent to adoption was signed before a notary public in Neshoba County on January 11, 1986, record 11–12. Only on June 3, 1986, however—well after the decree of adoption had been entered and after the tribe had filed suit to vacate that decree—did the chancellor of the chancery court certify that W. J. had appeared before him in Harrison County to execute the consent to adoption.

78. ICWA specifically confers standing on the Indian child's tribe to participate in child custody adjudications. Section 1914 authorizes the tribe (as well as the child and its parents) to petition a court to invalidate any foster care placement or termination of parental rights under state law "upon a showing that such action violated any provision of sections 1911, 1912, and 1913" of the ICWA. See also Section 1911(c) (Indian child's tribe may intervene at any point in state-court proceedings for foster care placement or termination of parental rights). "Termination of parental rights" is defined in Section 1903 (1) (ii) as "any action resulting in the termination of the parent-child relationship."

79. Ibid.

80. 511 So. 2d 918 (Miss. Ct. 1987).

81. Id. at 919.

82. Id. at 920.

83. The lower court may well have fulfilled the applicable ICWA procedural requirements. It clearly did not, however, comply with or even take cognizance of the substantive mandate of Section 1915 (a): "In any adoptive placement of an Indian child *under State law,* a preference shall be given, in the absence of good cause to the contrary, to a placement with (1) a member of the child's extended family; (2) other members of the Indian child's tribe; or (3) other Indian families" (emphasis added).

84. Ibid.

3

Research Design

The research described in this book began in 1972 when we contacted 206 families living in five cities in the Midwest who were members of the Open Door Society and the Council on Adoptable Children (COAC) and asked them whether we could interview them about their decision to adopt a nonwhite child. All but 2 of the families, for reasons unrelated to adoption, agreed to participate in the study. The parents allowed a two-person team composed of one male and one female graduate student to interview them in their home for 60 to 90 minutes at the same time that each of their children, who were between three and eight years old, was being interviewed for about 30 minutes. In total, we interviewed 204 parents and 366 children. The race, sex, and adoptive status of the children are shown in Table 3.1.

Seven years later we sought out these families again and were able to locate 71 percent of them. The remaining 29 percent of the families were unreachable through any of the channels we tried. We contacted local Open Door Societies and COAC officers and consulted membership lists of various other transracial adoption organizations. We asked for information from people who had helped us seven years before. All our leads in these cases resulted in returned "undeliverable" envelopes. While it is unfortunate that we were unable to locate all the original families, we are gratified that we could reach 71 percent of them seven years later.

One hundred and forty-three families received our questionnaire and a cover letter reminding them that they had participated in our study seven years earlier. We explained that we were interested in how things had progressed in the intervening period and that we hoped to interview their children three or four years hence. Ninety-three percent of the families contacted participated in the second survey. Ten of the 143 families did not. The questionnaire focused on their relations with their adopted child(ren), on the children born to them, on the children's racial identity, and on the ties that both the adopted and the

Table 3.1
Racial, Sexual, and Adoptive Statuses of Children Subjects

Racial Background	Adoptive Status				Total
	Adopted		Born to Family		
	Boys	Girls	Boys	Girls	
White	21	21	100	67	209
Black	75	45	---	--	120
American Indian, Asian, etc.	16	21	---	--	37
Total	112	87	100	67	366

nonadopted children had to their larger family units (that is, grandparents, aunts, and uncles), their schools, and their communities. This time, we interviewed only the parents by mail and telephone.

In the fall of 1983 and the winter of 1984, the families were contacted a third time, when we returned to our original research design and conducted personal interviews in the respondents' homes, including the parents and the adolescent children who were still living with them.

Of the 133 families who participated in the 1979 study, 88 took part in the 1984 survey. In addition, 8 families who had participated in the 1972 study but could not be found in 1979 were located in 1984 and participated. From among the 133 families who had been involved in the 1979 study, 28 had moved and could not be located or, in a few cases, when we did find them, we could not arrange to interview them. In 1 family, the only child who had been transracially adopted died in an auto accident. Eleven families declined to be interviewed, and in one city the interviewing team did not complete the scheduled interviews and we therefore lost 5 families. The refusal rate of 10 percent, while still low, was slightly higher than the 7 percent we had received in 1979.

Among the 11 families who did not wish to be interviewed, 2 had been divorced since 1979. The family members were separated, and some of them did not wish to "get involved." Three families had been interviewed by other researchers and felt that "enough was enough." One parent said, "We have gone through a number of family problems recently and this is not a good time for us. . . ." The other 5 families gave no reason.

Going back to the 1979 profiles of the 11 families who declined to be interviewed in 1983–84, we found that in 5 of the families the parents described problems between them and their children. These problems included: the child had a "learning disability that put a lot of stress on the family"; the child was "hyperactive and . . . experiencing identity problems"; the child was "retarded and having personality problems" or had "a severe learning disability and behavioral problems that [affect] school performance"; and "the adoption has not been accepted by the extended family." Another set of parents, who characterized their relations with their transracially adopted child as "negative," traced the problems to a brain injury that had resulted from an auto accident.

In 5 families the parents agreed to be interviewed but did not allow their children to participate for a variety of reasons; these included that only the transracially adopted children were still at home and the parents felt that they were too young (14 and 15 years old) to go through an interview that probed into the areas we were covering; that the children did not seem interested and the parents did not want to pressure them; and, in 1 family, the only child still at home stated specifically that she did not want to be interviewed.

In total, the 96 families had 394 children, 213 boys and 181 girls, 256 were still living at home, and 34 were away at school but considered the parents' home their home. The others had moved away, were working, or were married. Forty-three percent of all the children had been transracially adopted.

We interviewed 218 children. They represent 55 percent of the total number of children born to or adopted by the parents and 85 percent of the children still living at home. Of the 34 children who were attending colleges or universities and considered their parents' home their official residence, we were able to interview a few because they were home on vacation. Some of the children remaining at home were too young (not yet adolescents) to be included in this phase of the study. Fifty-four percent of those at home were transracially adopted. Among the transracially adopted children, we interviewed 61 boys and 50 girls, or 80 percent of those at home. Eighty-nine of the 111 transracially adopted children were American black. The others were Korean, Native American, Eskimo, and Vietnamese. We also interviewed 48 males and 43 females who were born into the families and 4 males and 12 females who were white adoptees.

The median ages of the children interviewed in the three categories were 14.9 years for the transracially adopted children, 16.8 years for those born to the parents, and 16.9 for the same race adoptees. Their ordinal positions in the family are shown below:

Position	TRA	Born	White/Adoptee
		(Percent)	
Only child	1.0	---	---
Oldest child	7.2	35.1	31.3
Middle child	10.8	15.4	12.5
Youngest child	47.7	12.1	6.3
Other position	33.3	37.4	49.9
Total	100 (111)	100 (91)	100 (16)

The third survey focused on how the family members related to each other, the racial identities of the adopted children, the adopted children's sense of integration with their families, the parents' and children's expectations concerning their future identity and bonds that the transracial adoptees are likely to have toward the mainly white-oriented world of their parents and siblings, and the ties that the transracial adoptees are likely to develop with the community of their racial and ethnic backgrounds or with some composite world. This volume reports the major findings of the three studies that began in 1972 and concluded in 1984.

4

Demographic Profiles of the Parents and Children

When we examined the parents' responses to the initial interview schedule in 1972, we were struck by the homogeneity of the families' social and economic status. Their educational backgrounds, for example, show that at least 62 percent of the mothers completed four years of college and 28 percent of them continued on to graduate school. Sixty-one percent of the fathers attended university past the bachelor's degree and 18 percent completed at least four years of college. Sixty-eight percent of the fathers worked as professionals. Most of them were ministers, social workers, or academicians. Among the remaining third, 12 percent were businessmen and the other 20 percent were clerical workers, salesmen, skilled laborers, or graduate students.

None of the mothers held full-time jobs outside their homes. Almost all of them explained that when they and their husbands made the decision to adopt, it also involved a commitment on the wife's part to remain at home in the role of full-time mother. Before they were married or before they adopted their first child, 46 percent of the mothers held jobs in a professional capacity and 3 percent were enrolled as graduate students. About 14 percent did not work outside the home before they gave birth to or adopted their first child.

The parents were shown a list of annual income categories and asked to place themselves in the appropriate one. The median income in 1972 was $16,500.

If, however, one were to predict the incomes of these families on the basis of the educational attainments of the male respondents, it is quite likely that one would predict heavier representation in the $25,000 and above category. The fact that 68 percent of the fathers worked in professional occupations would also lead one to expect incomes higher than those reported. But observing that a majority of the fathers chose such traditionally low-paying professions as the ministry, social work, youth work, and teaching, one can better understand the lack of status congruity represented by high occupational and educational achievement and relatively low income.

The average age of the mother was 34 and that of the father 36. The range for both parents in 1972 was between 25 and 50. They had been married for an average of 12 years; the shortest time was 2 years, and the longest was 25 years.

The Midwest is heavily Protestant, and so were the respondents in our sample. Sixty-three percent of the mothers and 57 percent of the fathers acknowledged belonging to some Protestant congregation. Lutheranism was cited by 19 percent of both mothers and fathers. Twenty-one and 22 percent of the parents are Catholics (which is commensurate with the national Catholic representation), 1 and 2 percent are Jewish (at least 50 percent less than the national representation), and the remaining 15 and 19 percent acknowledged no formal religious identification or affiliation. Most of the parents who acknowledged a religious affiliation also said they attended church regularly, at least once a week. The church played an important role in the lives of many of these families. Some reported that much of their social life was organized around their church and that many of their friends usually belonged to it, especially other families who had adopted nonwhite children. One of the families cited their affiliation with the church as the major factor in their decision to adopt. Mrs. J. explained her feelings this way: "I think when you are involved, when you consider yourself a Christian and are involved in an interracial congregation, it's silly for a person to preach something and not to do that themselves."

Another couple, a family with an income in 1972 of over $50,000 a year, described the church as the center of many of the social service activities in which the wife was engaged. Through their church, both parents became involved in an inner-city housing program and met and made friends with black families. The husband described their life-style this way:

Our whole life-style in the last several years has changed considerably. The church, and our working in the housing program, has really made us more aware of racial problems. The natural social climate of people like ourselves in the society is mostly one of skiing and hunting and fishing and the arts and parties. It is a rather superficial style of life, in large part, I think, because doctors by and large see so many problems in their work that they are not overly fond of coming home from death and dying to see more problems. So they are attracted to a social climate. Through the work with our church we have become aware of other problems. We've met other people in the church who seem more real. Once you start spending a lot of your time discussing problems of your country, the world, your city, race, it's a little difficult to stand around and talk about a skiing trip.

Political affiliations and activities were not as involving as the church for most of the families. About a third of the parents described themselves as independents, about 40 percent as Democrats, and 12 percent as Republicans;

the others had no preference or named a local party (in Minnesota it was the Farmer Labor Party) as the one they generally supported or had voted for in the last election. Only a small proportion, less than a quarter of the group, said that they belonged to a local political club or that they worked for a political candidate.

The socioeconomic characteristics of the families in our study closely matched those reported by Lucille J. Grow and Deborah Shapiro in their study of white families who had adopted transracially conducted in 1974. Although Grow and Shapiro's families were distributed across all regions of the United States, they found, as we did, that the parents were better educated than average. (A majority of the fathers had attended university past the bachelor's degree, and about half of the mothers had attended college for at least four years.)[1] Over half of the fathers held professional or technical positions. Grow and Shapiro also found that about two-thirds of the families were Protestant and that most of the parents were regular churchgoers. Religion played an important part in the lives of the families in the Grow and Shapiro sample, as it did in ours. Many of their respondents, like ours, traced their motivation for adopting a nonwhite child to their religious beliefs and church affiliation.

In both samples, the parents thought of themselves as liberals or independents, but with few exceptions (10 and 4 percent, respectively), the families lived in all-white or predominantly white neighborhoods. In other words, although in both surveys the parents claimed to be more liberal in their political views or affiliations than their socioeconomic status might lead one to predict, their choice of where to live was quite consistent with their status as middle-class, educated professional people.

BIRTH AND ADOPTION PATTERNS

The number of children per family ranged from one to seven, including biological children as well as adopted children. Nineteen percent of the parents did not have any biological children. All of those families reported that they were unable to bear children. The range of children born and adopted in all the families is shown in Table 4.1.

The families who adopted more than three children were in almost all instances ones in which the father or both parents were professionally involved in adoption services, youth work, or social work. They had had prior experience as foster parents, and some had foster children currently living with them. In a sense, their decision to adopt and their plans to make themselves available as foster parents were part of their professional roles.

Twenty-six percent of the families adopted their first child. Since 19 percent of these parents were unable to bear children, it turns out that only 7 percent of those who had children born to them had adopted their first child. In many cases, the fact that parents who were not infertile had had children born to them before they adopted was not a matter of choice, but a reflection of the

Table 4.1
The Number of Children, Number Adopted, and Number Born into Families

Total Number of Children	Percentage of Families		No. of Children Adopted	No. of Children Born into Family
1	3	3	1	–
2	16		1	1
		26		
2	10		2	–
3	2		3	–
3	6	26	2	1
3	18		1	2
4	3		4	–
4	2		3	1
4	9	24	2	2
4	10		2	2
5	1		5	–
5	1		4	1
5	1	11	3	2
5	4		2	3
5	4		1	4
6	1		4	2
6	1	4	2	4
6	2		1	5
7	3		4	3
7	1	5	2	5
7	1		1	6

policy of the adoption agency with which they were dealing. Unless a couple could produce medical evidence that they were unable to bear a child, most of them were "strongly advised" to have at least one child and then, if they were still interested in adoption, the agency would be willing to consider their candidacy.

Twenty-six percent of the time, the first adopted child is the oldest child in

Table 4.2
Racial Characteristics of First and Second Adopted Children

Characteristics[a]	First Adoption	Second Adoption
	(In Percent)	
American black	65	70
American Indian	11	3
Korean	5	9
Mexican/Puerto Rican	5	1
White	14	17
Total	100	100

[a]Forty-four percent of the parents described their children as mixed—black and white—and 17 percent described them as a combination of American black, American Indian, and Mexican

the family, 32 percent of the time he/she is the middle child, and 41 percent of the time he/she is the youngest child. Among those families who adopted more than one child (56 percent), the second adopted child occupied the "middle" position 35 percent of the time and the "youngest" position 65 percent of the time.

The distribution by racial characteristics of the first and second adopted children is shown in Table 4.2. American blacks made up the largest category of adopted children. They also comprised the category of children who were the most available for adoption.

Most of the families wanted a racially mixed child, but they did not have strong preferences concerning the specific characteristics of the mixture. Some of the families, but fewer than 10, said they felt that the problems of adopting a black child would be more than they were willing or able to undertake. One parent said, "At the time we weren't ready to adopt a black child. Taking an Indian child was less of a step."

Another parent said about their experience with adoption, "I was afraid of what my parents and other people would say. But I've changed, and by the time we adopted our second child I only wanted a Negro child."

Comments such as the above also came from parents who adopted Korean or American Indian children. But more typical responses were ones such as the following:

We wanted more children than two. We started worrying about the population explosion. We knew that there was not much of a possibility of our adopting a white child. We felt that we could handle a child that maybe some other people could not. We knew that there was a need for parents who would adopt a racially mixed child. Once we decided to adopt, we discussed who we would like to adopt and we both agreed that we'd like to adopt a minority child. I think part of the reason was that we had both spent two years in Africa in the Peace Corps. Seeing all these differences in people was interesting and exciting and not threatening. And we wanted to, if we could, incorporate those differences into our family. So we decided we would take a minority child and we weren't really specific as to what kind. We didn't think in terms of a black child or Indian child. We just thought whoever needed a home we would take. At the time, the hardest to place child was the black child, and so since we had been in Africa, that was no problem with us. We had some black friends with whom we were fairly close and we decided that was fine. We wanted any mixed race, Negro or Indian, any mixed race. We told the agency it made no difference as long as she is brown.

One of the families who adopted a black child felt that they had been propagandized and given misinformation by the adoption agency. Mrs. G. said:

We were all naive about our racial feelings. We wanted to do good works. We had all this input from agencies who said that no black families would adopt. We gained the impression that the children would stay in institutions for the rest of their lives. We believed that these agencies knew the truth and were telling it to us. Since we wanted to have a different kind of family, one with all kinds of people in it, and since we thought we could provide a good home and since we were interested in black people and black culture and since we had a feeling that we wanted to know more about black people and what their struggle was, we went about with the adoption.

Mr. and Mrs. G. felt that the agencies had deceived them and that, indeed, there are black parents who want to adopt black children. In other words: "We feel now that if a black child can find a black home, that is the ideal. If we were to adopt today, knowing what we know about the interest and availability of black parents, we would not adopt a black child and we would not help or advise anyone else to do it."

Among those families who adopted one child, 56 percent adopted a boy and 44 percent a girl. Among those families who adopted more than one child, 60 percent adopted boys and girls, 22 percent adopted only boys, and 18 percent adopted only girls. The sex ratio for all the adopted children shows that 41 percent of the families adopted only a boy, 32 percent adopted only a girl, and 27 percent adopted both sexes. The overall pattern thus reveals a slight preference for boys over girls. In almost every instance when parents expressed a preference for a boy or girl, it was because they wanted a child to match or complement a desired family pattern. For some, a girl was needed as a sister or a boy was wanted as a brother; for others, there were only boys in the family and the parents wanted a daughter, or vice versa. In only a few instances did childless parents indicate that they had had a sex preference.

The ages at which the first and second children were adopted are shown in Table 4.3. Note that 69 percent of the first-child adoptions were of children less than one year of age compared to 80 percent of the second-child adoptions.

Table 4.3
Ages of Children at First and Second Adoption

Ages	First Adoption	Second Adoption
	(In Percent)	
Less than 1 month	11	11
1 to 2 months	27	24
3 to 5 months	13	28
6 to 11 months	18	17
1 year to 1 year 11 months	11	10
2 years to 2 years 11 months	3	1
3 years to 4 years 11 months	6	2
5 years and older	8	7
No Answer	2	–

One explanation for the greater proportion of younger adoptions the second time around is that adoption agencies were more likely to provide families who had already proven themselves by their successful first adoption with the agencies' most desirable and sought after children than they were to place such children in untried homes.

In 1972, only a minority of the families we contacted had considered adopting a nonwhite child intentionally. Most of them said they had wanted a healthy baby. When they found that they could not have a healthy *white* baby, they had sought to adopt a healthy black, American Indian, or Korean baby, rather than an older white child or physically or mentally handicapped white child or baby. They preferred a child of another race to a child whose physical or mental handicaps might cause considerable financial drain or emotional strain. About 40 percent of the families intended or wanted to adopt nonwhite children because of their own involvement in the civil-rights movement and as a reflection of their general sociopolitical views. Eighty-one percent of the families had at least one child born to them before they adopted transracially. In many instances, the adoption agency told them to "come back" after they had borne a child.

In summary, the demographic characteristics for the first survey show that on the average families had between three and four children. Forty-four percent adopted one child, and 41 percent adopted two children. The large majority adopted after they had had at least one child (although not necessarily as a matter of choice). Black children were adopted by at least two-thirds of the families, followed by American Indian, Korean, white, and Mexican or Puerto

Rican children. When a family adopted one child, there was a slightly greater likelihood that it would be a boy, but when more than one child was adopted, 60 percent adopted both a boy and a girl. About 70 percent of the first adoptions and 80 percent of the second adoptions were of babies less than one year old.

Of the mothers whom we contacted seven years later, at least a third were working full-time outside their homes. For some of them, it was a matter of necessity; for others, it was a matter of choice. Among the women who returned to work by choice, almost all were engaged in professional positions of the type they had left before they adopted their first child. The women who worked by necessity were divorced and had become the heads of their households. Most held white-collar or secretarial jobs. One divorced woman went back to work driving a city bus, then moved into the company's public-relations department. The majority of the women chose to remain at home as full-time housewives and mothers.

In 1972, all the families were intact; there were no separations, divorces, or deaths. By 1979, two of the fathers had died. In 1 family, both parents had died and the older siblings were raising the younger ones. In 1 family, the parents were separated, and in 19 families, the parents were divorced. In 3 of those 19, the father had custody of the children.

Twenty-three families adopted one more child after 1972, and 12 families had another child born to them. Of the children who were adopted after 1972, 11 are white, 11 are American black, and the other 7 are Vietnamese refugees. Thirteen are boys and 10 are girls. Eighteen percent of the parents reported that at least 1 child had left home to attend college or to marry.

NEIGHBORHOODS, SCHOOLS, AND FRIENDS

In 1972, 78 percent of the families lived in all-white neighborhoods. Four percent lived in predominantly black neighborhoods, and the other 18 percent lived in mixed neighborhoods. Among the large majority who lived in all-white neighborhoods, only a few said they planned to move when their adopted children approached school age. Most of the parents saw no incongruity or problems between their family composition and their choice of neighborhood.

Little changed in that respect over the years. In 1979, 77 percent of the families still lived in all-white or predominantly white neighborhoods. The others lived in mixed communities. Several families who lived in white neighborhoods transferred their church memberships to mixed congregations in other neighborhoods. One mother said, "We did this chiefly to give our adopted daughter greater personal acceptance and support there also."

A few of the families who lived in mixed neighborhoods moved there because they wanted a better racial mix for their children. One parent in a mixed neighborhood reported that of the eight families on their block, four had adopted transracially. Several parents said that they planned to move into a mixed community before their adopted children become teenagers.

On the other hand, one parent said that his family had decided to leave a mixed neighborhood because their children were making such observations as "All blacks steal" and "Most black kids get into trouble with the police." The mixed neighborhood was less affluent than the one in which they had lived previously. The parents said that, indeed, many children were in trouble with the police and they were mainly black children.

Grow and Shapiro reported that the families in their survey tended to live in totally or predominantly white neighborhoods in relatively small communities. They also noted that "parents in neighborhoods that are not totally white were almost twice as likely as the families in white neighborhoods to report a high degree of satisfaction with their experience in adopting the study child."

Seventy-one percent of the parents reported that their children attended mixed schools, and 6 percent said the schools were mostly black. With one exception, all the children in this latter category lived with their mothers after their parents had divorced. A lower standard of living seemed to be the major factor for the child attending a predominantly black school, as opposed to a different ideological position or commitment.

Eighty-eight percent of both the fathers and mothers participated in the 1983–84 study. Among the remaining 12 percent, the mother served as the respondent most of the time. Returning to the families four and a half years after our second study, we found that 83 percent of the parents were still married to their original partners; six had divorced before 1979 and two after 1979. Three of the parents were separated. Half of the divorced couples had remarried. The mother had custody of the children in four families, the father in two, there was joint custody in two, and each parent had custody of at least one child in three families. In four of the families the father had died, and in one family both parents had died before 1979 and the children had been reared by older siblings.

The fathers' median age was 44.4 years and the mothers' 43.5 years. In 1984, 72 percent of the mothers were employed full-time outside their homes, almost all of them in technical and white-collar positions as teachers, nurses, and secretaries. Sixty-six percent of the fathers continued to work in professional fields as lawyers, ministers, teachers, professors, and doctors. Most of the others were in business. The median family income was $44,000 (based on 92 responses). The median for the mothers was $12,000 (based on 45 responses) and for the fathers $35,000 (based on 62 responses).

The strength and form of their religious attachments remained much the same as they had been in earlier years. Of the 80 percent who designated a religious preference, 19 percent were Catholics, 2 percent were Jews, and the others were Protestants, with Lutheranism named most often by those who reported a religious preference. Fifty-two percent said that they went to church at least once a week. Forty-eight percent of the mothers and 46 percent of the fathers

Table 4.4
Year in School, by Race and Adoptive Status

Year in School	TRA	Born	White/Adoptee
		(in percent)	
Less than 7 years	3	--	--
7 - 8 years	32	15	8
9 - 12 years	58	55	75
13-16 years	7	29	17
More than 16 years	--	1	--
Total	100	100	100

said that they prefer the Democratic over the Republican party; 53 percent of the mothers and 48 percent of the fathers described themselves as "liberals" as opposed to 8 and 16 percent, respectively, who labeled themselves "conservatives."

Ninety-three percent of the families lived in single-dwelling homes in residential neighborhoods. Seventy-three percent of the parents described their neighborhood as completely or almost completely white. Eighty percent of the parents reported that they had been living in the same house for at least ten years.

In 1983–84, the transracially adopted children were most likely to be the youngest children still at home, 81 percent of them, compared to 17 and 1 percent of the children born into the family and the white adoptees, respectively. All but 4 of the transracially adopted children were still in school at the time of the study; 15 of the children born to the families and 4 of the other adoptees were no longer in school. Table 4.4 shows the breakdown by years of those in school. Among the children at the precollege level, 83 percent of the transracially adopted children, 82 percent of those born into the family, and 80 percent of the white adoptees were attending public institutions. At the college level as well, most of the children were attending public universities, with no differences by adopted status.

The racial composition of the schools that the children attended was described by them as follows:

100–76 percent white	58
75–51 percent white	22
50 percent white	10
Less than 50 percent white	10

The nonadopted children and white adoptees were no more likely to have attended the predominantly white schools than were the transracially adopted children.

The next chapter describes the parents' thoughts about and evaluations of their decision to adopt transracially and their impressions of how they and their children have come through the experience.

NOTE

1. Lucille J. Grow and Deborah Shapiro, *Black Children, White Parents: A Study of Transracial Adoption,* (New York: Child Welfare League of America, 1974), p. 42.

5

The Parents' Experiences

Chapters 5 and 6 provide accounts of the transracial adoption experience first from the parents' perspective and then from the children's. Each account pulls together the experiences recounted for the first time in 1972 and reported again in 1979 and 1984. This chapter, which focuses on the parents' experiences, is organized by topics rather than chronologically, as the children's chapter is arranged. Thus, for example, the discussion of the parents' perceptions of their adopted children's racial identity encompasses the entire period of the study, from 1972 through 1984. The choice of topics was based on the issues reported in each of the three separate volumes. The order of the topics discussed is as follows:

- Reactions of family, friends, and neighbors to the decision to adopt transracially

- Provisions parents made for educating their children about their birth cultures

- Parents' perceptions of their children's school performance, interests, and aspirations

- Friendships and dating

- Children's racial identities

- Changes in the parents' lives, personalities, and identities as a function of the trans-racial adoption

- Parents' expectations about the future

- Birth records

- Advice parents would give

REACTIONS OF RELATIVES, FRIENDS, AND NEIGHBORS
TO THE DECISION TO ADOPT TRANSRACIALLY

Almost half of the parents reported that they had had social contacts with families who had adopted transracially before they adopted their first nonwhite child. For most of the families, the contact was a casual friendship or a professional relationship.

Only a handful (9 percent) of the 1972 respondents reported any negative changes in their relations with friends because of the adoption. Twenty-seven percent felt that some of their friends had drawn closer to them as a result of the adoption. For a few of the families, their friends served as role models and sources of information about transracial adoption. One couple reported that their adoption of a black child cost them the friendship of a couple they had considered their best friends. The others did not notice that the adoption made any change in their choice of friends or in the quality of their relationships.

Seven years later, the response pattern was much the same. The large majority of the respondents felt that there were a few changes as a result of the adoption. Fifteen percent said that they had drawn closer to some friends because of the adoption, and 5 percent said they lost a friend or circle of friends as a result of their transracial adoption. One mother said, "A close friend of mine told me, 'Your son is a safe person to act out your grand liberalism on. He is so handsome and such a good athlete.' " A few respondents commented that their friendships had become more diversified: "We have developed friends of different races that we would not have searched out."

The reactions of relatives, however, and the parents' responses to these reactions were more complicated. Twenty-eight percent of the parents perceived grandparents and aunts and uncles as approving and positive about their decision from the outset. Thirty-five percent said that most of their close relatives assumed an initially negative and disapproving stance but were coming around to the point where they acknowledged their own relationship to the adopted child and the families were on speaking, and generally friendly, terms. Both of these groups included relatives who were just plain mystified or surprised by their children's or nieces' or nephews' behavior. This was especially the case in families in which the couple had borne children.

Of the remaining 37 percent, 31 percent said that their close relatives still rejected the adopted child and were not reconciled with the parents. The other 6 percent reported that contacts had been resumed, but the parents felt that the relations were nervous and apprehensive in their interaction with the child and with them. One set of parents who were still not reconciled with their children's grandparent related an incident in which this grandparent had telephoned the adoption agency just prior to the time a black child was to be placed in his son's home and informed them that he "did not want them placing a nigger child in his family."

One mother explained that each of the three times they announced their plans to adopt a nonwhite child her parents were "shocked"; the shock lasted for approximately three weeks. Another told us that her mother believed "you are doing this [adopting a black child when she could bear her own children] to hurt me."

Some parents described comical instances in which the grandparents were at first shocked, hostile, rejecting, and so on, and then came to love and feel attached to their new grandchild. Their general attitude, however, as expressed in the language they used when talking about blacks or American Indians or Asians, did not alter at all. They still referred to blacks as "niggers" and to Asians as "gooks" or "chinks," and they still continued to make derogatory remarks about the laziness, dumbness, untrustworthiness, and so on, of such people.

Respondents who had become reconciled with their parents after a period of estrangement described elaborate arrangements they had worked out whereby they did not visit their parents at their parents' home (usually when it was in another city) or, if they visited their parents they did not sleep in their house.

None of the respondents reported accepting a compromise that would have involved the grandparents relating to the birth grandchildren but not to the adopted grandchildren. And none of the parents indicated that they had included their parents in the decision-making process. In other words, none of them told us that when they initially considered the idea of adopting a nonwhite child, or indeed when they had pretty much made up their minds to try to adopt such a child, they consulted with their parents or asked them for their opinion or advice. In almost all instances, the grandparents were informed of the parents' decision after the adoption agency had told them a specific child was available and it was only a matter of weeks (or even less) before the child would be placed in their home.

When we questioned these families seven years later about their relationship to family members, 12 percent reported that the rift had not healed. In some instances it had deepened and the family ties had been broken. About 10 percent said that only a scar remained as a result of the initial negative reactions. Parents and children, or siblings, had managed to patch things up. One husband said that his wife's parents had disowned her for almost a decade, but ties had been reestablished last year: "There is still tension, but it is decreasing." Another respondent said that her family cut her off for three years, but they have now resumed relations. One father reported that two of his sisters do not give Christmas or birthday presents to his children, but they do give presents to their other nieces and nephews. The father commented that this behavior causes some problems because of the closeness of the extended family: "When we get together for holidays and birthdays, we tell our kids that the hostility is directed to us as a family, and not to any individual members."

Fourteen percent of the parents said that the adoption had served to bring them closer to their own parents: "It enriched our relationships with family members. Our parents are as loving to their adopted child as they are to their other grandchildren." One mother said:

The adoption [of two black girls] did not affect our relations with our parents, but we believe it has changed their outlook about themselves. My husband's parents visited relatives in Sweden several years ago and found themselves staunchly defending the adoptions which they had originally been against. They now live in Florida and are outspoken in their Lutheran church about racial matters.

The large majority reported that the adoption had not resulted in important long-term change in their relations with parents and other relatives. They also felt that initial hostility and skepticism had long since disappeared.

Grow and Shapiro found that "the more contact the parents had with their relatives, the stronger the expression of satisfaction with the adoption." Our study revealed no relationship between satisfaction about adoption and the extent or quality of family ties.

Interestingly, unlike the direction of the ties with relatives and friends (where relations improved over time), more families reported negative reactions and difficulties with neighbors in 1979 than in 1972. In our earlier survey, 21 percent of the respondents felt that their neighbors' reactions were positive and that relationships were good. In 1979 only 6 percent of the respondents made that assessment. In 1972 6 percent of the families reported difficulties and negative reactions, but in 1979 that figure was 13 percent. In the earlier survey, all the adopted children were less than eight years old and many were preschoolers. Seven years later, however, some of the children were entering adolescence. They were all bigger, more visible, noisier, and more assertive. Two families reported receiving hate mail and suggestions that they move.

One family reported that after they brought their black child home, they received an ultimatum from the City Council ordering them to leave town. The family called the FBI for protection. They continued to live where they had been living, and although their relations with their neighbors were not especially friendly, they and their children did not become victims of insults or violence. Another family, who described their neighborhood as "exclusive," said that they were surprised that they had not received any hate mail, obscene phone calls, or insults scrawled on their house.

By the time we queried these families for the third time, in 1984, the "problem" had ceased to exist. None of the parents reported tensions with neighbors or friends or estrangements from siblings or parents that they traced to their decision to adopt transracially. When the issue came up in the interviews with the adolescents, we found no differences between the responses of the transracially adopted children and those born into the family. The transracial adoptees did not sense they were outsiders in terms of the extended family unit. They defined themselves as having at least as close ties with their grandparents and aunts and uncles as their "birth siblings." Such behavioral measures as frequency of visits and phone conversations confirmed the accuracy of the children's perceptions.

PROVISIONS PARENTS MADE FOR EDUCATING THEIR CHILDREN ABOUT THEIR BIRTH CULTURES

In 1972, we inquired about parents' efforts to help their adopted children identify with their own racial group. Eight percent responded that the children were still too young to do anything along those lines. Twenty-six percent said that they were doing very little, either by conviction or convenience. They emphasized that they were putting most of their efforts into living together as a family. Sixty-six percent claimed that they were doing various things in order to have their adopted child learn about and identify with the race into which he or she was born. The most frequently mentioned efforts involved bringing books, pictures, toys, and music, along with cultural artifacts associated with or helpful in describing the child's race, into their homes. In addition, they joined the Open Door Society and made arrangements for their child to play with other nonwhite children on a regular basis. Since such children were not usually available in their immediate neighborhood, this typically involved contacting Open Door Society families and then transporting children by car.

The following response on the part of a family who had adopted an American Indian child represents an elaborately worked out program:

We're reading a lot of books. We are also buying books so he will have easy access to them once he gets older. We just got some small pamphlets put out by the Vermillion Indians in South Dakota which have concepts of Indian culture in them. Probably on the four-, five-, six-year old level. We've had some contact with the Indian community. We've talked to a girl who called about COAC stuff, and we said we were interested. We arranged a picnic for Indian families and families that had adopted Indian kids. When the Sioux kids who were going around through the Youth Understanding Exchange were in town, we went over to see their show and talked with them. It's mostly a matter of trying to explain Indianness to him and letting him meet other Indians so he can see they are real people. We try to avoid TV shows that have Indians on them, unless there is a very unusual one and it has an historically correct view. It's hard at his age level. It goes through and gets lost. We went to the powwow last summer and the ones who were dressed up were fine, but the others he didn't think were Indians. I think we're doing okay so far. A year ago, I would have said no. But I think it's come this year.

A family with an Indian-black child suffering from phenylketonuria (PKU) described their efforts:

I guess we don't care. I don't think we are really hung up on the racial thing. We'd like for "C" to identify herself as a person. She's very pretty and it's too bad she feels so angry. Whether we can be so liberal if it comes to the point of her marrying a black man, I don't know.

We did try to get some information about Indians. We talk about Indian arts and crafts; we had a black friend who we helped through school. She did baby-sitting for us. We kept contact with her; we have been fairly close. We try to spot black neighbors, and we do keep up with COAC picnics where there are interracial families. We try to keep in contact with people who have mixed racial children. Where I [the father] work we have a few blacks, not many. we have international friends; we have Pakistani friends, Indian friends, from Jamaica.

I think as long as "C" is so angry, it's difficult to know. We would hope and pray that through the years other friends would help her. We had all these naive notions that by being positive about adoption, positive about people with other racial backgrounds and friends and children, that would help. We have bought some storybooks and tried to have things available to show blacks and whites. She very definitely thinks of herself as a black child in a white family and we might as well face it and accept it.

About 12 percent of the parents self-consciously and openly stated that they "are living and plan to continue to live" as they would have if they had not adopted a child of a different race. Those families did not bring artifacts or books that were representative of other cultures or ways of life into their homes, and they did not seek out black children for the purpose of providing special friendships for their nonwhite child. Their main objective was to bring their child into their life-style—to have him or her become a full-fledged member of their family. They have not changed, nor do they have any plans to change, their own life-style. The parents who assumed this position were as likely to have adopted a black child as an American Indian or Korean child. There was no homogeneity of response on the basis of the race of the adopted child.

Seven years later, in 1979, the range and types of responses were much the same. About a third of the families were doing little or nothing in the way of acknowledging or teaching their adopted children about their backgrounds. The other two-thirds helped mainly by exposing their children to books, magazines, music, television, and movies. Almost every family who adopted a black child commented that they all watched "Roots" together. Several families said that they attended a church in which all or a majority of the congregation were black. About 10 families had black godparents for their adopted children. One mother said, "I keep up a running verbal history lesson." Others noted that their children's school was doing an excellent job of integrating the curriculum, using a variety of multiracial and multicultural materials. Thirty-five percent of the families claimed that they observe the holidays of the particular groups from which their adopted children came.

One family wrote: "We observe Frederick Douglass's and Martin Luther King's birthdays. We have experimented with Ghanian, Moroccan, Irish, Russian, and American Indian recipes, and we have learned African and American Indian songs and music and a lot about African holidays."

Another family said, "We make a point of attending different ethnic groups' cultural events." One family with two sons born to them and two black adopted daughters spent two years in Liberia, where the father worked as an engineer.

Some families "did nothing" because they said they lacked the time. Most, however, did nothing because they did not approve of treating their adopted children as "special"—at least in the sense of catering to his or her exotic cultural background. One family said, "We do nothing because we are confused about what to do. We have no black friends." Another family stated their position as follows:

We try to watch TV programs like "Roots," go to movies, and read books about people with African heritage. We're not too great at observing any ethnic holidays in our family so we don't make a big thing about our adopted son's ethnic background either. I feel it would be inconsistent. If we did it for him we'd be obligated to look into Scotch, Cuban, Norwegian, German, Bohemian, Danish and Irish ethnic celebrations too. It would probably be a very good education and would be a good school project, but we have lots of other things to teach and do together with our children.

Almost all the families with adopted Korean children had Korean artifacts in their homes, experimented with Korean cooking, and read books about Korea. A few said they planned to visit Korea as a family when their son or daughter was older. One family was studying language tapes and children's song tapes from the library.

In 1984, the number of families who were involved in activities that enhanced the racial identity of their adopted child had diminished still further. About 37 percent said that they did not do anything special; an additional 13 percent said that they used to engage in various activities but gave them up several years ago. The rest of the families, about half of those whom we interviewed, described such activities as church attendance (in primarily black churches), observance of special holidays (for example, Martin Luther King's birthday), encouragement of friendships with blacks, and introduction into the home of music, books, and food that highlighted the children's racial heritage. One father told us that he was a clergyman and that he devoted a portion of his time to serving a biracial church. Another family encouraged their children to celebrate Black History Month and to read the works of W. E. B. Du Bois, Paul Robeson, and other black leaders. They also went to a black dentist. One family sent their adopted black son to an all-black private school.

Almost all of the parents (85 percent of them) believed that their transracially-adopted children had some knowledge and appreciation of their racial and ethnic background. They gained them mostly from books, courses in school, and television. Friends and participation in "ethnic activities" were thought by the parents to be much less important. Almost all of the parents (87 percent) said that they and their children discuss racial issues, attitudes, and instances of racial discrimination over the dinner table and in other informal settings, usually in the context of the children's friends, some event they had seen on television or read about in the newspaper, the activities of a political figure, and so on.

PARENTS' PERCEPTIONS OF THEIR CHILDREN'S
SCHOOL PERFORMANCE, INTERESTS AND ASPIRATIONS

Questions about the children's performance in school were not included in the first phase of the study because for the large majority they would have been inappropriate. The children were too young. When we raised the issue in 1979, 74 percent of the parents responded that their adopted children were doing well in school and that there were no academic problems or difficulties with teachers. Fourteen percent characterized their children as "slow learners" or as having a learning disability. Ten percent said their children were not motivated and were easily distracted. Two percent complained of problems with teachers.

Describing his nine-year-old black son, a father said:

"X" has never recovered from peer influence in the elementary (and at that time predominant black) school where it was "cool, man" not to know. He was far behind in reading, writing and mathematics. He is slowly progressing with the reading, is below average in sentence structure and spelling, and will probably fail his math. He has the ability, but it is a game of catch-up and he is not a worrier, content instead to ride things out. He is, however, an excellent musician and a very good athlete.

Describing their adopted black son, a mother commented:

"T's" teachers adore him. He is smart, friendly, considerate, and kindhearted. However, at times his behavior is so wild as to drive all the teachers and administrators to distraction.

Of her nine-year-old black daughter another mother said:

She gets along well with teachers and friends. She is a leader, very popular, president of her school. She has a glowing personality but is only an average student. She had a hard time in 1st grade.

In describing problems, a mother described the experiences of her two black adopted sons as follows:

"R," in 5th grade, is having the first good year in school since preschool. He has been the victim of prejudice in school; lack of expectations. His teachers wrote him off. Now he is an average student. Our younger son (nine years old, also adopted) has a severe learning disability. His school has two teachers for seven students. He is having his best year he has ever had.

By 1984, most of the children were in high school and college. We asked the parents about the grades of their adopted and birth children who were still living at home or who were attending college or university and for whom the parents' home remained the official residence. The grades shown in Table 5.1

Table 5.1
Average Grades among Oldest Children by Race and Adoptive Status

	TRA	Born	White/Adoptee
Mean Grade*	2.5	1.8	2.7**

*A = 1; B = 2; C = 3; D = 4; F = 5.
**Based on an N of 7.

are those received by the oldest child in the family. They were culled from all the schools attended by the children. The parents reported poorer grades for the oldest adopted (transracial and white) child than for the oldest child born into the family.

The mean grades reported by the parents in the three categories for the second child are shown in Table 5.2. The pattern is similar to that described for the oldest child in that the parents report higher grades for the child born into the family than they do for children in the other two categories. When we compared the 39 families who had a transracial adoptee as their third child and the 23 families whose third child at home was born to them, we found that again the parents reported higher grades for the child born into the family. (See Table 5.3.)

Almost all of the children who were still in high school or junior high school planned to go on to college. In discussing their oldest child who was still at home, 13 out of the 15 parents of the transracial adoptees said that their son or daughter had plans to go on to college, as did all 21 of the children born into families and all 5 of the parents of white adoptees. The parents in almost all instances said that they agreed with the education and career plans of their children. No major differences concerning future education were reported on the basis of the adopted status or race of the child.

We also asked the parents to describe the activities in which their children like to engage and in which they do well, whether they are leaders or followers

Table 5.2
Average Grades among Second Oldest Children by Race and Adoptive Status

TRA	Born	White/Adoptee
2.6	1.8	2.0*

*Based on an N of 6.

Table 5.3
Average Grades among Third Oldest Children by Race and Adoptive Status

TRA	Born	White/Adoptee
2.7	2.1	--*

*There were no such families.

or good mixers, whether they have stable friendships, and the racial character-istics of their children's friends and dates.

Regarding the children's favorite activities and those in which the parents perceived them as doing well, sports was clearly the favorite for all three groups, followed by music and socializing with friends. The parents also saw their children as doing best in sports. As the percentages in Table 5.4 indicate, there are no big differences among the three categories of children save that the parents perceived the oldest child born to them as having more academic and intellectual interests.

We also asked about the socializing skills and leadership qualities the parents perceive their children as having. (See Table 5.5.)

With little difference by ordinal position or adoptive status, most parents perceive their children as "good mixers." But again, the responses about the oldest child born into the family are somewhat different. The oldest birth child is more likely to be perceived as a loner than are children in any of the other categories.

As the percentages in Table 5.6 show, parents are more likely to see their children as leaders than as followers, and they are more likely to see the oldest child born into the family as a leader than the children in the adoptive catego-ries or other ordinal positions.

FRIENDSHIPS AND DATING

Queries to the parents about their children's friendships were also included only in the second and third phases of our study. In 1979, we asked the parents: "Has your adopted child had problems making friends, belonging to peer groups, dating, and other peer-type relations?" Eighty-five percent of the parents said their adopted children had no difficulty making friends and belonging to groups. Most of the parents said their adopted children had not yet started to date.

Over 90 percent of the parents said that their birth children had experienced no problems with peers because they had a nonwhite sibling. One parent, the father of five birth and two adopted children, explained at some length:

Table 5.4
Favorite Activities, by Race, Adoptive Status, and Ordinal Position in Family

Favorite Activities	Categories of Children								
	TRA			Born			White/Adoptee		
	1st	2nd	3rd	1st	2nd	3rd	1st	2nd*	3rd*
	(in percent)								
Sports	41	55	36	23	48	47	33	--	--
Music	10	13	7	13	12	11	12	--	--
Social Activities	13	11	11	10	4	16	16		
Academic, Intellectual	10	6	--	20	8	--	--		
Arts/Crafts	--	--	11	10	--	--	8		
Other	26	15	35	24	28	26	31		
Total	100	100	100	100	100	100	100	--	--

*Ns were too small.

Our children have all been superb in handling any comments that might arise. I suspect that few problems have arisen, since we never heard about them at home. There is one qualification, when the children first entered the public school system here—they attended a predominantly black school and so they soon learned how to survive in that scene. The need to protect each other simply brought them closer together and the pressures were due partly to the fact that they were white and partly to the fact that they were bi-racial and living with a white family. Apparently they learned street survival methods well and benefited from the experience.

The mother in the same family wrote:

In a community like ours, our children were probably helped. It was the "in thing" to do here.

A father observed:

Our daughter has more problems with her birth brother's long hair than with her non-white brother.

Table 5.5
Socializing Skills, by Race, Adoptive Status, and Ordinal Position in Family

Child is a Good Mixer	Categories of Children								
	TRA			Born			White/Adoptee		
	1st	2nd	3rd	1st	2nd	3rd	1st	2nd*	3rd*
	(in percent)								
Yes	72	72	76	54	76	95	67	--	--
No, loner	14	13	7	25	16	--	18	--	--
Both	10	13	3	13	--	--	8	--	--
Neither	4	2	14	8	8	5	7	--	--
Total	100	100	100	100	100	100	100	--	--

*Ns were too small.

Table 5.6
Leader versus Follower, by Race, Adoptive Status, and Ordinal Position in Family

Leader/ Follower	Categories of Children								
	TRA			Born			White/Adoptee		
	1st	2nd	3rd	1st	2nd	3rd	1st	2nd*	3rd*
	(in percent)								
Leader	48	45	61	58	52	50	38	--	--
Follower	34	32	25	19	16	22	23	--	--
Both	11	13	11	19	16	22	16	--	--
Neither	7	10	3	4	16	6	23	--	--
Total	100	100	100	100	100	100	100	--	--

*Ns were too small.

Table 5.7
Racial Characteristics of Dates, by Adoptive Status, among Oldest Children

Race of Dates	TRA	Born
	(in percent)	
White only	72	84
Black only	14	--
Black and white	14	9
Other	--	7
Total	100	100

In 1984, the majority of the parents reported that their children's friends were white. But among the transracially adopted children, parents also noted that a substantial minority had only black friends or both black and white friends. Among the white children (those born as well as those adopted) the percentage of parents reporting that they had only black friends was between 0 and 4.

Concerning the stability of their children's friendships, there was practically no variation: between 75 and 100 percent of the parents reported that their children maintained friendships over a long period of time.

Many of the parents claimed that their children did not date; they were too young. For example, half of the parents describing their oldest transracially adopted child who was still at home said that the child was not into dating, nor were one-third of the oldest children born into the family or 40 percent of the white adoptees. For the second and third children, the percentages of those not dating were higher (for example, 70 percent among the transracially adopted children and 52 percent among those born into the families). We reported the racial characteristics of the dates only for the oldest transracially adopted child and for the oldest child born into the family still living at home. The large majority of the transracially adopted children and the birth children dated whites (See Table 5.7).

CHILDREN'S RACIAL IDENTITIES

Much of what we learned about the children's racial identities, awareness, and attitudes about race in the first phase of our study came from the children's responses to the subjective tests that made use of dolls, puzzles, and pictures. These responses are reported in Chapter 6. Here we describe how the parents perceived their adopted children's racial identities beginning in 1972.

Seventy-nine percent of the parents who had adopted a white child said that the child considered himself white. Thirty-eight percent of the parents who

Table 5.8

Parents' Perceptions of First Adopted Child's Racial Identity, by Race of Child

Parents' Responses	White	Black	American Indian-Asian Other
		(in percent)	
Too Young	7	38	30
Confused	11	11	11
White	79	5	11
Black	--	38	8
American Indian	--	--	15
Asian	--	--	7
Mexican, Puerto Rican	--	--	14
Don't know	3	8	3
Total	100	100	100

adopted a black child said that the child considered herself black, and 36 percent of the parents who adopted an American Indian, an Asian, or a child from some other racial category said that the child identified with that category. The parents' responses to questions concerning their perception of their adopted child's racial identity are shown in Table 5.8.

Even though objectively there is no difference between the age ranges of the white and nonwhite children, Table 5.8 shows that 38 and 30 percent of the parents of nonwhite children claimed that their child was too young to have acquired a racial identity, compared to 7 percent of the parents of a white child. We interpreted this as meaning that parents who had an adopted black, American Indian, or Asian child were less sure of their child's racial identity than were parents of white children.

The parents' responses to the question: "With which race would you like to see your adopted child identify?" may also be interpreted as being ambivalent, because 11 percent of the parents who were talking about a white child said that they had no preference, compared to 24 percent who were describing a black child and 34 percent who were describing an American Indian or Asian child. Thirty-one and 35 percent of the parents who were describing black and American Indian or Asian children said that they wanted them to identify themselves as members of their own race; the others had no preference or wanted them to identify with their own race *and* the race of their adopted family or with the human race.

It appears then that, save for approximately one-third of the parents who said specifically that they wanted their child to identify with the race that matched the child's physical characteristics, the preferences of the other parents had little likelihood of being fulfilled. It is not realistic for a black child in the United States to have two racial identities, and identifying with the human race has not proven to be a useful substitute thus far in American society, which still places important distinctions on racial characteristics.

One family talked about their son's identity in the following manner:

That's the problem I was talking about before. I guess it's not so much what we would like. It's that we just don't identify with the black community. We're not against the black community; it's just we don't have the background. We don't think we'll be able to instill in "D" the identity of the black community—we're not going to raise him deliberately as a white person, but I'm sure he will be one just because we are. What I hope is that when he decides to try out his blackness, and I'm sure he will—to see how he is accepted by the black community—I hope we will be in a close enough relationship that I can learn from him.

More typical responses about their child's racial identity as an adult are the following:

It's his decision, not ours. Hopefully, we will raise him with an identity toward both groups because he is both white and Negro and if he wants to identify with one group, that's his decision. I would hope that as a mulatto child, and since there are many mulatto children, that he might feel a part of a new kind of race, and of having the potential of both races within him, such as exists in Hawaii where the people are all mixed races. I would feel better if he chose to identify with the blacks than if he chose to identify with the whites, because I really feel that if he tries to pass for white, we have not done our jobs as parents. But if he wants to identify with blacks, this is legitimate because legally he is a Negro child and as far as society now exists in 1972, he is a Negro child. To most whites, he is not a mixed race. So therefore, I can't say what society will be like in twenty years from now, but as it is right now, hopefully he will identify with the Negro race simply because that's what he is now. Society views him as Negro.

I think he should identify with Indians. He is Indian. There's no reason why he shouldn't. I don't feel that identifying with one means he has to reject the other, however; I think it will depend a lot upon where he's living. If there are other Indians around, he'll probably identify with them. I think, too, he'll probably have fairly close contact with both. I don't think he can avoid that his family is white and most of the people in town are white. I would guess that if there is an Indian group, he will be a member of it. And after that, I have no idea how close . . .

He's Indian; hopefully he'll feel proud of being an Indian and be interested in being with other Indians. Maybe somewhat resentful that he didn't grow up with other Indians and therefore seek them out. I don't think there's any guessing as to how big a thing it will be in his mind. It will probably depend a lot upon what happens in the next ten or fifteen years—in terms of general society as much as anything else.

Another family who adopted an American Indian commented that they really did not see much likelihood of their child identifying with the Indian culture because there is no contemporary American Indian culture and it would be foolish and harmful to identify with the white community's definition of this culture.

Later in the interview, we asked the parents: "What is your guess about the future; when your child is an adult with which racial group do you think he or she will identify?" Twenty-six percent of the parents who had adopted a black child said black, and 22 percent of the parents who had adopted an Asian or American Indian child thought their child would retain that identity as an adult. Not all the remaining parents thought their child would become a "white adult"; indeed, only about 35 percent in both groups said they thought he or she would become "white." The remaining 40 percent or so felt that the child was too young for them to look that far ahead into the future or said that they were hopeful that the child would identify with both black and white, Indian and white, or Korean and white. On further probing, it turned out that practically all the parents who expected their adopted child to identify with the race into which he or she was born also believed that the child's physical characteristics: skin pigment, hair, eyes, nose, and so on, would make it impossible for him or her to become "white."

Seven years later we again asked the parents with which racial category they thought their children identified. The parents' responses in 1972 and 1979 are reported in Table 5.9.

Note first that all but 3 percent of the parents were able to answer the question. In 1972, 41 percent could not answer because they did not know or did not believe that their children had acquired racial identities; and, among the 60 percent who did answer, 40 percent thought that their children identified as black. By 1979, 45 percent thought their children identified themselves as black. Twenty-three percent said their children viewed themselves as both black and white. Thus, in 1979, 60 percent more parents said that they thought their children perceived themselves as black or partly black than they did seven years earlier.

One mother described her son's identity as "reluctantly black." She wrote:

We have urged him to accept that he is black. We have tried to make him proud of his black heritage. He now accepts that he is black, but I think he'd be happy to pass for white.

In another family of three children, the father described his two adopted children's racial identifications. His adopted son was seven and a half and black; his adopted daughter was nine and part black, part Indian, and mostly white.

Table 5.9
Parents' Perceptions of Their First Adopted Child's Racial Identity

	1972	1979
	(in percent)	
White	19	15
Black	24	45
American Indian	5	7
Korean	3	2
Holds mixed identity	8[a]	23[b]
		5[c]
Child is too young to have acquired a racial identity	30	--
Child is confused but beginning to wonder about the matter	8	--
Do not know	3	3

[a]Includes black and white or American Indian and black.
[b]Black and white.
[c]Korean and black.

"J" has some problems feeling secure with the toughest black kids in our neighborhood. He has been reluctant for them to know his parents are white for fear they'll tease him. So far he is learning to hold his own despite his fears. He's been practicing judo to build his self-esteem. He has also expressed twice a desire to be white so that he wouldn't be the only different [one]. "I know I look good brown, but will I always have to be brown?" We [the family] assure him we like him brown even if he is the only brown one—we wanted him that way. This seemed to help. "K" [nine years old] finds the subject of race and her racial identity pretty painful. In many ways she would like to be white, period. Her skin is white, her hair golden brown and "straight." She can pass for white with many people. There is much ahead for her to work through and choose. In some ways she prefers staying young so she won't have to grow up, and she occasionally talks baby talk.

A similar theme came through in a family with three sons, one of whom is adopted and black. The family lived in an all-white neighborhood. The father said of his son's identity:

"M" is mixed, but doesn't like to be called black. He says he wishes he were white like us or sometimes says we should have another black in the family. . . . I hope he does pursue his heritage if he feels unsettled at all about it when he's older. My only disappointment really is when he says he doesn't want to be black or thinks that that's bad. We've tried to promote "Black is beautiful" and white is beautiful, but I know children occasionally do call him names like "nigger" and he must be somewhat hurt by it. He usually calls them a name in return and plays with one of his good friends.

A mother commented:

I tend to forget that she is black. A couple of years ago her little brother hit her on the foot with a hammer. At the hospital emergency room we had to wait a long time for X-rays. People kept coming up to us and asking if this was the little girl who got her foot hammered. They would look at me in what I thought was a strange way. I finally figured out that they thought I had hit her with the hammer. For months it bothered me. I mentioned it to a friend who suggested that the people at the hospital were probably just curious about a white mother with a black child.

A father observed:

I don't think American society really has a classification of racially mixed, but that is how the boys identify themselves. When we adopted the boys, I thought that we as a family would have more identification with black culture than has happened. Our girls [who were born to them] have a greater awareness of racial matters than they otherwise would and that seems positive to us. We think all four children like themselves and regard themselves as persons of worth capable of good relationships, of assuming normal responsibilities, and of being members of a caring family.

Between 1972 and 1979, the increased percentage of parents who perceived racial awareness in their children and a belief that their adopted children had acquired a racial identity (as black or black and white, as opposed to nothing) represented a major change over the seven-year time span.

In the 1984 survey, we phrased our questions about their children's racial identities as follows:

1. Did you have an identity that you wanted or expected [name of child] to assume?
2. Have those expectations changed over the years? If they have, how and why?
3. At the present time, with which racial group does [name of child] identify? Does he/she consider him/herself [black, white, Korean, et cetera]?
4. At the present time, do you perceive [name of child] as [black, white, other]?

We separated the parents' responses to the first question into two categories: their descriptions of their expectations for the transracially adopted child and for their white adopted child. Table 5.10 shows the parents' responses for the first and second transracially adopted and the first white adopted child.

The parents' responses about their first and second transracial adoptees are similar, and both are somewhat different from their responses about their white adoptees. For the latter, more of the parents (understandably) expected the child

Table 5.10
Parents' Expectations about Adopted Child's Identity

Response Categories	Categories of Children		
	1st TRA	2nd TRA	1st White/ Adopted
	(in percent)		
We wanted our child to share the family's identity	12.2	7.1	28.4
We wanted our child to identify with his/her racial and ethnic background	23.2	26.2	--
We wanted the child to be interracial	3.6	4.8	--
We had no expectations or desires about the child's identity	50.0	47.7	43.0
Other responses (e.g., Christian, physically and intellectually able, successful woman)	6.1	7.1	14.3
No answer	4.8	7.1	14.3
Total	100	100	100

to share the family's identity. But the largest group of parents reported that they had no expectations or desires about the identity to be assumed by their adopted child. Note also that fewer parents expected their second transracially adopted child, as opposed to their first, to share the family's identity. Perhaps the experience of having a child of another race or ethnic background in their family sensitized them to that issue.

When we asked directly whether their expectations about their transracially adopted children had changed over the years, we found that for at least two-thirds of the parents they had not changed. Six percent of the parents said that they had changed their expectations for their first transracially adopted child, and 10 percent for the second transracially adopted child. In both cases the parents had shifted toward a desire for their children to assume their black identity. The higher percentage for the second transracial adoptee supports the

Table 5.11
Parents' Perceptions about How Child Identifies Him/Herself

Categories	Categories of Children		
	1st TRA	2nd TRA	White/Adoptee
	(in percent)		
Black	48.8	47.6	--
White	26.8	28.3	58
Native American	2.4	4.8	--
Asian	4.9	2.4	--
Mixed	4.9	9.6	7
None	2.4	--	7
Other	2.4	--	--
Irrelevant	--	--	7
Don't know	3.6	2.5	7
No answer	3.8	4.8	14
Total	100	100	100

notion that the parents had become more sensitized to the importance of ethnic identity.

Responses to Questions 3 and 4 are shown in Tables 5.11 and 5.12.

About 63 percent of the parents believe that their transracial adoptees identify with the ethnic/racial background of their birth, be they black, Asian, Native American, or mixed. But 27 percent believe that their nonwhite children identify themselves as white. All of these children had black and white birth parents. For the white adoptees, the parents report that one child (representing 7 percent of the group) identifies himself as mixed when, according to the parents, both of his birth parents were white.

Table 5.11 describes how the parents perceive their children. Note that roughly the same percentage of parents perceive their child as black, Native American, Asian, and white (for the white adoptees) as they report for their children's assessment. What is different in the two charts is the smaller percentage of parents who perceive their black children as white. In other words, the parents, unlike the children, do not identify their children who have black and white birth parents as white. The parents are more likely to view those children as having a "mixed" identity or to consider the racial/ethnic identity irrelevant.

Table 5.12
Parents' Current Perceptions of Child's Identity

| | Categories of Children | | |
Categories	1st TRA	2nd TRA	White/Adoptee
	(in percent)		
Black	42.7	45.2	--
White	10.7	9.6	64
Native American	1.2	4.8	--
Asian	4.9	7.1	--
Mixed	8.5	14.3	--
None	6.1	7.1	--
Other	2.4	--	--
Irrelevant	20.8	7.1	14
No answer	2.7	4.8	22
Total	100	100	100

Thus the data in Tables 5.11 and 5.12 indicate that the parents are not imposing (at least explicitly) a "white" identity on their "black and white" transracial adoptees.

In the study done by Ruth G. McRoy and Louis A. Zurcher of 30 black adolescents who had been transracially adopted and 30 black adolescents who had been adopted by black parents, the parents were asked to "denote their children's racial background."[1] Eighty-three percent of the inracial adopted parents (black parents with black children) listed their child's background as black/black and 17 percent as black/white. Among the white parents who adopted black children, 27 percent reported their child's racial background as black/black, 57 percent as black/white, and the other 16 percent as black/Mexican, Indian, Korean, or Latin American. McRoy and Zurcher commented that 60 percent of the parents of transracial adoptees "seemed to have taken a color-blind attitude to racial differences between the adoptee and family."[2] They described these families as living in predominantly white communities with their adopted children attending predominantly white schools. They reported that 20 percent of the parents of transracial adoptees acknowledged the adoptees' racial identity and the need to provide black role models for them. Those parents enrolled their child into an integrated school, moved to a neighborhood on the fringes of the black community or to an integrated neighborhood, or became members of a church located in the black community. Their children expressed an interest in contact with other blacks and often discussed racial identity issues with their parents and peers.

Another 20 percent of the transracial families had adopted several black children and acknowledged that their family was no longer white but interracial. They enrolled their children in integrated schools. Racial discussions and confrontations in the home were common. The children were taught to emphasize their black racial heritage.

Comparing the parents' responses in our study against the McRoy-Zurcher data, we note that even after combining all of the parents who responded "none," "irrelevant," and "no answer" to the question of how the parent identifies the child, we come up with only 31 percent who might fit the "color-blind" response that is reportedly 60 percent of the responses of families with transracial adoptees in the McRoy-Zurcher study. And even after including the 10 percent who said that they identify their transracial adoptee as white, we still report a smaller percentage of parents who appear to overlook the "race issue."

We asked the parents in our study whether any of their transracially adopted children talked to them about slurs or insults that they might have received because of their color or racial background. Sixty-five percent of the parents said that their children had told them about at least one incident. Eight percent of the parents thought their children might have encountered such experiences but chose not to talk to them about it. The incidents that were reported to the parents by their children almost always involved name calling ("nigger," "jungle bunny," "chinkman," "Pearl Harbor," "gook," and so on) by other children. One family told us that some children in school had put up a sign on the wall that read: "KKK" and "Kill the Nigger Dog." The principal found out who was involved and suspended those pupils. Seven parents said that the incident related by their children involved an insulting remark by a teacher or the parent of a friend.

Almost all of the parents reacted to their child's report by discussing the experience and trying to help the child deal with it. They explained to the children that as they grew up they were likely to encounter other such experiences and some would perhaps be of a more serious nature. In those instances in which other adults were involved (teachers or parents of friends), the parents went to the school or to the home of the parent involved. On one occasion when the parent called on a mother who had pushed the son to the floor and called him "nigger," the mother's response was: "You should not have adopted a nigger." The parents did not believe that these incidents, hurt and angered as the children were by them when they occurred, were likely to leave lasting impressions or scars.

CHANGES IN THE PARENTS' LIVES, PERSONALITIES, AND IDENTITIES AS A FUNCTION OF THE TRANSRACIAL ADOPTION

A theme that we kept coming back to in our interviews with the parents was how their decision to adopt a child of a different race might have changed each of them as individuals and as a family. During the first phase of the study, 63 percent of the parents claimed that some changes had occurred in their personality and in their attitudes. An additional 19 percent recognized changes in themselves, but attributed them to the fact that they had become parents for the first time. Most of the 63 percent who attributed the changes in themselves to the fact that they had adopted transracially claimed that they had become more racially and socially sensitive. They felt that they had become more aware of manifestations of prejudice, and they believed more strongly than they did before in the importance of treating people alike and in not emphasizing distinctions that stemmed from racial characteristics.

A few parents said the adoption had made them realize how prejudiced they had been and to some extent still were. The difference was now that they were parents of a black child, they felt they must face up to their prejudice and in most instances do something about it. One family put it this way: "We have to work extra hard to stomp out this residue of racial bigotry in ourselves."

Another family, however, insisted, "We just don't identify with the black community. We don't care much about racial attitudes. We know we will not be accepted by the black community. I guess the big change is that we are much more aware of our feelings and we do try less often to think of ourselves as white."

Most of the families talked about how adopting a black or Indian child had made them "color-blind," meaning that they no longer noticed or tended to separate people by color.

For the most part, whatever changes the parents reported in themselves did not result in institutional changes. Respondents did not claim that they had joined new organizations or stopped attending those to which they had belonged. The main organizational or institutional change that occurred in their lives was that they joined the Open Door Society. A few families mentioned that they had established closer ties to their church or that they had joined another church, one in which they felt their adopted child would be more readily accepted.

When they were asked directly: "Did your racial identity change after you adopted [name of child]?" 70 percent said that it did not—that they still considered themselves white. About 30 percent said that the adoption had the effect of making them lose their sense of identity with any objective racial category and that they now identified only with the human race. In about 5 percent of the families, the identity of one parent shifted to the race of the adopted child and that of the other remained unchanged.

The same question was asked about the identity of the family. Sixty-nine of the parents said that their family's racial identity had changed as a result of the adoption. The most common response was that the family perceived its racial identity as "mixed"; 44 percent responded in this way. Twenty-two percent said that the family now identified with the human race and that it had no racial identity in the manner in which the term is typically applied. The race of the child they adopted was not related to the parents' responses.

The couple who had spent some time in Africa in the Peace Corps had thought about their white identity quite a lot and were uncomfortable with it. The mother said:

I became concerned, I think, with being a "Wasp" when I was in Africa because I saw the great discrepancies there between people. I felt I was in the minority and I felt a hatred towards whites, particularly Americans. America is not well loved abroad. So I think I was more aware when I was in Africa than I am now.

When we returned to the families in 1979 and asked the parents: "What race do you consider your family to be?" 45 percent answered "mixed" or "interracial," 22 percent answered "human," 3 percent answered "no racial category," and the others said "white." A mother wrote:

We consider ourselves a black family. I have become constantly aware of blackness and have taught black history courses at local schools and gave pulpit editorials at church. At the same time, I know where my white friends are coming from. They have moved on to women problems, but I continue to feel black ones.

While the mothers felt this more than the fathers, it was by no means only a mother's or woman's response.

In response to a follow-up question: "Did your own racial identity change after the adoption?," 30 percent answered that it did. In essence, these parents said that they no longer identified themselves as white. They felt that as parents of black children, they had either internalized the experience of being black or become part of the black consciousness.

Regarding other changes that the adoption might have produced in the parents, 72 percent said that it had affected them in important ways. With seven years' hindsight, not all of them saw the effect in a positive light. Nine percent of the parents noted that the problems they were having with their adopted children made them feel inadequate, giving them a negative feeling about themselves and a sense of failure. A still smaller group was bitter at having undertaken something that wasn't working as well as they had hoped and anticipated.

For the large majority, however, the changes were positive. They felt a sense of fulfillment. They said that the transracial adoption gave their lives new purpose, that it offered challenges to which they responded energetically. They felt rewarded by the relationships they had with their adopted children. It made some parents' lives more interesting because it introduced the possibility of greater variety of people and friends. One mother wrote: "I appreciate the larger variety of children brought around by our children. They expand my husband's and my own group of friends as we get to know them and their families."

Another mother wrote: "I was 38 at the time we adopted transracially. That experience changed me from an ordinary housewife to an active civil rights worker and community program developer."

Some parents commented on their changed reactions to racial issues in American society: "I have a more personal investment now in the reality and effects of racism in our culture." Not unexpectedly, only 20 percent of the mothers said that the adoption had no effect on their personalities, while 37 percent of the fathers felt that way. A mother wrote:

The other children [there were four older children, all of whom were born into the family] are able to have good relationships with minorities and are able to accept all people because they share this love for their brother. It is really hard to put into words all the good things I feel. I do realize that as he grows older there will be problems, but at this point I feel there are none that we can't help him work out.

Another wrote:

I have done in life what I wanted to do and what I felt was right. No one else was standing in line to take him. No one was even interested in looking at him.

On another dimension, a mother explained:

I had been sent to a juvenile detention home when my own parents were divorced. I saw in my decision to adopt transracially that I was taking a child no one wanted. I wish that I had been wanted enough to be adopted by some family.

A father made this observation:

As a consultant to the city's school system, I lead several hundred field trips a year. I know kids all over town. I get a lot of positive strokings in public. But at home, I can't manage my older son. I have not succeeded in opening him up. It shakes my faith in myself.

Along these same lines, another father said:

He shakes my self-confidence. My job draws very positive vibrations from hundreds of teachers and thousands of students. Thus, when he unloads on me about not caring or runs away, it is a real blow.

At the end of the interview, another father commented about his 12-year-old Indian son:

He is a healthy child. In a one-on-one setting, he and I do very well. I like him as a companion on trips. He is very alert to his surroundings and eager to fill in gaps about how things work, etc. If I were to set up an ideal environment for him, it would include lots of space (a farm), pets, a workshop where he could putter and tinker. Trees and fields and places to be active and/or quiet. He would have a lot less opportunity to watch TV and lot more situations involving teamwork and concern for others.

In the 1984 survey, we asked the parents if the adoptions had affected their relations with their spouses. Thirty-nine percent said they felt no effect. About 40 percent said that they thought the adoption had brought them closer to each other. They now shared goals and commitments to a life-style they had not anticipated when they married. A few of the respondents said the closeness resulted from a need to close ranks in the face of a common adversary. One parent expressed it this way:

We have four kids. If we ever run out of a topic of conversation, we can always discuss our son "B"; his problems have driven us to despair, but his beauty, intelligence, personality, and love are also the light of our lives.

On the other hand, 20 percent of the parents were concerned that the adoptions had caused marital strains. The problems of coping with their adopted children had been more than they had anticipated. The parents often found themselves on opposite sides of an issue affecting their relations with the adopted children.

Forty-five percent of the fathers reported that the adoption had no effect on their relations with their wives. Only 33 percent of the mothers felt the adoption had no effect. The mothers were more inclined to see the adoption as having had positive effects on their relations with their husbands. Forty-one percent of the mothers observed positive effects, as opposed to 33 percent of the fathers.

Grow and Shapiro reported that 33 percent of the mothers and 25 percent of the fathers in their study perceived no change in their marital relationship as a result of the transracial adoptions. Four percent of the mothers and 5 percent of the fathers thought their marriages had suffered. The large majority (63 percent of the mothers and 70 percent of the fathers) said they felt they had happier marriages as a result of the transracial adoptions.

The 1984 survey also asked the parents to think back and describe "what aspects of your life you lived differently as a result of your decision to adopt a child of a different race." One-third of the parents said that they did not change the pattern of their lives at all; they did nothing differently. For the rest, learning about black and Native American cultures (for example, foods, art, history, ceremonies), seeking out blacks as friends, sending their children to interracial schools, and attending black churches were the changes most of them cited that bore directly on the *transracial* aspect of their decision to adopt. But the parents also mentioned "buying a bigger house, having less discretion about moving, and having fewer outside activities."

A couple who adopted one child when they were over 40 and did not have any born to them said, "It thrust us into a younger group of people because we joined groups in which our daughter's friends' parents were involved. We also joined with them in racial protest. It totally enriched our lives." Families reported such observations as: "We learned more internal tolerance." One family commented, "We spend half of our lives talking to social workers." Others reported attending black churches, taking classes in Korean cooking, attending powwows in the Southwest. The bottom line was: "We developed an awareness of racial issues in a white society." One family reported that they went to the Human Relations Commission because of harassment from their neighbors. They also felt as if they were "living in a fishbowl all the time." Another family remarked, "Our racial awareness preceded our decision to adopt transracially. The adoption would have never occurred if we had not had the awareness."

The parents were also asked: "If you had an opportunity to start over again, what things about your living arrangements would you do differently after you adopted [name of first transracially adopted child]?" Nearly half (44 percent) said that they would not have changed their lives in any significant way. The others talked about moving into a biracial neighborhood and living in a bigger house. Some parents mentioned living in a less affluent neighborhood. And one parent said, "We would not have done it. Knowing what we do today, we would not have adopted transracially."

We concluded after analyzing the parents' responses in 1984 that at this stage of their lives, when most of their children were adolescents or young adults, many of them were not inclined to reflect on how they would have changed their lives. Perhaps it takes greater distance, more years to have elapsed after the children have left the family home and have been out on their own, before the parents are willing to contemplate and confess to what they "might have done."

Consistent with the parents' reticence to imagine a different kind of life for themselves and their children, the large majority (80 percent) claimed that the campaign waged by the NABSW and Native American groups in the early and mid-1970s against transracial adoption had bothered them, but did *not* cause them to alter their behavior or their decision to adopt a black or Indian child. Among the 20 percent who reported stronger reactions, the most common was anger at the attacks on them. Most said that they considered the NABSW arguments to be "without foundation," "a bunch of bullshit"; "it was wrong because it resulted in children not being adopted." One family told us, "When we tried to adopt a second black child, we were told 'forget it.' We then adopted 'A,' who is Puerto Rican.'' Another said, "What parents can offer is so much better than what our daughter would have had—a home instead of an institution or going from one foster home to another.'' Yet another set of parents admitted that their decision not to adopt another black child was a result of the campaign: "We are not sure we would have adopted had we been exposed to their arguments earlier. We decided not to adopt a third child as a result of the stance of the black social workers.'' Others said that the attacks on them made them feel guilty. But the position of the NABSW also had the effect of strengthening their desire to know people of different races and to think more about race.

Only 8 percent of the parents thought the campaign had any effect on their adopted children. Those who did said that the children shared their anger at what they viewed as the unfairness and the wrongheadedness of the attacks. One parent said, "If anything, it made us more secure because we talked about ethnic and racial backgrounds much more than we would have if the black social workers had not launched their attack.''

PARENTS' EXPECTATIONS ABOUT THE FUTURE

Toward the end of each of the three phases of the study, in 1972, 1979, and 1984, we asked the parents to look into the future and tell us what they foresaw about their relationship with their adopted children, how they would fare as a family, and how their children would be treated by the larger community. When the children were very young, we asked especially about what would happen when the children reached adolescence. Seventy percent of the parents said that they had given this question considerable thought before they adopted and had decided to adopt even though they recognized that their family and their child might be confronted with serious problems. About 12 percent of the parents expressed the hope that American society would change significantly so that the prejudice and discrimination that they recognized currently existed would be diminished to the extent that their child would not suffer. In support of this hope, they pointed to the changes that had occurred institutionally in the United States (largely as a result of the Supreme Court decision in *Brown v. Board of Education*) and in the informed attitudes and feelings that they had seen manifested since the end of World War II. One family said simply, "We're betting on a good world.''

But the great majority expected that their adopted child would experience rejection by many groups that comprise white society and that the rejection would be especially strong on the part of the parents of the child's white friends. They also expected that adolescence would be the first time their child would undergo a crisis about his or her identity. Overwhelmingly, however, the parents believed that the type of home life they provided for their children before they reached adolescence and the emotional security with which they would endow them would see them through the crisis.

The following observation was made by parents who had adopted a black boy:

He'll have a lot of problems. First, he'll have the normal problems, which are tremendous of course; and then added to that he'll have the racial problems out here in a white community especially. There are some people who don't favor social integration on a one-to-one basis. These people are afraid of their daughters being impregnated by black males. They are afraid of a black touching them. There are all kinds of weird fears. He'll have conflicts with bigoted teachers. There are Archie Bunkers in the school system and in the teaching profession, just as there are in all professions. Maybe more so in our community because it's 98 percent white. They are not made aware of their own deficiencies. So they go on reinforcing them year after year and maybe go through their entire lifetimes without realizing they're an Archie Bunker. But when "D" comes along, he's going to make them aware of that. I presume we'll have problems with sex and problems with teaching, and problems with certain homes where he wants to go; those will all be negative aspects.

Most of the parents believed that by the time their adopted children become adults, they would have worked out their relations with the larger society and they would feel secure and well adjusted. Twenty-five percent believed that their children would be able to marry anyone they chose and that color would not present exclusive barriers. The others would not commit themselves and claimed only that their child would find his or her place and would make a workable adjustment. How many of these statements were wishful thinking on the parents' part and how many of them were deliberate convictions was hard to determine.

For whatever weight one may wish to attach to it, it is worth noting that the parents in the Grow and Shapiro survey also conveyed this sense of optimism about the future in general and about the ability and motivation of their adopted children to adjust to the complex status their color and adoption had imposed on them.

In the 1979 survey, we asked the parents to:

Think ahead a few years to when your adopted child is an adult. Do you anticipate that he/she will live mostly in the community in which he/she has been reared, or will he/she seek out a community whose racial or ethnic characteristics match his or her background?

Do you anticipate that your adopted child will marry a person whose racial or ethnic characteristics match his or hers?

In response to the first question, 38 percent of the parents felt that adulthood was a long way off and were not prepared to guess about the type of community their adopted children would choose. Among those who did answer, very few expected their children to live in a black community. Slightly more than 50 percent thought their children would live in the same type of community in which they had been reared: white middle-class neighborhoods. The other 12 percent thought their child would seek out a mixed neighborhood, the type one is likely to find in university communities such as Madison, Wisconsin, or Ann Arbor, Michigan. According to the parents, that was the type of community in which their child was reared, the one he/she was accustomed to and comfortable in. The children's lack of experience in black neighborhoods would make it difficult for them to adjust. Those parents who answered that their children would live in a white community also said that their children were accepted as white or were being reared as white people. One mother reported that her nine-year-old black son wanted to move to the African plains when he grows up and live self-sufficiently with nature and animals in a treehouse.

Sixty-four percent of the parents would not speculate on their children's future spouse. The third or so who did venture a response were divided almost evenly among white, mixed, and black. One mother, who had commented that the family did not do much in the way of observing black culture, said, "I hope maybe a black woman might be able to give him the cultural background his parents can't." A father wrote:

Our children have been raised in a home atmosphere where race has no bearing on relationships. I suspect she [a black nine-year-old daughter] will feel free to seek out someone on the basis of personality, not race; and given the greater freedom of women to do the initiating today, I suspect she will have a relatively easy time of it.

In 1979, it seems that most of the parents hoped that they could delay giving hard thought to these matters until they became pressing. Their responses indicate that about 25 percent of the parents expected their adopted children to pass as white. Those children were of mixed background and probably looked as white as their nonadopted siblings.

When we asked essentially the same questions five years later, the reality of the choices involved was much closer. Of those parents who wanted to express their views on these issues (28 percent did not), 50 percent said they thought their adopted child would live in the same type of community as that in which the child was reared (predominantly white and middle-class), 22 percent believed that the child would live in a mixed racial/ethnic community, 9 percent felt that the child would seek out the ethnic or racial community whose characteristics matched his/her racial background, and 11 percent thought that the racial or ethnic composition of the community would not be an important criterion for the child. The remaining 8 percent of the parents mentioned location, city size, or other physical characteristics of the community.

In response to our query about the racial characteristics of the person their adopted son or daughter was likely to marry, 46 of the parents said that they could not answer the question because they did not know. Among those who were willing to venture an opinion, 44 percent believed that their transracially adopted child would marry a person whose racial characteristics matched his or

Table 5.13
Parents' Expectations about Future Relations with Their Children

Child's Status	Mean Score*
First TRA	1.75
Second TRA	1.62
Third TRA	1.63
First child born to parents	1.40
Second child born to parents	1.71
Third child born to parents	1.56
First white adopted	1.75
Second white adopted	2.00

*The lower the score, the closer the expected relationship.

hers and 24 percent said that since their child had grown up in a white community, the child was likely to choose a person from that community. Sixteen percent said that "race" would not be a crucial consideration in their transracially adopted child's choice of a marital partner. The others felt that their transracially adopted children were not likely to choose a person of their own racial ethnic background because they had met so few of them and were unlikely to encounter many in the future, or they believed that the transracially adopted child would marry a white person but offered no explanation.

Still focusing on the future, we asked the parents about the quality of the relationship that they expected to have with their children, both the birth and the adopted ones, after the children left home. Using a four-point scale, we asked whether they thought the relationships would be (1) close, (2) fairly close, (3) fairly distant, or (4) distant. Table 5.13 describes the mean scores.

On the basis of these ratings, neither the adopted status of the child nor his/her ordinal position in the family appeared to be a significant predictor of the quality of the relationships the parents felt they were likely to have with their children in the future. The only exception was the first child born into the family. The parents expected to have the closest ties with that child.

As for the parents' expectations of how close their transracially adopted and birth children were likely to be and how close the transracially adopted children were likely to be with each other, we found that the parents held remarkably similar expectations for each of the five types of relationships. (See Table 5.14.)

The parents did not expect the transracially adopted children to be closer to

Table 5.14
Parents' Expectations about Future Relations among Siblings

Siblings' Relationship	Mean Score
First adopted/first born	2.0
First adopted/second born	2.0
Second adopted/first born	2.1
Second adopted/second born	1.8
Among adopted children	1.9

each other than to the siblings who were born to the parents. Ordinal position also seems not to have affected the parents' expectations about sibling closeness.

BIRTH RECORDS

In our 1979 survey of the parents, we introduced the delicate and controversial topic of birth records. At that time only 4 states permitted adult adoptees to examine their original birth certificates. The other 46 states all had statutes regulating an adult adoptee's access to his or her own birth records.

In the realm of federal law, the Indian Child Welfare Act of 1978 was designed to prevent denial of tribal rights to which Native American adoptees may be entitled. The law granted all such adoptees over the age of 18 access to the tribal identification of their biological parents, but did not allow the release of any personal information on the identities or whereabouts of the biological parents.

At both its 1979 and 1987 conventions, the Delegate Assembly of the NASW issued similar statements regarding open records. In 1987, the position adopted was the following:

The identifying nature of the information shared is based on law or the agreement of the parties effected . . . The needs and right of adoptees to know their birth origin should be recognized and respected. This right extends to requests from adult adoptees for identifying information . . . The social work profession, along with social agencies, has a responsibility to initiate and support appropriate changes in the law . . . that would facilitate the sharing of identifying information between adult adoptees and birth parents when both parties are in agreement.[3]

In 1988, the Child Welfare League's *Standards for Adoption Service, Revised* included the following statement:

Within relevant statutes, child welfare agencies should assist adopted persons who have reached the age of majority in their search for information about, or their wish to establish contact with, birth parents, siblings, or other members of their birth family, provided that these persons are willing. Agencies should advocate the development of state and provincial laws that permit adopted adult individuals be given all identifying information, with the birth parent(s) consent, or after an unsuccessful diligent attempt has been made to locate the birth parents, as prescribed by law.[4]

The pronouncements of the NASW, like those of the CWLA, are not binding on any social agency. But both groups' positions carry a certain degree of moral authority. Essentially, both organizations advocated changes that would facilitate access when the consent of the principals involved had been granted.

In the 1987 volume, we presented a list of the 50 states plus the District of Columbia categorized by statutory division vis-à-vis their positions on open records. The following is an update of those categories. In the interval, 6 states changed their statutes in regard to open records (Alaska, Indiana, Kentucky, Maryland, Missouri, Utah). All of them left the most restrictive category, "Confidential Records." Alaska, Kentucky, and Missouri opted for the two least restrictive categories, and Indiana, Maryland, and Utah moved into the "Registry" or the second most restrictive category. There were no shifts by any state into a more restrictive category regarding the adoptee's right to have his/her records opened.

CONFIDENTIAL RECORDS

(Records are sealed unless adult adoptee requests that his/her records be opened. Then it is left to the court to decide whether the request is for a "good cause.")

Arizona
Delaware
District of Columbia
Georgia
Hawaii
Iowa
Mississippi
Montana
New Jersey
New Mexico
North Carolina
Oklahoma
Rhode Island
Vermont
Virginia
Washington
West Virginia
Wyoming

REGISTRY

(Adult adoptees and birth parent[s] register. The court then serves as an intermediary in arranging for the two partners to get together.)

Arkansas
California
Colorado
Florida
Idaho
Illinois
Indiana
Louisiana
Maine
Maryland
Massachusetts
Michigan
Nevada
New Hampshire
New York
Ohio
Oregon
South Carolina
South Dakota
Texas
Utah

SEARCH AND CONSENT
(Adult adoptees employ the services of an agency to search for birth parents. If agency is successful and birth parent[s] agree, the agency arranges a meeting.)
  Connecticut
  Kentucky
  Minnesota
  Missouri
  Nebraska
  North Dakota
  Pennsylvania
  Tennessee
  Wisconsin

OPEN RECORDS
(Adult adoptees can demand to see their records from the court.)
  Alabama
  Alaska
  Kansas

Our 1979 study asked the parents: "In the last few years, there has been quite a lot of discussion about open records. Has your adopted child(ren) asked you directly or tried to find out in any other way about his or her biological parents and family?"

We reported that 47 percent of the parents said that their adopted children expressed mild interest, 16 percent told us that their children expressed strong interest, and 37 percent said that their children expressed no interest or curiosity about their birth parents. We also commented on the parents' own attitudes on the issue, noting that parents' reactions were heavily in favor (by about eight to one) of the adopted children's right to know and need to find their birth parents. Nearly all of the parents said that they would help their children locate information about their birth parents after they were 18 or 21 years old.

In the 1984 survey, we asked both the parents and the adoptees about their interest in birth records. The parents were asked:

1. Has your adopted child asked you directly or tried to find out in any other way about his or her birth parents and family? If yes, please explain.

2. What is your position about revealing information concerning your adopted child(ren)'s birth parents?

3. Do you have any information about your adopted child(ren)'s birth parents that you will *not* reveal to him/her? If yes, please explain.

Table 5.15 shows the parents' responses to the first question. According to the parents, about half of the adoptees have shown no interest in their birth parents. Approximately 30 percent asked about them but expressed no desire to locate their birth parents, and about 20 percent have told their parents that they would like to try to locate their birth parents.

Seventy-two percent of the parents believe the adoptees should have access to all the information available on the birth records when the adoptee is an adult. Twelve percent said that they have already supplied their adopted chil-

Table 5.15
Parents' Reports about Adopted Children's Interest in Birth Parents

Degree of Interest	Categories of Children*	
	1st TRA	2nd TRA
	(in percent)	
Have not asked or shown any interest	50.8	43.4
Have not asked but parents have given them information	10.2	3.3
Asked, but parents felt threatened	3.4	--
Asked about them, but show no interest in locating	26.6	31.2
Want to find one or both parents	7.3	18.8
No answer	1.7	3.3
Total	100	100

*The white adoptees are not included because the N's are too small; six children know their birth parents.

dren with all the information they had about the birth parents. Three percent believe that the records should remain closed. Five percent did not answer. The remaining 8 percent placed some conditions on release of the information (for example, medical need, mutual desire).

Seventy-eight percent of the parents said that there was no information that they have not or would not reveal to their children. Those who would withhold or have withheld information did so because the child was born out of wedlock, the mother was in prison, or siblings were born to the same mother.

ADVICE PARENTS WOULD GIVE

At the end of the interviews with the parents in 1972 and 1984, we asked them: "If a family similar to your own in terms of religion, income, and education living in the community asked you to advise them about whether they ought to adopt a nonwhite child, what would your advice be?" Each time, over 85 percent of the families said, in essence, "Go ahead and do it." In 1972, save for 7 percent who answered that as a mater of principle they would not advise anyone on such an important personal decision, all but 3 percent said they would urge the family to adopt. The 90 percent in our survey was almost identical to the percentage (91 percent) of respondents in the Grow and Shapiro survey who also said they would urge both white and black parents to adopt transracially.

Forty percent warned that the family should be very clear in their own minds that they are not making their decision because of their belief in "some social cause," "civil rights," "racial equality," or what have you. The decision should be made on the basis of how much they wanted a child and because they believed they could offer the child a good home. Slogans, causes, and political ideology should have no place in their decision. Most of the parents mentioned as bad motives "proving you are liberal," "wanting to do something noble," and "taking a stand against the population explosion." The good motives were the "selfish ones, including wanting a child very badly."

Some of the parents were quite eloquent in describing what they mean:

A couple should take a child because the child needs a home and because they are selfish enough to want that child. Many of the people I've talked to have this noble ambition that they are finally doing something great for the world. But if you don't want this child very, very selfishly, as much as you want a natural child, you cannot raise him properly. At least I don't feel you can. You've got to want your adopted child every bit as much, if not more, than your natural child. And it's got to be a very selfish desire—not something you're doing for the world. Because when you get down to the nitty-gritty problems of living every day, suddenly you're not thinking about the world, you're thinking about you and the child and your relationship.

The first thing I would tell them is to look into it; contact an agency first of all. The second thing is to sit down and talk for a while and just throw out questions. How are your parents going to accept this child? How do you feel about a nonwhite child? What facilities do you have in your home for a nonwhite child? How conscious are you of race and the racial problems? Questions like that do really get them thinking. Lastly, I think I'd tell them of the joys, because I think that any parent who goes into a nonwhite adoption should be aware of all of the problems first. Because it is not the easiest way to have children. I feel that parents should be fully aware of the problems they will face, for example, how does a parent feel when someone slights their child? Do they take it personally? Like I look on a person who says something with pity; I don't take it personally. But I think this is something parents have to think about and look through.

Even families who had children with unexpected physical and mental problems maintained that they still believed in adoption. The family with the severest problem urged that the couple obtain as much information about the child, adopt as young a child as possible, and be sure of their own self-image.

Only one family said flatly, "We would not help any white family adopt a black child. We feel now that if a black child can find a black home that is ideal. If it were us today, knowing what we know, we would not do it."

In 1984, 8 percent of the parents would not advise anyone as a matter of principle. Six percent would advise against transracial adoption, and 1 percent were not sure what advice they would offer. The most negative reaction we heard was:

We would urge couples not to have anything to do with transracial adoption. We know several close friends who have adopted nonwhite children, and in none of the cases has it worked out. The transracially adopted children have left home and gone to live in a black community. We are glad we did it, but would not recommend it.

Eighty-five percent of the parents would urge transracial adoptions. One-third of them warned, as did 40 percent in 1972, that the family should have their motives and values straight, by which they meant that people should not adopt transracially because they think it is a "political cause." "Do not do it as part of a crusade," a mother warned. "Examine your motives," said many of the parents repeatedly. "Be sure of your own expectations and feelings about why you are doing this. Be open and committed to children. Do not adopt because you are trying to prove a point." "If they have to ask, they may be in trouble," was another reaction.

Forty-seven percent advised: "Adopt if you love and want children. Be sure you have a commitment to adoption." Or: "If a family really wants to do it, they should. It has been a good decision for us. Not without problems, but no child is." "They should decide whether they want a child, not a nonwhite child." "Pray about it. Keep your motives straight. Don't do it to wave a banner, but because you need a child to love." "Make sure you are not doing it out of white liberal guilt. It is not a status symbol; it is a commitment for a very long time."

But among those parents, about 25 percent warned that families have to be prepared to handle "the race issue" and specifically the "transracial adoption" issue. A family who said that they had serious reservations about adoption per se emphasized that "a child has to be young enough for bonding."

Another family made some specific recommendations. The parents advised:

Learn as much about the natural heritage of the child you are thinking about adopting as possible. Be prepared for problems different from those of biological birth kids. Take a hard look at realities, not just the liberal romantic aspects of adoption. Don't go into a transracial adoption naively or romantically. Transracial adoption at the time we did it was popular. Now, some families are having problems with their children. All things considered, though, we'd do it again.

Several other families stressed the importance of learning about the racial heritage of the child and of being prepared to teach adopted children about their heritage: "An adoptive couple should agree ahead of time how to handle the race issue." Another family said, "A couple should strive to make themselves aware of the *real* racial attitudes of their family, friends, and community, because these attitudes will affect them, as well as their nonwhite adopted child."

Twelve years later, we find 85, rather than 90, percent of the families surveyed still willing to advise others like themselves to go ahead and adopt transracially. Stung as they were by the attacks of the NABSW and other groups and tarnished as many have been by the experience of parenting, they still believe that what they did was right and good for their children.

NOTES

1. Ruth G. McRoy and Louis A. Zurcher, *Transracial and Inracial Adoptees,* (Springfield, IL: Charles C. Thomas, 1983), p. 129.
2. Ibid., p. 130.
3. *NASW News* 25, no. 1 (January 1980): 20.
4. Child Welfare League of America, *Standards for Adoption Services,* (New York: Child Welfare League of America, 1988), p. 4.

6

The Children's Experiences

STUDIES OF RACIAL IDENTITY AND ATTITUDES OF CHILDREN

Unlike Chapter 5, on the parents' experiences, this chapter is arranged chronologically. The first part reviews studies of young children's racial identities and attitudes. The next part describes the responses of the children in our study to the projective materials we gave them in 1972, when they were between three and seven years of age. The last part focuses on the children's responses to the interviews conducted in 1984, which asked about their performance in school and their future educational plans, their friends, their racial identity, their place in the family, their self-esteem, and their expectations about the ties they are likely to have to their families in the future.

Empirical studies of young children's racial attitudes and identity extend over more than five decades. Judith D. R. Porter states that Bruno Lasker in 1929 was the first "serious investigator" to study the racial awareness of preschool children.[1] But Porter claims that Lasker's conclusion that "children up to the age of eight are ignorant of racial differences" is questionable, because "he studied not the children themselves but adults' reminiscences of childhood experiences and teachers' observations of elementary school subjects."[2]

A decade after Lasker's study, Ruth Horowitz studied a sample of nursery school children and found that they had a sense of social awareness. Her observations, however, were based on 24 subjects.[3]

The work of Kenneth B. and Mamie P. Clark, which began in the late 1930s, involved the use of white and brown dolls to study the racial preferences, awareness, and identity of white and black children.[4] Their early work serves as a benchmark for most of the subsequent studies of young children's racial

Table 6.1
Percentage of Children Selecting the White Doll

Request for	Percent Selecting White Doll
1. Doll most like to play with	67
2. The nice doll	59
3. The bad doll	17
4. The doll that is a nice color	60
5. The doll that looks white	94
6. The doll that looks colored	6
7. The doll that looks Negro	20
8. The doll that looks like you	33

Source: Kenneth B. Clark and Mamie P. Clark, "Racial Identification and Preference in Negro Children," in E. Macoby, T. Newcomb, and E. Hartley, eds., *Readings in Social Psychology* (New York: Henry Holt, 1947), p. 171, Table 1; p. 175, Table 5.

attitudes and awareness. The basic design the Clarks employed involved presenting black subjects between the ages of about three and seven with white and brown baby dolls and asking the children, "Give me the doll that . . ."

1. You like to play with best
2. Is a nice doll
3. Looks bad
4. Is a nice color
5. Looks like a colored child
6. Looks like a Negro child
7. Looks like a white child
8. Looks like you

Items 1 through 4 were intended to measure racial attitudes; Items 5 through 7, racial awareness; and Item 8, racial identity. With variations, such as the introduction of a third doll with skin lighter than that of the brown doll or the use of dolls other than baby dolls, this technique for measuring young children's attitudes and awareness about race has been used up to the present time by researchers in the United States, New Zealand, South Africa, and England.

The Clarks' basic results are shown in Table 6.1.

On the items that measure racial preferences or attitudes (1 through 4), most

Table 6.2
Percentage of Children Selecting the White Doll, by Age

Request for Doll	Age of Respondent Percentage Selecting White				
	3	4	5	6	7+
Play with the best	55	76	74	71	60
Nice Doll	58	76	72	53	52
Looks Bad	19	24	11	15	17
Nice Color	58	72	78	56	48
Looks White	77	86	94	97	100
Looks Colored	13	17	7	4	0
Looks Negro	29	35	30	17	7
Looks Like You	61	31	52	32	13

Source: Kenneth B. Clark and Mamie P. Clark, "Racial Identification and Preference in Negro Children," in E. Macoby, T. Newcomb, and E. Hartley, eds., *Readings in Social Psychology* (New York: Henry Holt, 1947), p. 172, Table 2; p. 176, Table 6.

of the children exhibited a white bias. On the items that measure awareness (5 through 7), almost all the children indicated their ability to differentiate skin color. On the item that measures identification (8), two-thirds of the children identified themselves accurately.

When the children were divided into homogeneous age categories, the Clarks found that older children were more likely to identify themselves correctly and to distinguish the white doll from the brown doll. But age made little difference in the attitude items. The older children were as likely to express pro-white attitudes as were the younger ones. (See Table 6.2.)

Skin shade, however, did differentiate responses on some of the preference items and on self-identity. As the percentages in Table 6.3 indicate, the lighter-skinned children were more likely to prefer and to identify with the white dolls than were the darker-skinned children. Responses to the awareness items revealed little difference by skin shade.

The Clarks concentrated their studies on black children, mostly in segregated southern schools, more than 50 years ago. Their basic findings, however, that black children prefer white to black, have been replicated in practically every study of young children's racial attitudes.

H. J. Greenwald and D. B. Oppenheim thought that part of the explanation for the high percentage of incorrect self-identification among the children in the Clarks' studies may have been the lack of an appropriate doll with which the

Table 6.3
Percentage of Children Selecting the White Doll, by Skin Shade

	Skin Shading		
Request for Doll	Light	Medium	Dark
Play with the best	76	67	61
Nice doll	67	56	60
Looks bad	13	17	18
Nice color	70	53	65
Looks white	94	92	96
Looks colored	9	6	4
Looks Negro	20	21	18
Looks like you	80	26	19

Source: Kenneth B. Clark and Mamie P. Clark, "Racial Identification and Preference in Negro Children," in E. Macoby, T. Newcomb, and E. Hartley, eds., *Readings in Social Psychology* (New York: Henry Holt, 1947), p. 173, Table 3; p. 176, Table 7.

lighter-skinned black children could identify.[5] They decided to repeat the Clarks' experiment, but instead of having only two dolls (dark brown and white), they used three dolls (dark brown, medium brown, and white). In addition, the questions the experimenters asked were more open-ended, for example: "Is there a doll that . . . ," instead of, "Give me the doll that . . ." Their subjects were 75 nursery school children between the ages of three and five. Thirty-nine were black and 36 were white. The results are reported in Table 6.4.

Greenwald and Oppenheim concluded on the basis of the responses shown that "these similarities to the previous researchers' results indicate high reliability over time. . . . Apparently then, different samples and sample sizes, the difference of an entire generation, the use of different dolls and also white examiners did not bring about appreciably different answers to the basic questions."[6]

But changes did occur with regard to the identification item. As the results in Table 6.5 show, only 13 percent of the black children misidentified themselves, compared to 36 percent of the Clarks' northern black sample. The use of a light-skinned black doll, then, played a role in reducing the percentage of misidentification. The authors concluded that "Negro children do not manifest an unusual tendency to misidentify themselves. However, the similarity of the evaluative responses in all the studies corroborates the unpopularity of the Negro's skin color among children."

Mary Ellen Goodman studied the racial attitudes of four-year-old black chil-

Table 6.4

Black and White Children's Responses to Initial Questions about Racial Dolls

Questions	Dolls	Negro Children	White Children
		(In Percent)	
1. Doll want to play with	Dark	28	22
	Medium	13	4
	White	56	63
2. Doll do not want to play with	D	14	31
	M	56	51
	W	12	4
3. Doll that is good	D	35	20
	M	15	3
	W	50	69
4. Doll that is bad	D	21	26
	M	50	51
	W	10	3
5. Doll that is nice color	D	31	18
	M	8	8
	W	56	71
6. Doll that is not nice color	D	17	37
	M	62	57
	W	13	3
7. Doll that looks like white child	D	5	0
	M	3	17
	W	90	78
8. Doll that looks like colored child	D	73	54
	M	19	54
	W	5	6

Source: H. J. Greenwald and D. B. Oppenheim, "Reported Magnitude of Self-Misidentification among Negro Children—Artifact?" *Journal of Personality and Social Psychology* 8 (1968): 50, Table 1.

dren attending nursery schools in a city in the northeastern part of the United States. She reported in 1952:

Basically our Negro children are out-group oriented. Through all the individual variations there runs this common thread. . . . These children share a fundamental orientation—a sense of direction away from Negroes and toward Whites.

Our Whites are in-group oriented. Individual orientations among them are as great as among the Negroes but this they have in common. . . . Racially speaking they are complacent about the self. Their basic orientation—their sense of direction is around and within the orbit of the White world.[7]

Goodman concluded on this note:

Table 6.5
Percentage of Black and White Children's Selections of the Doll That Looked Like Them

Doll Colors	Negro Children by Skin Color			Total Negro Children	White Children[a]
	Light	Medium	Dark		
Greenwald and Oppenheim					
Dark Brown	22	50	43	41	19
Mulatto	56	19	50	38	25
White	11	25	0	13	47
(N)	(9)	(16)	(14)	(39)	(36)
Clark and Clark Study					
Dark Brown	20	73	81	63	--
White	80	26	19	36	--
(N)	(46)	(126)	(79)	(253)	--

[a]White children misidentified themselves more than black children in the present study ($X^2 = 16.29$, df = 2, p < .0001).

Source: H. J. Greenwald and D. B. Oppenheim, "Reported Magnitude of Self-Misidentification among Negro Children—Artifact?" *Journal of Personality and Social Psychology* 8 (1968): 51, Table 2.

It is all too clear that Negro children not yet five can sense that they are marked, and grow uneasy. They can like enormously what they see across the color line and find it hard to like what they see on their side. In this there is scant comfort or security; and in it are the dynamics for rending personality asunder.[8]

Twenty years later, in 1972, J. Kenneth Morland, who had been studying young children's racial attitudes for about a decade, reported the results of his study in Lynchburg, Virginia. The major purpose of the 1972 study was to determine children's racial attitudes as racial balance was being instituted throughout the Lynchburg public school system.[9] The study involved 116 children (aged three, four, and five) in nursery schools and 103 children in kindergarten and primary grades (first through third), who were interviewed by means of a series of pictures.

Racially the children were divided as follows: nursery school level, 58 white and 58 black; kindergarten and primary grades, 53 white and 50 black. The nursery school children were interviewed in school and the kindergarten and primary grade children at home. White interviewers interviewed white children, and black interviewers interviewed black children.

The children were shown six pictures, which had the following characteristics:

Picture 1   Six white children, three boys and three girls, sitting around a table eating cookies and drinking punch

Picture 2   Same as Picture 1, but the children are black

Picture 3   Six men, three black and three white, in a group holding paper cups

Picture 4   Same as Picture 3, but the people are women

Picture 5   Six girls, three black and three white

Picture 6   Same as Picture 5, but the children are boys

Morland asked the children essentially the same questions about the pictures that the Clarks had asked their subjects about the dolls and added the following: "Which man looks most like your father?" and "Which woman looks most like your mother?"

Morland reported that the major findings of this study were: (1) Black children do not show as favorable an attitude toward their own race as white children show toward theirs. (2) Blacks are more likely to accept whites than whites are to accept blacks. (3) Compared to whites, blacks are less likely to prefer their own race, to say they would rather be children of their own race, to identify their mothers and fathers with members of their own race, and to say that children of their own race are prettier, better students, and nicer than whites. (4) On only one measure, self-identity (that is, which child the respondents said they looked most like), did black children show no significant difference from white children. (5) Preschool blacks were less likely than in-school blacks to accept members of their own race, to prefer members of their own race, to say that they looked like members of their own race, and to say that they would rather be members of their own race. In-school and preschool children did not differ significantly on any of those measures. The data supporting these conclusions are presented in Tables 6.6 through 6.10.

In concluding his report, Morland commented:

A major finding of this study of racial attitudes among Lynchburg school children is support for the existence of an American norm that each racial-ethnic grouping of Americans should have a favorable view of itself. The movement toward this assumed norm was seen in a clear-cut way among the black American children studied. Preschool black respondents preferred, identified with and had a strong bias for whites. However such preference identification and bias were significantly less among blacks in kindergarten and primary grades, and by the end of high school black Americans showed a highly favorable evaluation of and no social distance from "Black American." [10]

A few years earlier, in 1969, Morland had applied essentially the same ap-

Table 6.6
Racial Preference of In-School Children, by Race

Racial Category of Respondents	Prefer Own Race	Prefer Other Race	Preference Not Clear
	(In Percent)		
Black (N=50)	54.0	26.0	20.0
White (N=103)	78.6	6.8	14.6

$X^2 = 13.11$; df $= 2$; p$<.01$

Source: J. Kenneth Morland, *Racial Attitudes in School Children: From Kindergarten through High School* (Final Report, Project No. 2-C-009) (Washington, DC: U.S. Department of Health, Education, and Welfare, National Center for Educational Research and Development, 1972), p. 7, Table 4.

Table 6.7
Acceptance of Other Race by In-School Children, by Race

Racial Category of Respondents	Acceptance	Non-Acceptance	Rejection
	(In Percent)		
Black (N=50)	86.0	8.0	6.0
White (N=103)	66.0	15.5	18.5

$X^2 = 6.94$; df $= 2$; p$<.05$

Source: J. Kenneth Morland, *Racial Attitudes in School Children: From Kindergarten through High School* (Final Report, Project No. 2-C-009) (Washington, DC: U.S. Department of Health, Education, and Welfare, National Center for Educational Research and Development, 1972), p. 6, Table 2.

Table 6.8
Responses of In-School Children, by Race, to the Questions "Which Girl Is the Prettiest?" and "Which Boy Is the Best Looking?"

Racial Category of Respondent	Children of Own Race	Children of Other Race	Neither or Not Sure
	(In Percent)		
Black (N=50)	46.0	28.0	26.0
White (N=103)	62.1	7.8	30.0

$X^2 = 11.31$; df $= 2$; p$<.01$

Source: J. Kenneth Morland, *Racial Attitudes in School Children: From Kindergarten through High School* (Final Report, Project No. 2-C-009) (Washington, DC: U.S. Department of Health, Education, and Welfare, National Center for Educational Research and Development, 1972), p. 11, Table 13.

Table 6.9

Responses of In-School Children, by Race, to the Questions "Which Girl Is the Best Student?" and "Which Boy Is the Best Student?"

Racial Category of Respondent	Children of Own Race	Children of Other Race	Neither or Not Sure
	(In Percent)		
Black (N=50)	36.0	40.0	24.0
White (N=103)	57.3	11.6	31.1

$X^2 = 16.548$; df $= 2$; p$<$.001

Source: J. Kenneth Morland, *Racial Attitudes in School Children: From Kindergarten through High School* (Final Report, Project No. 2-C-009) (Washington, DC: U.S. Department of Health, Education, and Welfare, National Center for Educational Research and Development, 1972), p. 12, Table 14.

proach to a study of racial awareness among Hong Kong Chinese children.[11] He compared the responses of the Chinese children to those made by white and black children in Connecticut and Virginia. The children ranged in age from four to six. Table 6.11 compares the responses of American Caucasian, American black, and Hong Kong Chinese children to the question: "Would you rather play with these children or with those?"

The responses indicate that all three groups differed from each other, but that a majority of the whites and Chinese preferred their own race, while a majority of the blacks preferred the other race.

When the children were asked, "Which child do you look most like?" and "Which child would you rather be?" the three groups differed significantly

Table 6.10

Responses of In-School and Preschool Black Children to the Question "Which Child Would You Most Rather Be?"

School Level	Rather Be One of the Blacks	Rather Be One of the Whites	Rather Be Neither, or Not Sure
	(In Percent)		
In-school blacks (N=50)	64.0	32.0	4.0
Pre-school blacks (N=58)	34.5	58.6	6.9

$X^2 = 9.4$; df$=2$; p$<$.01

Source: J. Kenneth Morland, *Racial Attitudes in School Children: From Kindergarten through High School* (Final Report, Project No. 2-C-009) (Washington, DC: U.S. Department of Health, Education, and Welfare, National Center for Educational Research and Development, 1972), p. 9, Table 9.

Table 6.11
Racial Preference of American Caucasian, American Negro, and Hong Kong Chinese Children

Racial Groups	Prefer Own Race	Prefer Other Race	Preference Not Clear
	(In Percent)		
American Caucasian[a]	82.0	12.0	6.0
American Negro	28.0	53.3	18.7
Hong Kong Chinese[b]	65.3	25.3	9.3

[a] Significant difference from each of other two groupings at the .001 level by the X^2 test.
[b] American children chose between Caucasian and Negro; Hong Kong children chose between Caucasian and Chinese.

Source: J. Kenneth Morland, ''Race Awareness among American and Hong Kong Chinese Children,'' *American Journal of Sociology* 75, no. 3. (November 1969): 365, Table 3.

from each other. Both times, however, the white children were the most likely to select the child of their own race. (See Table 6.12.)

Morland concluded:

The findings show that Hong Kong Chinese children differed significantly from both the American Caucasian and American Negro children on racial preference and on two measures of self-identification. The Hong Kong children, unlike the American Negro children, preferred and identified with members of their own race. In this way they were like the American Caucasian children, who also preferred and identified with their own

Table 6.12
Percentage of Children Answering "Own Race"

Racial Group	Item A -- Look Like	Item B -- Rather be
	(In Percent)	
American white	77	77
American black	47	33
Hong Kong Chinese	36	54

Source: J. Kenneth Morland, ''Race Awareness among American and Hong Kong Chinese Children,'' *American Journal of Sociology* 75, no. 3. (November 1969): pp. 366–67, Tables 4 and 5.

race. However, the extent of such preference and identification among the Hong Kong children was significantly lower than among the American Caucasians. This pattern of response of the Hong Kong children in preferring and identifying with their own race in a less extensive way than American Caucasian subjects but in a more accepting way than American Negro subjects could be logically expected in a society with races in parallel positions. In such a society there is no dominant race to maintain its superior position and no subordinate race to show unconscious preference for and identification with the dominant race.[12]

In *Black Child, White Child,* Judith D. R. Porter's 1971 study of preschool children's racial attitudes and identities, the subjects were 175 white and 184 black children who attended 16 kindergarten and nursery schools in the Boston area. They came from middle-, working-, and lower-class (Aid to Dependent Children) families. Porter concluded that ''even before they [preschool children] have a sophisticated knowledge of racial categories, children of both races have a positive evaluation of 'white' and a negative feeling about 'brown.' Color associations and their cultural connotations are important influences on these preferences.''[13]

A major intervening variable introduced in Porter's study was social class. In addition to race, age, and sex, she wanted to know how socioeconomic status affected racial attitudes and identity. In the analysis of variance in Table 6.13, preferences are reported on the basis of responses to the doll selection items by the race, age, sex, and social class of the respondent. Porter's findings show that more white children in each sex, age, and class category preferred dolls of their own race than did black children.

Controlling for the effects of various segregated and integrated environments, Porter found that light-skinned children exhibited more own-race preferences in segregated settings than did dark-skinned children. But in desegregated settings, light-skinned children exhibited fewer own-race preferences than did dark-skinned children. (See Table 6.14.)

In 1967, J. E. Williams and J. K. Roberson reported the results of their study of 111 white children aged three through seven who responded to 24 sets of pictures.[14] Each set contained two pictures of the same object, but colored differently. In half of the sets one of the objects was white and the other black. The other 12 sets were dummies and were colored red, green, blue, orange, and so on. A two-line story was attached to each set of pictures, and each story ended with the experimenter asking the child to choose the object that was *bad, dirty,* or *pretty.* The adjectives were adopted from the evaluative scales developed by Charles E. Osgood, George J. Suci, and Perry H. Tannenbaum in *The Measurement of Meaning.*[15] The children's scores as reported by the Williams-Roberson study are shown in Table 6.15.

Note that 75 percent of the children consistently attributed a positive adjective (pretty, nice, good) to the white pictures and negative adjective (bad, mean, ugly) to the black pictures. According to the authors, age did not significantly affect the children's responses.

Table 6.13
Attitudes toward Own Race: Controlling for Sex, Social Class, Race, and Age

Race of Respondents[a]	Males Middle Class			Working Class			Lower Class		
	3 yrs	4 yrs	5 yrs	3 yrs	4 yrs	5 yrs	3 yrs	4 yrs	5 yrs
White	1.39[b]	1.29	1.31	1.50	1.31	1.24	1.39	1.33	1.26
	N-3	N-14	N-23	N-1	N-8	N-12	N-3	N-4	N-11
Negro	1.72	1.67	1.82	1.53	1.56	1.51	1.83	1.63	1.67
	N-3	N-7	N-10	N-5	N-17	N-15	N-1	N-12	N-5
Females									
White	1.46	1.27	1.28	1.33	1.19	1.19	1.17	1.31	1.25
	N-8	N-21	N-20	N-3	N-11	N-9	N-1	N-12	N-10
Negro	1.58	1.69	1.58	1.53	1.58	1.71	1.44	1.63	1.81
	N-4	N-18	N-4	N-11	N-24	N-7	N-7	N-14	N-6

[a]Total race effect, controlling for age, sex, and class: white = 1.30, Negro = 1.64, $p < .01$.
[b]1 = high own-race preference; 2 = low own-race preference.

Source: Judith D. R. Porter, *Black Child, White Child: The Development of Racial Attitudes* (Cambridge, MA: Harvard University Press, 1971), pp. 64–65, Table 5.

Joseph Hraba and Geoffrey Grant, in 1970, reproduced the Clark and Clark doll selection study, using as their subjects black and white nursery school and kindergarten children in Lincoln, Nebraska.[16] Their findings showed: (1) White children were significantly more ethnocentric on Items 1 and 2 ("Which doll would you most like to play with?" and "Which doll is the nice doll?"). (2) There were no significant differences between black and white children on Item 3 ("Which doll looks bad?"). (3) Black children were more ethnocentric on Item 4 ("Which doll is a nice color?"). (See Table 6.16.)

In their conclusion, Hraba and Grant asserted that their findings indicated that important changes were occurring among black children and that future studies would show even more strongly that blacks are proud of their identity.

The main trends in this discussion reiterate the observation that racial attitudes, racial awareness, and racial identity are formed at an early age (about three or four) and that, for most children in the United States, the desirable color is still white. Preschool black children attach more positive and attractive qualities to white than they do to black or brown. But changes are occurring in

Table 6.14
Attitudes toward Own Race: Controlling for Color, Class, and Social Contact

Setting	Light-Skinned		
	Middle	Working	Lower
Segregated	1.65	1.53	1.61
	N=11	N=5	N=10
Desegregated	1.77	1.61	1.73
	N=11	N=18	N=3
	Dark-Skinned		
Segregated	1.76	1.58	1.68
	N=17	N=26	N=17
Desegregated	1.50	1.52	1.55
	N=6	N=30	N=13

1 = high own-race preference; 2 = low own-race preference.

Source: Judith D. R. Porter, *Black Child, White Child: The Development of Racial Attitudes* (Cambridge, MA: Harvard University Press, 1971), p. 102, Table 15.

the attitudes and perceptions of black children. They are occurring mostly among black children already in school and especially among those past the primary grades. Morland reported more positive attitudes toward being black among his older black respondents than among his preschool black children. Hraba and Grant reported mixed results for the doll preference items and concluded that the consensus about white being better, more attractive, and more positive was beginning to crack.

It is important to emphasize that all the studies referred to were conducted with white and black children who lived in racially homogeneous families. None of the studies described attitudes or identity among the unusual category of children who were the subjects of our research: the adopted black child and the white sibling in a "white" family.

In the next section, we report these children's responses to some of the same tests that have been applied to more typical populations of children. The purpose of our research was not to replicate the earlier studies, because the idea of replication when the populations involved are so distinctive is foolish. But we thought it would be useful and helpful to be able to compare the responses of our subjects with the responses of black and white children who live in typical family settings. Should our children respond in a substantially different

Table 6.15
Percentage of White Children Who Attributed Positive and Negative Adjectives to Black and White Pictures

Adjectives	White Pictures	Black Pictures
	(In Percent)	
Pretty	87	13
Clean	85	15
Nice	84	16
Smart	82	18
Good	81	19
Kind	76	24
Ugly	17	83
Dirty	16	84
Naughty	18	82
Stupid	18	82
Bad	15	85
Mean	10	90

Source: J. E. Williams and J. K. Robertson, "A Method for Assessing Racial Attitudes in Pre-school Children," *Education and Psychological Measurement* 27 (1967): 685, Table 4.

way from that reported in most of these other studies, it would certainly be reasonable to assume that their family situation is an important factor (perhaps *the* crucial factor) in explaining the differences. For example, should our white subjects prove less ethnocentric in their attitudes and should our black subjects exhibit more own race preferences, the fact that these children are siblings must be considered important, because other conditions such as age, sex, and stimuli were not obviously altered.

RACIAL IDENTITY AND ATTITUDES OF TRANSRACIALLY ADOPTED CHILDREN AND THEIR SIBLINGS

Three separate tests or sets of materials were employed for the purpose of measuring the children's racial identity, awareness, and attitudes. The first set of materials included three baby dolls; one doll looked like a white baby, another like an American black baby of medium or dark complexion, and the third like a light-skinned black baby or an American Indian or Asian baby. All dolls were dressed identically—they were clothed only in a diaper. The chil-

Table 6.16
Hraba and Grant Results (1970) Compared with Clark and Clark Results (1939)

Dolls	Clark and Clark (1939) Blacks	Hraba and Grant (1969) Blacks	(1939-1969) X^2 Blacks	Hraba and Grant (1969) Whites
(Play with)				
1. White doll	67 (169)	30 (27)	36.2 p<.001	83 (59)
Black doll	32 (83)	70 (62)		16 (11)
(Nice doll)				
2. White doll	59 (150)	46 (41)	5.7 p<.02	70 (50)
Black doll	38 (97)	54 (48)		30 (21)
(Looks bad)				
3. White doll	17 (42)	61 (54)	43.5 p<.001	34 (24)
Black doll	59 (149)	36 (32)		63 (45)
(Nice color)				
4. White doll	60 (151)	31 (28)	23.1 p<.001	48 (34)
Black doll	38 (96)	69 (61)		49 (35)

Individuals failing to make either choice are not included, hence percentages add up to less than 100.

Source: Joseph Hraba and Geoffrey Grant, "Black Is Beautiful," *Journal of Personality and Social Psychology* 16, no. 30 (1970): 399, Table 1.

dren were allowed to look at, hold, and play with the dolls for a few minutes while the interviewer arranged the equipment. Then the three dolls were put on the floor or on a table and the formal interview began. The interviewer asked the child to point to the doll that:

1. You like to play with the best

2. Is a nice doll

3. Looks bad

4. Is a nice color

5. Looks like a colored child

6. Looks like a black child

7. Looks like a white child

8. Looks like you

Following these items, a second set of dolls was introduced. The second set differed from the first in that three of the dolls were boy dolls and three were girl dolls. The three boy dolls were dressed identically. They were supposed to represent boys between about six and eight years old. The girl dolls were also dressed identically and represented girls within the same age range. The skin shades were the same as those of the baby dolls. The girl subjects were exposed to the girl dolls and the boy subjects to the boy dolls.

The main reason for introducing these older sex-typed dolls was to increase the likelihood that we were offering meaningful and effective stimuli for the older children in the sample. Even with the inclusion of the "older" dolls, there remained the possibility that boys who were seven years old would find the dolls of little interest and that questions about which ones they would like to play with best, were nice, or looked bad might evoke random responses. We thought, however, that we could improve the chances of obtaining mean- ingful responses from the older children, especially the boys, if the dolls looked like children their own age. The same eight questions were asked about the boy and girl dolls that were asked about the baby dolls.

Following the questions about the dolls, the children were shown 24 sets of pictures, each of which was pasted on a six-by-eight piece of cardboard. This instrument was adopted from the Williams and Robertson study cited in the previous section. Each set contained two pictures of the same object (animals, toys, umbrellas, airplanes, and so forth), but colored differently. In half of the sets, one of the objects was white and the other black. The other 12 sets were dummies, and the pictures were colored red, green, blue, or orange—any color except black or white. A two-line story was attached to each set of pictures, and each story ended with the interviewer asking the children to choose the object that was *bad, dirty,* or *pretty.* The adjectives were adopted from the evaluation scales developed by Osgood, Suci, and Tannenbaum and reported in *The Measurement of Meaning.* The full set of adjectives is: *pretty, mean, clean, bad, nice, stupid, smart, naughty, good, dirty, kind,* and *ugly.* These items provided another measure of the children's racial attitudes.

In the third task, each child was asked to arrange and identify family mem- bers from puzzles constructed especially for the study. Fifteen figures were cut out of plywood, and each of five figures was described to the children as rep- resenting different family roles that could be fitted into five molds cut from a common plywood board. There were three mother figures, identical in size, in shape, and in the clothing painted on them. The only difference was that one's skin color suggested she was white, another's skin color suggested she was black, and a third's skin color suggested she might be, for example, American Indian or someone from Korea. There were three fathers, three sisters, and six brothers (two representing each skin color) whose color matched that of the three mothers. The children's task was to arrange a family with five people in it and to identify the figures that looked like their mother, their father, their sister(s), or their brother(s). They were also asked to arrange families of four people and then to select a friend from one of the remaining figures. They were asked to choose which child looked most like them and with which little girl or boy they would most like to play. The children's responses to the various tasks connected with the puzzles provided measures of racial awareness, racial attitudes, and racial identity.

Findings: Dolls

The first set of results describes the children's responses to the dolls. Remember that in studies reported earlier we found that white children as well as black and other nonwhite children tended to exhibit white racial preferences. These results were reported first by the Clarks in the late 1930s, and then by Goodman, Greenwald and Oppenheim, Porter, and Morland.

On the racial awareness and identity dimensions, there was not as much consensus. The most common pattern indicated that black children are more aware of racial differences, but that white children identify themselves more accurately than do black children. Since the concept of identity includes affect, as well as cognition, and since black children are more ambivalent about their skin color, these results do not appear to be inconsistent.

The major hypothesis in this study was that the atypical environment in which the children were being reared would affect their responses in such a manner as to mute the typical white preferences and reduce differences in responses about awareness and identity that are attributable to race. Specifically, we expected that both the nonwhite and the white children would not have as strong a preference for white as had been reported for other white and black children, that the nonwhite children would not have a greater sense of racial awareness than the white children, and that the white children's racial identity would not be any more accurate than that of the nonwhites. For each dimension then, we anticipated that the nature of the children's family setting would have a sufficiently strong impact so as to alter the pattern of responses away from those most often cited.

Responses to the Dolls

Each respondent received a score based on the number of times he or she attributed a *positive* quality to the white doll. A child received one point each time he or she selected the white doll in response to: "Which doll would you: (a) like to play with the best? (b) think is a nice doll? (c) think is a nice color? and (d) did not select the white doll as the doll that looked bad." Each respondent could have a score that ranged from 0 to 4. The *higher* the score, the more times the respondent indicated a preference for the white doll by selecting it.

The mean scores of 1.6 for the white children, 1.8 for the black adopted children, and 1.7 for the American Indian/Asian children demonstrate that none of the children manifested a white racial preference. Out of a possible score of

4, which would have meant that the white doll was selected in response to each question, the average score was 1.7. Such a score means that none of the children selected the white dolls even half of the time. All three categories of children manifested the same choice patterns.

We also divided the children into homogeneous age categories and compared racial preference scores by age as well as race. We found that the ages of the children within each racial category did not make a significant difference in their preferences.

The sex of the children also did not prove to be a significant differentiating characteristic. Among the white children, the mean score for the boys was 1.6 and for the girls 1.7. Among the black children, the boys' and girls' mean scores were both 1.7. Among the American Indian or Asian children the boys' mean score was 1.9 and the girls' 1.6.

The children's responses were also divided, according to the interviewer's perception of the shade of the subject's skin color, into light, medium, and dark. Practically all the children described as having light skin by the interviewers were Caucasians. The children whom the interviewers described as having medium skin were black and American Indian or Asian, and the children whom the interviewers described as dark-skinned were almost all black. The racial preference scores by light, medium, and dark skin shades show that skin shade did not affect preferences for white or nonwhite dolls to a significant extent. On the whole, the mean scores of the light children were not noticeably different from those of the medium and dark children: 1.8, 1.8, and 1.9, respectively.

In the one skin shade category in which the frequencies were large enough to make comparisons among racial groups, the preference scores were the same for the black and American Indian or Asian children of medium skin shade. Thus the light, medium, and dark children all responded to white dolls with about the same degree of positiveness. The white dolls were not given a preferential or more desirable status than the nonwhite dolls by any category of respondents.

To summarize, the children's responses to the racial preference items using baby dolls as stimuli showed no bias in favor of white. Neither on the basis of race alone, race and age, race and sex, or race and skin shade did any of the children exhibit white racial preferences.

The children's responses to the same four items when the stimuli were boy and girl dolls followed much the same pattern. The racial preference scores showed no significant difference between white and nonwhite children, and none of the groups exhibited a preference for the white dolls. On the whole, neither age, sex, or skin shade made a significant difference in the preference scores for the boy and girl dolls. The older American Indian and Asian children (five through seven) exhibited less of a preference for the white dolls than did the younger children in that racial category. But aside from that, there were no differences by racial categories.

Table 6.17
Percentage Making Correct Racial Identification of Baby Dolls, by Race and Adoptive Status

Correct Identification		White Children	Black Children	Indian-Asian Children
		(Percentage Making Correct Identification)		
White doll*		82 (161)	72 (105)	76 (35)
Colored doll:	Lighter	43	45	52
	Darker	47 (165)	44 (107)	48 (33)
Black doll:	Lighter	33	39	43
	Darker	56 (170)	43 (108)	46 (33)

*$X^2 = 2.83$; df = 2; p < .05.

Racial Awareness

The next set of comparisons measured racial awareness, that is, the children's ability to classify the dolls into appropriate racial categories. Table 6.17 describes the percentage of children in each racial category who correctly identified the baby dolls that look like a colored child, a black child, and a white child, and Table 6.18 reports the same comparison for the boy and girl dolls. The similarity of percentages across racial categories shows that in only one instance (Table 6.18) did one group of children make more accurate identifications than did any other. The white children were more likely to identify the white dolls correctly than were the black, American Indian, and Asian children.

Additional analysis however, revealed that practically all the mistakes in identification were made by children who were less than five years old, for both the baby and boy or girl dolls. (See Tables 6.19 and 6.20.)

Even among the younger-than-five children incorrect identifications were distributed randomly across racial categories. The three- and four-year-old black children provided no more accurate identifications than the three- and four-year-old white children did. The sex of the respondents did not significantly differentiate accuracy of identification for either the baby or the boy and girl dolls, save for the black girls' more accurate identification of the baby dolls.

Racial Identity

On the identity dimension, the selection of the doll that looked most like the respondent, 76 percent of the white children selected the white baby doll, 76

Table 6.18
Percentage Making Correct Racial Identification of Boy and Girl Dolls, by Race and Adoptive Status

Correct Identification		White Children	Black Children	Indian-Asian Children
		(Percentage Making Correct Identification)		
White doll*		85	68	58
Colored doll:	Lighter	41	41	28
	Darker	50	43	49
Black doll:	Lighter	28	30	49
	Darker	60	57	30

*$X^2 = 17.8$; df = 2; p < .01.

percent of the black children selected either the lighter or the darker brown doll (31 and 45 percent, respectively), and 59 percent of the American Indian and Asian children selected the lighter- or darker-skinned doll (21 and 38 percent, respectively). The largest proportion of children in the last-mentioned category

Table 6.19
Percentage Making Correct Racial Identification of Baby Dolls, by Age and Race

Correct Identification	White Children					Black Children					Indian-Asian Children				
Age	3	4	5	6	7	3	4	5	6	7	3	4	5	6	7
White Doll*	55	70	90	100	100	67	65	67	100	88	50	73	80	100	92
Colored doll:															
Lighter	37	44	57	52	24	36	44	33	25	38	50	73	100	50	8
Darker	47	33	41	48	76	49	37	56	75	62	33	27	0	50	92
Black doll:															
Lighter	21	17	30	36	48	50	29	33	25	38	50	36	50	25	55
Darker	47	55	67	59	48	30	46	56	75	62	50	46	50	75	36

*$X^2 = 4$; df = 6.3; p < .05.

Table 6.20
Percentage Making Correct Identification of Boy and Girl Dolls, by Age and Race

Correct Identification	White Children					Black Children					Indian-Asian Children				
Age	3	4	5	6	7	3	4	5	6	7	3	4	5	6	7
White Doll*	55	65	91	90	100	45	66	100	100	92	70	36	67	100	93
Colored doll:															
Lighter	32	43	42	55	29	38	34	45	42	54	30	27	22	40	36
Darker	52	37	48	42	71	36	49	55	58	46	50	46	56	40	64
Black doll:															
Lighter	25	23	42	23	35	23	38	46	25	23	30	46	45	20	36
Darker	35	47	55	74	65	52	55	36	75	77	40	18	33	60	57

*$X^2 = 4$; df $= 12.9$; $p < .01$.

identified themselves with the white doll (41 percent), and the smallest proportion identified themselves with the lighter-skinned brown doll, the doll that objectively bore the greatest resemblance to them. The major difference then was between the American Indian and Asian children and the white and black children. But the fact that the American Indian and Asian children had the lowest percentages of correct self-identifications probably results less from their ambivalence or self-rejection than from our failure to provide them with an appropriate model with which to identify.

On the whole, more accurate self-identifications were made by the older children in each racial category. (See Table 6.21.) Sex did not significantly affect the accuracy of identifications. (See Table 6.22.)

Table 6.21
Correct Self-Identification, by Age and Race, of Baby Dolls

Ages	White					Black					Indian-Asian				
	3	4	5	6	7	3	4	5	6	7	3	4	5	6	7
								Lighter					Lighter		
	60	74	90	86	90	24	33	22	25	75	25	-	25	25	55
								Darker					Darker		
						46	44	67	50	25	42	64	25	50	18

Table 6.22
Correct Self-Identification, by Sex and Race, of Baby Dolls

White		Black		Indian–Asian	
Boys	Girls	Boys	Girls	Boys	Girls
		Lighter		Lighter	
71	81	31	32	10	28
		Darker		Darker	
		45	44	45	33

The skin shades of the respondents closely matched the skin shades of the dolls they identified as looking like them. Sixty-two percent of the light-skinned children selected the white baby; 60 percent of the medium children selected the lighter and darker colored dolls. Seventy-two percent of the dark-skinned children selected the two colored dolls.

The identifications of the boy and girl dolls followed a similar pattern. The older the child, the more accurate the identification, irrespective of race, and white and black girls made more correct self-identification than did boys. The respondents' skin shades matched the identity choices for the boy and girl dolls even more closely than they did for the baby dolls.

Summary of Responses to Dolls

On the basis of all the responses to the items in which dolls were used to measure racial attitudes, awareness, and identity, we found no consistent differences among the three racial categories. There was no consistent preference for the white doll among the black, white, and American Indian or Oriental children. There was no indication that the black children had acquired racial awareness earlier than the white children, and there was no evidence that the white children were able to identify themselves more accurately than the non-white children.

 This was the first study of racial attitudes and identity among young children in American society that reported no white racial preferences. Our results suggested that the unusual family environment in which these children were being reared may have resulted in their acquiring atypical racial attitudes and in their not sharing with other American children a sense that white is preferable to other races. But the children's responses also demonstrated that their atypical racial attitudes did not affect their ability to identify themselves accurately.

Pictures

The next group of tests examined the children's responses to the 12 sets of black and white pictures. The six negative adjectives that could be used to characterize the black and white pictures were: *bad, stupid, naughty, dirty, mean,* and *ugly*. The six positive adjectives were *pretty, smart, good, clean, nice,* and *kind*. Each subject received two scores ranging from 0 to 6 on the basis of the number of times he or she attributed a *positive* adjective to either the black or white picture and the number of times he or she attributed a negative adjective to either the black or white picture.

For example, if a respondent associated five of the positive adjectives with white pictures and one with a black picture, he or she received a score of 5 on the "white" positive dimension and a score of 1 on the "black" positive dimension. Similarly, if he or she associated three negative adjectives with white pictures and three with black pictures, he or she received a score of 3 on the "white" negative dimension and a score of 3 on the "black" negative dimension. Table 6.23 summarizes the scores by race and adoptive status.

Note two facts about the information in Table 6.23. First, there are no significant differences in scores among the three racial categories, and second, irrespective of their own racial designation, the children were more likely to identify white objects with positive adjectives and black objects with negative adjectives. Unlike the doll situation, then, in this context we found that children in each of the racial groupings exhibited a pro-white bias.

Dividing the children according to the interviewer's perception of their skin shade into light, medium, and dark did not significantly alter the response pattern described above. The dark-skinned children, all of whom were black, did not evaluate white and black objects differently than the medium-skinned children, most of whom were black.

The children's responses were also divided into homogeneous age categories. Only among the black children did age affect scores. The older black children were more likely to associate black pictures with positive adjectives and white pictures with negative adjectives than were the younger children. Scores for the white, black, and American Indian or Asian children within homogeneous age categories are shown in Table 6.24.

The six- and seven-year-old black children expressed more positive attitudes toward the black images than did younger children of the same race. More positive attitudes toward black images on the part of older black children are consistent with the findings of Rosenberg and Simmons.[17] They found that black high school students had higher self-esteem than white high school students did and that older black youths had higher self-esteem than younger blacks. They attributed the higher self-esteem to the influence of the civil-rights movement and to the slogan "black is beautiful."

On the whole, we did not find that the black children in our study evaluated the black images more positively than the white ones. Like their white and

Table 6.23
Mean Positive and Negative Scores for Black and White Pictures, by Race and Adoptive Status

Black and White Picture Scores	White Children	Black Children	Indian-Asian Children
Positive			
Black pictures	2.1	2.3	2.2
White pictures	3.9	3.7	3.8
Total	6.0	6.0	6.0
Negative			
Black pictures	4.1	3.8	4.3
White pictures	1.9	2.2	1.7
Total	6.0	6.0	6.0

American Indian or Asian siblings, they had higher positive scores for the white images and higher negative scores for the black images. The fact, however, that the seven- and eight-year-old black children in our sample (they represented the oldest age category) divided their positive and negative scores almost evenly between black and white suggests that by the time they are teenagers black children may evaluate black images more positively than white images.

Sex made a difference only among the white children. White girls evaluated black images more positively than did white boys, and white girls evaluated black images less negatively than did white boys. White boys were the most positive in their evaluation of white images. (See Table 6.25.)

Finally, we compared the responses of our white subjects to those reported by the children in the Williams and Robertson study discussed previously. The two sets of data are summarized in Table 6.26. The results show that for 10 out of the 12 items, white children reared with black or nonwhite siblings responded differently from white children reared in typical environments. A higher proportion of the children in the Williams and Robertson study associated white with positive and black with negative attributes than did the white children in our study. The only two adjectives for which there were no significant differences were *clean* and *dirty*.

The age ranges of the children involved in the two studies were very similar. The children in the Williams and Robertson study (1967) were between three and seven; ours were between three and eight. One might argue that geography

Table 6.24
Mean Positive and Negative Scores for Black and White Pictures, by Age and Race

Black and white Picture scores	White Children (age)				
	3	4	5	6	7
Positive Scores					
Black pictures	2.1	1.3	1.7	2.2	2.7
White pictures	3.9	4.7	4.3	3.8	3.3
Negative Scores					
Black pictures	3.9	4.8	4.3	4.4	3.5
White pictures	2.1	1.2	1.7	1.6	2.5

	Black Children (age)				
	3	4	5	6	7
Positive Scores					
Black pictures	1.9	1.5	2.1	2.4	3.1
White pictures	4.1	4.5	3.9	3.6	2.9
Negative Scores					
Black pictures	3.9	4.1	4.2	3.7	2.8
White pictures	2.1	1.9	1.8	2.3	3.2

	Indian-Asian Children (age)				
	3	4	5	6	7
Positive Scores					
Black pictures	1.9	1.6	2.1	3.0	2.4
White pictures	4.1	4.4	3.9	3.0	3.6
Negative Scores					
Black pictures	4.4	4.6	4.7	4.2	3.9
White pictures	1.6	1.4	1.3	1.8	2.1

Table 6.25
Mean Positive and Negative Scores for Black and White Pictures, by Sex and Race

Black and White Picture Scores	Girls			Boys		
	White	Black	Indian-Asian	White	Black	Indian-Asian
Positive Scores						
Black pictures	2.6	2.4	2.1	1.8	2.1	2.2
White pictures	3.4	3.6	3.9	4.2	3.9	3.8
Negative Scores						
Black pictures	3.7	3.8	3.4	4.4	3.9	4.2
White pictures	2.3	2.2	1.6	1.6	2.1	1.8

can explain most of the differences. White children in Chapel Hill, North Carolina, are more likely to express ''southern'' and therefore more antiblack attitudes than would a random selection of white children from Illinois, Minnesota, or Wisconsin. Therefore, it is the difference in geography rather than in family patterns that is the major explanation. We cannot prove the weakness of such an argument because we do not have responses from typical white children living in Illinois, Wisconsin, Michigan, and so on. But from all the data we have seen on racial attitudes in all regions of the country, we doubt that children in North Carolina, especially those who live in a university community, are likely to express opinions that are more pro-white than those of children in the Midwest.

On the basis of the results of these studies, it appears that children who were reared in the special atmosphere of biracial or multiracial families had different responses to stimuli concerning race than did American children reared in typical environments. The tensions usually associated with sibling rivalry seemed not to have sufficiently negative effects as to result in negative attitudes toward the race or races of their siblings. Families who have adopted transracially seem to have succeeded in providing their young children with perspectives and attitudes toward color, and presumably race, different from those held by children reared in more typical family settings. Fewer of the white, as well as the nonwhite, children in transracial homes associated the term *white* with the positive, attractive, and desirable characteristics attributed to it by white as well as black children in the rest of American society.

Puzzles

The third set of tasks each child was asked to perform involved putting to-gether and taking apart puzzles constructed especially for the study. A child was given three puzzles, each containing five figures, which he/she was told were a mother, a father, two sons, and a daughter. The figures in each group of five were all painted the same shade: white, dark brown, or yellowish-brown. All the mothers, for example, were the same size and had the same clothes painted on them; similarly with the fathers, brothers, and so on. The only difference among the three mothers and other figures was the shade of their skin.

The children were asked to perform several tasks with the puzzles. The first task was to arrange one family composed of five members. In doing so the children could select five figures of the same skin shade or five figures of different shades. It turned out that over two-thirds of all the children, those who were themselves white, black, or American Indian, arranged a family made up of persons of different skin shades. They put together families with white mothers and brown fathers (or the reverse) and with brown or white children.

The pieces were then scattered, and the children were asked to put together a family that represented their family. In response, 77 and 74 percent of the white children picked the white mother and father figures, but only 48 and 56 percent of the black children and 55 and 53 percent of the American Indian or Asian children selected the white mother and father figures. In fact, of course, all the children have white parents. Nevertheless, about half of both the black and American Indian or Asian children selected parental figures whose skin shades more closely matched their own. (See Table 6.27.)

The same choice pattern repeated itself when the children's responses were divided into the light, medium, and dark skin shade categories. The medium and dark children were much less likely to select the light mother and father than were the light-skinned children.

Neither age nor sex had any effect on the children's selections. Younger black and American Indian or Asian children were as likely as older children in these categories to select the skin shades that matched their own. Boys' selections were similar to those of girls.

The parent figures were removed, and the subjects were next asked to choose from among three sets of nine children's figures those figures that looked like them and like their brother(s) and sister(s). The children's choices are described in Table 6.28.

On self-identity, 71 percent of the white boys and 61 percent of the white girls selected the white figure and 78 of the black boys and 76 percent of the black girls selected the dark or the medium-brown figure.

Among the American Indian or Asian children, 58 percent of the boys and 59 percent of the girls selected the medium and dark figure, but a large minor-

Table 6.26
Percentage of White Children Who Attributed Positive and Negative Adjectives to Black and White Pictures in Two Studies

Adjectives	Simon		Williams-Roberson	
	White object	Black object	White object	Black object
	(189)		(111)	
	(In Percent)			
Pretty	70	30	87	13
Clean	82	17	85	15
Nice	58	42	84	16
Smart	59	41	82	18
Good	59	41	81	19
Kind	58	42	76	24
Ugly	37	63	17	83
Dirty	12	88	16	84
Naughty	31	69	8	82
Stupid	46	43	18	82
Bad	33	67	15	85
Mean	33	67	10	90

ity selected the lightest of the children figures. The American Indian or Asian children, like the white and black children, identified themselves correctly in the matching of the sex of the figures with their own. We do not believe that the selection of the light figures by approximately 40 percent of the American Indian or Asian children should be attributed to errors of cognition. Rather, we

Table 6.27
Percentage Selecting Light Mother and Father Figures, by Race and Adoptive Status

Puzzle Selections	White Children	Black Children	Indian-Asian Children
Your Mother	77	48	55
Your Father	74	56	53

Table 6.28
Self and Sibling Selections, by Sex and Race

Puzzle Selections	White Boys	White Girls	Black Boys	Black Girls	Indian-Asian Boys	Indian-Asian Girls
	(In Percent)					
Self						
Light	71	61	21	14	42	41
Medium	17	26	31	35	42	35
Dark	12	13	47	41	16	24
Brother						
Light	36	43	51	50	38	14
Medium	29	32	20	18	25	50
Dark	35	25	29	32	37	36
Sister						
Light	53	44	53	32	33	50
Medium	21	28	23	48	42	20
Dark	26	28	24	20	25	30

are more inclined to believe that just as the dolls did not provide good enough models for these children, the puzzle pieces also were not appropriate enough stimuli. They failed to provide the children with appropriate figures with which to identify.

The figures in Table 6.28 show that, unlike the selection of parental figures, the choices of brothers and sisters were not biased in favor of any racial category. There was no tendency for white children to overselect whites or for blacks to over- or underselect blacks. The children's selections were most probably based on their real-life situations, since we know that 83 percent of the nonwhite children have at least one white sibling and that all the white children have at least one nonwhite sibling.

The final set of tasks involving the puzzle figures asked the children to select the boy and the girl they would most like to play with and then the boy and the girl they would most like to have visit them. These choices are described in Table 6.29. Race appears not to be a prominent concern in the children's selection of friends. There is no indication from the percentages in Table 6.29 that white children overselected white figures or that black children over-selected white figures. The friendship choices, like the sibling choices, seem unaffected by color.

Table 6.29
Friendship Selections, by Sex and Race

Puzzle Selections	White		Black		Indian-Asian	
	Boys	Girls	Boys	Girls	Boys	Girls
	(In Percent)					
Girl play						
Light	44	28	66	44	33	22
Medium	39	37	27	17	34	22
Dark	17	35	7	39	33	56
Boy play						
Light	33	48	39	16	45	33
Medium	33	23	29	52	33	33
Dark	34	29	32	32	22	34
Girl visit						
Light	38	40	47	38	50	50
Medium	31	50	23	31	25	25
Dark	31	30	30	31	25	24
Boy visit						
Light	44	30	43	21	55	31
Medium	34	43	26	41	18	54
Dark	32	27	31	38	27	15

When the responses were compared by skin shade, there was also no systematic preference for either light- or dark-skinned children. Sex probably would have been an important predictor of friendship choices, but the task confronting the children was to select the boy and the girl with whom they would like to play and visit, and therefore the children did not have to make a choice on the basis of sex.

To summarize the results of the various experiments described in this section, it appears that black children reared in the special setting of multiracial families did not acquire the ambivalence toward their own race reported in all other studies involving young black children. Our results also show that white children did not consistently prefer white to other groups, and there were no significant differences in the racial attitudes of any of the categories of children. Our findings did not offer any evidence that black children reared by white parents acquired a preference for black over white. They showed only that black children perceived themselves as black as accurately as white children

Table 6.30
Year in School, by Race and Adoptive Status

Year in School	TRA	Born	White/Adoptee
	(In Percent)		
Less than 7th grade	3	--	--
7 - 8 grade	32	15	8
9 - 12 grade	58	55	75
13 - 16 grade	7	29	17
More than 16th grade	--	1	--
Total	100	100	100

perceived themselves as white. The American Indian and Asian children had lower scores, but we thought it likely that their scores were an artifact of poor equipment and faulty design rather than a measure of their sense of identity.

There was only one instance in which the black children showed less awareness, or perhaps ambivalence, regarding their identity than did the white children, and that was in the matter of selecting puzzle figures with skin shades that matched those of their own parents. The black, as well as the American Indian and Asian children, erred more than the white children in selecting figures whose skin shades matched their own rather than the figures whose skin shades more closely resembled those of their parents. They did not make this error in selecting figures that represented either themselves or their siblings.

Writing in 1975, we said the practice of transracial adoption was having a significant, perhaps even a revolutionary, impact on the racial identity and attitudes of young black and white children. However, it was still too early to predict with any degree of accuracy what was likely to happen to these children in later years, during adolescence and adulthood. It might be that the attitudes and prevailing tones of the larger society would have sufficient impact so as to alter or confuse the identity and attitudes formed within the relatively unique setting of these multiracial families.

Children's Experiences as Adolescents and Young Adults

We did not interview the children in the second phase of our study, in 1979, so the next time we encountered the children directly was in 1984. By then, they were all adolescents and young adults. All of the children who participated in the 1984 survey had been involved in the initial study in 1972.

All but 4 of the transracial adoptees were still in school in 1984; 15 of the children born to the families and 4 of the other adoptees were no longer in school. Table 6.30 shows the breakdown by years of those in school.

Among the children at the precollege level, 83 percent of the transracially adopted children, 82 percent of those born into the family, and 80 percent of the white adoptees were attending public institutions. At the college level as well, most of the children were attending public universities, with no difference by adopted status.

The racial composition of the schools that the children attended were described by them as follows:

Racial Composition of Schools (in percent)

76–100 percent white	58
51–75 percent white	22
50 percent white	10
Less than 50 percent white	10

There was no greater likelihood of the transracially adopted children attending schools that had a smaller percentage of white students than the other respondents.

School Performance and Future Educational Plans

The table below reports the average grades, according to the adolescents, that they received in school at the end of the last school year.

	Mean Grade Last Year*
TRA	2.5
Black	2.4
Born	2.0
White/Adopted	2.0

* We converted an A to a score of 1, a B to a 2, a C to a 3, a D to a 4, and an F to a 5.

The plans of the transracially adopted children and the children born into the families who are still in high school or junior high are quite similar; 75 percent of the transracially adopted children said that they plan to go on to college or university, and 13 percent plan to attend some other type of school (trade, design, and so forth). The others either plan to work or do not have a clear idea of what they want to do after high school. Given that the median age of the children in this category is not quite 15, it is not unusual for 12 percent to claim that they have not decided what they will do three or four years hence.

Among the children born into the families, 94 percent expect to pursue college or university education and 4 percent plan to attend some type of trade school. Of the 10 white adoptees who were still at the precollege level, 1 expects to travel, 1 expects to work, 2 have not decided, and the others plan to go on to college or university.

There was a large and varied range of occupations that respondents said they expected to go into when they completed their schooling. The most frequently cited areas of interest were law, business, teaching, and computers, although each of the four categories was mentioned by only 10 percent or less of the respondents. Adopted status made no difference in any of the choices.

The bases for their choices were "interests" and "skill," followed by "aptitude," "enjoyment," "wanting to help people," and "like children." Only 3 percent said that they were interested in a particular occupation or profession because they could make a lot of money in that field.

Parents or teachers did not seem to be an important consideration in making future plans; 6 percent of the respondents mentioned them as having significant influence. But 83 percent said that they thought their parents agreed with or supported their interests and preferences. When we asked the adolescents whether they thought their parents supported or agreed with their brothers' and sisters' choices, the transracially adopted children, more than the children born into the families, said they believed that their parents approved of their siblings' choices (70 percent for the brothers and sisters). Among the children born into the families, 60 percent thought their parents approved of their transracially adopted brothers' plans and 50 percent that their parents approved of their transracially adopted sisters' plans. However, 22 percent also said that they did not know their parents' reactions because their brothers or sisters had not expressed clear preferences about their future plans.

Interests and Friendships

Early in the interviews we asked the adolescents a series of questions about their interests, the kinds of activities in which they thought they excelled, special qualities that they attributed to themselves, the clubs they belonged to, and their friends.

For all three categories of adolescents, sports was the favorite activity named most often by 61 percent of the transracially adopted children, 44 percent of the children born to the family, and 38 percent of the other adoptees. Music, reading, and crafts were some of the other activities named, but never by more than 15 percent of any category of adolescents. Not surprisingly, of all activities, sports was named most frequently (by 64 percent of the transracially adopted children, 34 percent of the children born to the families, and 38 percent of the other adoptees).

We asked, "Are there some qualities about you that you think are special?" As shown in Table 6.31, most of the respondents answered that they did have special qualities. The majority focused on relational and personality characteristics rather than on talents or skills; though the transracially adopted children emphasized the former qualities to a somewhat lesser extent than did the other

Table 6.31
Qualities That Respondents Think Are Special, by Race and Adoptive Status

| Qualities | Categories of Children | | |
	TRA	Born	White/ Adoptee
	(In Percent)		
None	19.8	11.0	--
I am a good friend	21.6	24.2	31.3
People trust me, like to talk with me, think of me as a caring person	19.8	35.2	31.3
Physical skills	9.0	2.2	--
Special talent, other skills	12.6	5.5	--
Being adopted	2.7	--	6.3
Other	14.5	21.9	31.1
Total	100	100	100

adolescents. The fact that the transracially adopted children are on the average two years younger than the children in the other categories could account for the weaker emphasis on personality and interpersonal qualities.

Most of the respondents claimed not to belong to any clubs either at school or outside of school. The largest group who did were the transracially adopted children, 31 percent of whom belonged to sports clubs. We also asked specifically about membership in clubs or organizations that represented an ethnic or racial type; 89 percent of the transracially adopted children reported no affiliation, as did 92 and 94 percent of the other adolescents.

Close friendships followed same sex lines, as is usually the case among all age groups in the United States. Thus 88 percent of the transracially adopted children chose same sex persons as their good friends, as did 84 percent of the adolescents in the other categories. But friendships within and across racial lines revealed different patterns among the three categories. The preferences are shown in Table. 6.32.

The percentages in Table 6.32 show that black transracially adopted children are almost as likely to choose white friends as are children in any of the other categories. The black children show a slightly greater tendency to select blacks as friends than do the white children or the transracially adopted children of American Indian or Korean backgrounds. The opportunities for selecting black rather than white children as friends are obviously much smaller for all cate-

Table 6.32
Friendship Choices, by Race and Adoptive Status

Friend	TRA (Black)	TRA (Other)	Born	White/ Adoptee
		Category of Children		
	(In Percent)			
	Friend #1			
White	73.2	76.0	88.6	68.8
Black	14.6	4.0	5.7	12.5
Other	6.7	4.0	3.4	12.5
No Answer	5.5	16.0	2.3	6.2
	Friend #2			
White	70.8	72.0	79.5	81.3
Black	19.1	12.0	10.2	6.3
Other	4.5	--	5.7	--
No Answer	5.6	16.0	4.6	12.4
	Friend #3			
White	61.8	56.0	71.6	81.3
Black	25.8	12.0	8.0	--
Other	3.4	--	8.0	--
No Answer	9.0	32.0	12.4	18.7

gories of children given the distribution of blacks in the communities in which the respondents live.

A 15-year-old black girl (of mixed parentage) commented, "I hung around white kids until sixth grade; after that I made black friends because everyone was saying I was white when I knew I wasn't. I also kept my white friends."

A 20-year-old respondent who described herself as "black and white" and who was homecoming queen in her high school described a series of incidents with blacks in high school who "hassled" her when she insisted that she was both black and white. But she also described one event in which a group of black girls whom she had feared came over to her and told her that they were glad she was homecoming queen because they felt that she was representing them. On a different occasion one of the black girls at school asked her, "Are you ashamed to be black?"

I said no. Then she asked why I didn't have any black friends and I said I'd be anyone's friend, I didn't care what they are, but I also explained that I was adopted into a white family. They didn't know that. The girls used to think I was acting white. If they said anything to me face to face I'd explain why I talked without slang and my family situation and my neighbors.

On the other hand, one 14-year-old black said:

I feel like a black person. I talk more to my black friend because he knows what I am talking about.

A young woman born into her family explained that she has had hassles with people whom she considered to be her friends because she had a black sister and because she dated black men:

"Some of the people I thought were my friends have proven to have prejudiced attitudes."

About half of the respondents in each category said that they met their friends in the schools they attended. The neighborhood was named as the next most likely place.

In addition to querying the adolescents about their friends, we also asked them whom they dated and how parents (their own and those of the dates) reacted to the dating. Fifty-three percent of the transracial adoptees said that they date (although 8 percent do so only in groups), as do 62 percent of the adolescents born into the families (10 percent only in groups) and 60 percent of the white adoptees (12 percent only in groups). The smaller percentage among the transracial adoptees is probably explained by the fact that on the average they are two years younger than the children born into the families. The percentages among the white adoptees may not be meaningful because the frequencies on which they are based are so small. The racial characteristics among those who date are described in Table 6.33.

The transracial adoptees are more likely to choose blacks as dates than as "good friends"; 38 percent said that they date blacks (thought not exclusively), compared to 20 percent or so who named a black as their third closest friend. Sixteen percent of the birth and 14 percent of the adopted white respondents also report that they date blacks, which, while lower than the cross-race dating reported by the transracial adoptees, is nevertheless higher than what one is likely to find among a group of white adolescents in comparable communities.

Most of the respondents report that they have encountered no problems with either their own parents or those of their dates about their choice of date. But 29 percent of the transracial adoptees said that they have encountered difficulties, twice as often from the parents of the date than from their own. Nineteen

Table 6.33
Dating Choices, by Race and Adoptive Status

| | Categories of Children | | |
Race of Dates	TRA	Born	White/Adoptee
	(In Percent)		
Whites exclusively	60	78	86
Blacks exclusively	11	6	--
Blacks and whites	27	10	14
Whites and ethnics	2	6	--
Total	100	100	100

percent of the white adolescents also reported difficulties and, again, primarily (70 percent of the time) from the parents of the person whom they were dating. At the end of the interview, a transracially adopted black girl offered this observation: "I think it is a good idea for people to intermarry because then, someday, everyone will be the same color." Another 17-year-old black adolescent complained, "When I'm with my white girlfriends and we run into a group of guys, a lot of the guys are kind of prejudiced. No one asked me to the prom."

Race and Family

Having focused thus far on the respondents' accounts of their schooling, activities, interests, and friendships, we shift now to the adolescents' perception of their families and their place in the family. We asked all of them: "In what ways is your family similar or different than your friends' families?"

Most of the adolescents saw their family as similar to those of their friends in income level and socioeconomic status. That dimension was mentioned more often than any other by the transracially adopted children and the children born into the families. Those characteristics were followed by the quality of the relationships, the families' values, and the number of children. The differences that the adolescents saw between their own family and the families of friends were in their decision not to adopt transracially (the difference cited most often by all three categories of respondents), the greater or lesser freedom parents allowed their children (there were as many respondents who said "more freedom" as there were respondents who said "less freedom"), the quality of family relationships, and the number of children. What we found most interesting about the comparisons between friends and respondents' families is the lack of difference in the perceptions of transracially adopted children and the children born into the families concerning both the similarities and the differences among their own and their friends' families.

There were some issues that could only be discussed with the transracial adoptees. For example, we asked them, "Can you tell me how it feels being [black, Korean, and so forth] in a white family? Does it give you any problems, or is it all straightforward?" Seventy-one percent of the transracially adopted children answered that it gave them "no problems." They did not think about it; it was something that by this time they took for granted. Most others thought it embarrassing when they had to introduce their parents to new friends or when they were in public and everyone with them was white.

One 16-year-old black adoptee said that she is embarrassed by her "white parents" in front of her black friends:

My friends tease me when my parents come to school for conferences. They say, "Oh, my God, is that your mother? Ha, ha, your mother didn't want you." They also say I'm not as good as they are because my mom and dad are white. They said I don't act like a black person. It hurts me and makes me feel sad.

A 17-year-old black girl who described herself as "basically white inside" commented:

Just being black in a white family is special—it draws a lot of attention to me, not all good. I feel more comfortable with whites; I'm uncomfortable around blacks. I don't act the same as they do or talk the way they do. I don't like the same music or activities.

Another 19-year-old black said:

When I was eight or nine years old I did not want to show my parents to my friends.

The transracially adopted children were also asked, "Have there been times you wished you were of the same racial background as your parents?"

Sixty percent of the respondents answered that "there has never been such a time." Among those who said that there have been such times, no one reason was given by more than 4 percent of the respondents. Such explanations were offered as: "It's upsetting when I'm at a family gathering and everyone is saying who looks like who and I wonder who I look like," and, "When I'm with aunts, uncles, grandparents, and other members of the extended family." For example, a black daughter described a trip she took with her family to visit an aunt in South Dakota. She said, "There weren't any blacks there and I heard a lot of names. I've dealt with things like that before, but being the only black person there really made me feel like I wished I was white or any other color than black." Other reasons offered were: "At school, when I have to introduce my family to strangers"; "When shopping with my mother"; and "I dislike having to explain to my friends why my parents are different."

All of the children were asked, "Have there been times in your life when you wished you were another color?"

Forty-three percent of the transracially adopted children and 44 percent of the children born into the families said, "Never." Specifically, the times mentioned by both groups were at school and playing sports. It is interesting, and consistent with our observations about the transracially adopted children's sense of belonging to their family, that they were no more likely to wish they belonged to "another" race than were their white siblings. A 20-year-old son born into his family who has one black brother said, "I'd like to be a chameleon so I could be the color that was most useful at the time."

A 16-year-old black girl commented at the end of the interview, "I really don't see my family as a white family. Each of us is color-blind. Each person has his or her own personality." In another family, a child born into the family said about his black brother, "I don't look on him as a person of a different race. I look at him as a brother." A 14-year-old black girl commented, "Race doesn't matter; love is what is important."

One of the transracially adopted children who expressed herself most vehemently and most negatively about her racial identity was an 18-year-old American Indian girl. She said:

It bothers me that I'm Indian. People don't look up to Indians. The whites always fought the Indians, and the Indians got beat. We aren't looked up to. There is nothing special about being Indian.

Later on, when talking about her plans for the future, she said:

I'm not going to live on an Indian reservation, and I'm not going to live in Minneapolis where all the blacks are. I don't like being with Indians, and I don't want to be associated with blacks. They all stick together. You don't try to mix with them; they'd beat you up. Josh [her black brother] and I were beaten up five years ago by blacks. I want to live in a white community. I'm going to college, and I plan to live in a dormitory. After college, I'd like my kids to grow up in a white community.

A 20-year-old Korean, who had been adopted when he was 10 years old, reported:

When I was in Korea, I wished I was a full Korean. I took more abuse over there than blacks receive here. I used to get into fights every day because of my American background. When I was the number one student in third grade, the school would not give me my award in public, the way they do for all the number one students in a class, because they said, "You are an American." The book they gave me said "Number One" in it, but there was no publicity about it.

The transracial adoptees were asked to remember if they experienced incidents in which "people were nasty or unpleasant about your racial background.'' Thirty-nine percent of the respondents said that they never experienced such an incident. The most frequently cited event among those who did was name calling in school (46 percent). Twenty-six percent cited insulting remarks made to them on the street or in a public place. The remaining 28 percent cited incidents such as when friends told jokes insulting to blacks in front of them, challenges to fight because of their color, and insulting remarks by teachers. But no more than 5 percent of the transracial adoptees mentioned any one specific incident. Of those who described a certain event, half of them said that it occurred over two years ago. Sixty-three percent said that they told their parents about it. According to the respondents, most of the parents comforted them but ''played down the incident'' and did not take any action. Over half of the respondents also said that they did or said nothing to the perpetrator of the act.

The transracially adopted children were less likely to report that they and their parents ''discuss race, racial differences, racial attitudes, and/or racial discrimination,'' as shown in the responses below.

Percent Reporting Race Discussed

TRAs	54.0
White/Born	79.3
White/Adopted	75.0

But there were no differences among the three categories of respondents to the following question: ''When you sit back and think about how the world is organized, do you think in terms of racial categories, e.g., there are black, white, yellow, et cetera, people?''

Percent Answering "Yes"

TRAs	22
White/Born	22
White/Adopted	23

One direct way to find out how important ''race'' is to the respondent's identity was to ask, ''Imagine someone is meeting you at a train station who has never seen you before. How would you describe what you look like?''

We divided the adolescents by their adopted status and by sex, because on this matter especially we thought boys and girls might differ. The results are shown in Table 6.34.

Clearly, sex is not important, but race is. The white children (those born and adopted) are much less likely to mention the fact that they are white than are the transracial adoptees, of whom about 50 percent mentioned race as an identifying characteristic.

In the study by Ruth G. McRoy and Louis A. Zurcher, the authors assessed

Table 6.34
Mentions of Race and Sex in Self-Descriptions, by Race and Adoptive Status

Characteristics Mentioned	TRA		White/Born		White/Adoptee	
	Male	Female	Male	Female	Male*	Female
			(In Percent)			
Race	46.7	54.0	6.3	2.3	--	8.3
Sex	--	--	--	2.3	--	8.3
Race and Sex	3.3	4.0	6.3	2.3	--	--
Neither	46.7	40.0	85.4	88.4	--	75.0
Other/No Answer	3.3	2.0	2.0	4.6	--	8.3
Total	100	100	100	100	--	100

Categories of Children

*Frequencies are too small: N = 4.

racial identity by a content analysis of the responses of 30 transracial and 30 black inracial adoptees' self-descriptions to the "Twenty Statements Test." In the Twenty Statements Test, respondents are given the opportunity to answer the question "Who am I?" 20 times. The results reported by McRoy and Zurcher are consistent with ours, insofar as they also found that the transracial adoptees were more likely than the inracial adoptees to refer to race in their self-descriptions. Twenty-seven percent of the inracial adoptees did so, as opposed to 56 percent of the transracial adoptees.

In our study, the differences were 52 percent for the transracial adoptees (combining the male and female responses) as opposed to 8 percent for both the white born and white adoptees. This is lower than the percentage for black inracial adoptees in the McRoy-Zurcher study but demonstrates the greater salience of race among minority group respondents.

We also asked:

Which of the following statements fit how you really feel?

   (a) I am proud to be (select one): black, brown, Indian, Korean, white, other. Or,

   (b) I do not mind what color I am. Or,

   (c) I would prefer to be _____.

Sixty-six percent of the black transracial adoptees answered that they are proud to be black or brown, 6 percent said that they are proud to be of "mixed background," 17 percent said that they did not mind what color they are, and 11 percent said that they would prefer to be white. Among the 22 Korean,

Native American, Vietnamese, and other transracial adoptees, 82 percent said that they are proud to be whatever their racial heritage is and 9 percent said that they would prefer to be white.

Among the respondents born into the families, 84 percent said that they are proud to be white, 9 percent said that they do not mind what color they are, and 7 percent told us that they would prefer to be black, Spanish-American, Native American, or "different than I am." Seventy-five percent of the white adoptees said that they are proud to be white, 19 percent said, "I don't mind what color I am," and 6 percent said that they would prefer to be black.

McRoy and Zurcher reported that when the adoptees were asked to indicate whether they perceived themselves to be black, white, or mixed

seventeen (56%) of the TRAs referred to their racial background as being either mixed, part white, black-white, human or American; nine (30%) referred to themselves as black; three (10%) as white; and one responded Mexican. Inracial adoptees typically referred to themselves as black.[18]

Family Integration and Commitment

When we first began this project in 1972, we did not focus on the children's sense of belonging to their adopted families. We did not foresee that questions of family integration, loyalty, and commitment would be crucial. But in the 1984 survey we included items that probed how integrated into the family the adopted children felt themselves to be and how committed both the adoptees and their parents are to their relationship. The most consistent and perhaps the most important finding that emerged from that survey is the sense of belonging felt by the transracial adoptees to their adopted families—the mothers and fathers are their parents and the brothers and sisters their siblings; they are not viewed as substitutes or proxies for "real" parents or "real" family. Even though the adoptees "look" different from their parents and siblings, they believe and feel themselves to be part of their adopted family.

Indeed, on every measure we included in the 1984 study the transracial adoptees responded consistently and strongly that they belonged to and felt a part of their family and expected to continue to be family members in good standing when they left the parental home and organized their own lives. The transracial adoptees were not "doing time" in their adopted homes; they plainly viewed the familial bonds as permanent and powerful.

The most direct evidence we have for these observations is the transracial adoptees' responses on (1) the Family Integration Scale; (2) questions asking: "To whom would you go when you feel [happy, sad, et cetera]?"; and (3) expectations about future closeness to parents and siblings.

We report first the responses to the Family Integration Scale. This scale was adopted from the survey of the British Adoption Project (BAP) by Owen Gill and Barbara Jackson, which they conducted in 1980–81.[19] The study included 44 families, 36 of whom had adopted transracially and 8 in which at least one parent was black. The data referred to from the Gill and Jackson study are based on the 36 transracial adoption families. The distribution to each of the items by the four categories of respondents is described in Table 6.35.

We also computed mean and median scores for the four categories of respondents. The possible range was from 32 to 8; the lower the score, the higher the sense of family integration.

	N	Median	Mean	Standard Deviation
TRA	22	15.4	15.4	3.66
Black	89	15.3	15.2	4.27
Born	88	14.7	15.4	3.17
White/Adopted	16	15.5	16.7	4.00

The summary statistics as well as the percentages for each item shown in Table 6.35 fail to reveal any differences among the four categories of respondents. The transracial adoptees perceive themselves as having the same type of relationship with their family as the other children.

In reporting the results of their study, Gill and Jackson said:

The responses to these statements appear to show a general picture of family integration of these children with only a small number of children obtaining relatively low scores. There does, however, appear to be a difference between boys and girls on some of these questions. The four children showing the lowest family integration scores are all boys.[20]

We compared our transracially adopted children and children born into the families by sex and also compared both groups against the Gill and Jackson respondents. (See Table 6.36.) On six of the eight items, there are greater differences between the boys and girls in the Gill and Jackson study than there are among our respondents. On the whole, our study showed no strong differences between the transracially adopted boys and girls (save that the boys' percentages are consistently higher) and between the boys and girls born into the families.

The next set of items asked: "Who knows best what you are really like as a person and to whom would you go if . . . ."

1.   Of all the people in the family and outside, who
     knows best what you are really like as a person?

                              Percent Responded

                              Family Member*
     TRA   54.2

     Born   59.4

     White Adoptees   43.9

*For the transracial adoptees and children born into the family, the responses include 2.7 and 3.3
percent, respectively, who answered "a grandparent."

2.   If you were really happy about something that has gone
     right for you, which person inside or outside the family
     would you want to be the first to know?

                              Percent Responded

                              Family Member

     TRA   66.6

     Born   67.3

     White Adoptees   56.4

3.   If you were really worried about something personal, to
     whom would you go to talk about it?

                              Percent Responded

                              Family Member

     TRA   46.8

     Born   45.1

     White Adoptees   25.1

4.   If you were wrongly accused of stealing something from

      a local shop, to whom would you go to sort things out?

                                        Percent Responded

                                        Family Member
                            _____

        TRA   60.3

        Born   68.2

        White Adoptees   31.0

The responses of the transracially adopted children and the children born into the families are almost identical. The white adoptees are less likely to turn to a family member. (Remember that on the average the white adoptees are two and a half years older than the transracial adoptees, but the same age as the children born into the families.)

The third measure of the strength of familial ties exhibited by the adolescents is shown in their responses to the following question: "Looking ahead to a time when you will not be living in your parents' house, do you expect that you will feel close to them (e.g., discuss things that are bothering you or that you consider important)?" We divided the respondents by sex as well as adopted status because of the popular belief that daughters are likely to feel closer to their parents than sons. Our results, shown in Table 6.37, showed that there were no real differences by sex or adopted status.

We also asked, "After you and your [brother and/or sister] have moved out of your parents' house, do you expect that you will be close to one another (e.g., talk on the phone a lot, spend time with each other, discuss things that are important to each of you)?"

We computed means for older and younger siblings of the same and opposite sex. As in the findings reported for the parents, there were no real differences by sex or adopted status. (See Table 6.38.)

As expected, there was a significant positive correlation between the family integration scores and the expected future closeness to parents and siblings among the three categories of respondents. (See Tables 6.39 and 6.40.)

Further evidence for our contention that the transracial adoptees are as integrated into their families as the children who were born into them is the lack of differences in their responses to questions about the ties and feelings they have toward grandparents, aunts and uncles, and other members of their extended family. Among the transracial adoptees 82 percent have at least one grandparent still alive and 71 percent said that they feel close to their grandparents. Among the birth children 84 percent have grandparents who are still alive and 53 percent feel close to them, and among the white adoptees 87 percent have grandparents who are still alive and 57 percent feel close to them. Forty-four percent of the transracial adoptees, 50 percent of the birth children,

Table 6.35
Family Integration Scale, by Race and Adoptive Status

	Categories of Children			
Family Integration Items	TRA	Black	Born	White/Adoptee
	(In Percent)			
I enjoy family life:				
Strongly agree	40.4	40.4	46.6	37.5
Agree	53.7	51.7	50.0	50.0
Disagree	2.7	3.4	3.4	12.5
Strongly disagree	2.7	3.4	--	--
No answer	.5	1.1	--	--
I would like to leave home as soon as possible when I'm able to:				
Strongly disagree	10.0	9.0	14.8	18.8
Disagree	48.2	47.2	47.7	31.1
Agree	34.2	37.1	29.5	31.3
Strongly agree	6.1	5.6	8.0	18.8
No answer	1.5	1.1	--	--
People in our family trust one another:				
Strongly agree	27.6	29.2	27.3	25.0
Agree	51.7	48.3	55.7	56.3
Disagree	19.7	20.2	17.0	18.7
Strongly disagree	.5	1.1	--	--
No answer	.5	1.2	--	--
Most families are happier than ours:				
Strongly disagree	23.2	25.8	31.8	18.8
Disagree	69.3	66.3	63.6	68.8
Agree	4.4	4.5	4.5	12.4
Strongly agree	2.6	2.2	--	--
No answer	.5	1.1	.1	--

Table 6.35 (continued)

I am treated in the same
way as my brother and sister:

Strongly agree	30.3	32.6	26.2	6.8
Agree	49.1	49.4	50.0	56.3
Disagree	13.1	12.4	22.7	18.1
Strongly disagree	7.0	4.5	1.1	18.8
No answer	.5	1.1	--	--

Most children are closer
to their parents than I am:

Strongly disagree	24.6	27.0	29.5	31.3
Disagree	53.5	53.9	54.5	31.3
Agree	16.2	14.6	14.8	31.3
Strongly agree	5.2	3.4	1.2	6.1
No answer	.5	1.1	--	--

If I'm in trouble, I know
my parents will stick by me:

Strongly agree	37.5	37.1	45.5	37.5
Agree	56.1	56.2	48.9	56.3
Disagree	5.4	5.6	5.6	6.2
Strongly disagree	.5	--	--	--
No answer	.5	1.1	--	--

My parents know what I am
really like as a person:

Strongly agree	20.2	22.5	20.4	12.5
Agree	62.3	60.7	68.2	62.5
Disagree	14.4	12.4	9.1	18.8
Strongly disagree	2.6	3.4	2.3	6.2
No answer	.5	1.1	--	--

157

Table 6.36
Family Integration Scale, by Adopted Status and Sex

Family Integration Items	TRAs M	TRAs F	Born M	Born F	Gill/Jackson M	Gill/Jackson F
	(In Percent)					
Emjoy family life						
% Agree*	96.8	90.0	98.0	95.4	71.0	90.0
Would leave home						
% Disagree	62.3	52.0	58.4	69.8	57.0	57.0
Trust one another						
% Agree	78.7	78.0	85.4	81.4	57.0	73.0
Happier than ours						
% Disagree	96.8	88.0	93.8	97.7	57.0	95.0
Treated same as siblings						
% Agree	83.6	70.0	81.2	71.1	43.0	100
Closer to parents						
% Disagree	80.3	74.0	83.3	86.0	43.0	82.0
Stick by me						
% Agree	95.1	90.0	95.8	93.0	71.0	86.0
Know me						
% Agree	86.9	76.0	89.6	88.4	71.0	82.0

*The Strongly Agree and Agree responses were combined to match the Gill and Jackson categories.

Table 6.37
Future Closeness to Parents

	TRA	Born
	Mean Scores*	
Males	2.2	2.1
Females	2.5	2.2

* 1 = very close; 2 = close; 3 = fairly close; 4 = not at all close.

Table 6.38
Future Closeness to Siblings

	TRA	Born
Older Siblings of Same Sex		
Males	2.6	2.5
Females	2.6	2.3
Older Siblings of Opposite Sex		
Males	2.6	2.3
Females	2.6	2.7
Younger Siblings of Same Sex		
Males	2.4	2.4
Females	2.5	2.1
Younger Siblings of Opposite Sex		
Males	2.5	2.6
Females	2.9	2.0

and 38 percent of the white adoptees said that they visit or talk over the phone with their grandparents at least once a month. Essentially, the same pattern was repeated in response to questions about the adolescents' ties to their aunts and uncles. Thus, in their relations with extended family members, the transracial adoptees define themselves as having at least as close ties with their relatives as the children born into the families. The transracial adoptees do not sense that they are outsiders or that they are not accepted.

Self-Esteem

In a 1968 study conducted in Baltimore of 1,917 pupils in 26 schools, in grades ranging from 3 to 12, Morris Rosenberg and Roberta G. Simmons mea-

Table 6.39
Family Integration Scores and Future Closeness to Parents

TRAs	Born
$r = .37$	$r = .36$
$p = .000$	$p = .000$

Table 6.40
Family Integration Scores and Future Closeness to Siblings

TRAs	Born
r = .41	r = .33
p = .000	p = .01

sured "self-esteem" among black and white respondents by asking the pupils to respond to the seven items listed below.

- I feel I have a number of good qualities.
- I feel I do not have much to be proud of.
- I take a positive attitude toward myself.
- On the whole, I am satisfied with myself.
- I wish I could have more respect for myself.
- At times I think I'm no good at all.
- I certainly feel useless at times.[21]

These seven items were lifted from an earlier study conducted in New York State by Rosenberg of high school juniors and seniors in which he measured self-esteem by including these three additional items.

- I am a person of worth, at least on an equal plane with others.
- All in all, I am inclined to feel that I am a failure.
- I am able to do things as well as most other people.[22]

Rosenberg and Simmons are careful to explain what they mean by self-esteem in the following paragraphs.

The aspect of the self with which we are concerned in this study is one concisely described by Gardner Murphy as "the individual as known to the individual." . . . Thus, the individual's conscious beliefs, opinions, attitudes, values, and feelings about himself are encompassed in this definition.

Our chief, though not exclusive, concern is the individual's positive or negative orientation toward this object, his favorable or unfavorable attitudes toward it, and the associated emotional reactions . . . When we characterize a child as having high self-esteem [we mean] that he considers himself a person of worth. He has fundamental respect for himself, appreciating his own merits, even though he is aware of faults in himself which he hopes and expects to overcome. The person with high self-esteem does not necessarily consider himself better than most others, but neither does he consider himself worse. Low self-esteem means that the individual lacks respect for himself, considers himself unworthy, inadequate or otherwise seriously deficient as a person.[23]

Table 6.41
Self-Esteem, by Age and Race

Self-Esteem	8-11 Black	8-11 White	12-14 Black	12-14 White	15-19 Black	15-19 White
			(In Percent)			
Low	20	39	23	37	15	35
Medium	35	31	37	31	31	27
High	45	30	40	32	54	37
N=100%	508	211	320	257	292	187

Source: Morris Rosenberg and Roberta G. Simmons, *Black and White Self-Esteem: The Urban School Child,* Arnold M. Rose and Caroline Rose Monograph Series (Washington, DC: American Sociological Association, 1971), p. 5.

They reported the self-esteem scores for black and white children by age as shown in Table 6.41.

We see that in each age group a greater percentage of black children have high self-esteem than do white children. Rosenberg and Simmons comment on these results as follows: "These data thus clearly challenge the widespread assumption that black children are conspicuously low in self-esteem."[24]

When they compared the grades on report cards for the black and white children by self-esteem scores, they found that while grades made a difference, they made less of a difference for black than for white pupils. The pupils' socioeconomic status functioned in the same way as grades; namely, it bore upon the self-esteem of white children but had no effect on that of blacks.

After examining a great number of other factors that might influence self-esteem, Rosenberg and Simmons concluded that one factor provided an important, indeed crucial, explanation for why black children do not have lower self-esteem despite "the immense disprivileges" to which they are subject. That factor is the role of "significant others." Using a six-item scale that included how the respondents believe their friends, kids in their class, teachers, and mothers perceive them, Rosenberg and Simmons found a strong association between the respondents' self-esteem, on the one hand, and their belief that significant others hold positive attitudes toward them, on the other. Table 6.42 describes that relationship.

Rosenberg and Simmons concluded:

We thus see that significant others do play a most important role in the formation of the child's self-esteem—more important, indeed, than virtually any of the other factors we have considered. Furthermore, as we examine various measures of association, we find that the relationship between significant others' attitudes and self-esteem appears to be

Table 6.42
Self-Esteem and Attitudes Attributed to Significant Others, by Race

Self-Esteem	Blacks				Whites			
	Attitudes of significant others perceived as:							
	Favor-able			Un-favor-able	Favor-able			Un-favor-able
	1	2	3	4	1	2	3	4
	(In Percent)							
Self-Esteem								
Low	4	26	26	38	38	32	41	61
Medium	26	36	38	39	19	28	36	28
High	70	51	36	23	43	40	23	12
N=100%	(50)	(409)	(252)	(69)	(21)	(286)	(116)	(33)

Source: Morris Rosenberg and Roberta G. Simmons, *Black and White Self-Esteem: The Urban
School Child,* Arnold M. Rose and Caroline Rose Monograph Series (Washington, DC:
American Sociological Association, 1971), p. 144.

somewhat stronger among black than among white children. But with regard to the
perceptions of significant others we have seen, the black children are at no serious
disadvantage. These are the influences which really count for the black children and
which so effectively serve to protect their self-esteem.[25]

Since most of our respondents were adolescents in their junior and senior
years of high school, we used the original 10-item Self-Esteem Scale to see if
the black children in our study were likely to score higher or lower than the
white children. As shown in Table 6.43, we also separated out the white adoptees from the white adolescents who had been born into the families and the
other transracial adoptees from the larger group of black adoptees.

The highest possible score was 40 and the lowest 10. The lower the score,
the higher the self-esteem. Only the scores of respondents who answered all
ten items were included in computing the means and medians shown below.

Categories of Respondents	N	Median	Mean	Standard Deviation
Black	86	17.8	18.1	3.49
Other TRAs	17	18.0	18.3	3.66
Born	83	18.1	18.0	3.91
White/Adoptee	15	18.0	18.5	3.16

There are no meaningful differences among the four categories of adolescents on their overall self-esteem scores. Unlike the black and white respondents in the Rosenberg and Simmons study, the black adolescents in our study did not score higher on "self-esteem."

McRoy and Zurcher also reported self-esteem scores, which they measured by using the self-esteem component of the Tennessee Self-Concept Scale. High scorers on the self-esteem component of the Tennessee Scale like themselves and feel that they are persons of worth. Low scorers evaluate themselves negatively and doubt their worth as individuals. The mean for the scale's norming samples who are white, nonadopted individuals was 345.6. McRoy and Zurcher reported means of 348.9 for the transracial adoptees and 348.7 for the inracial adoptees. Thus their data, as did ours, revealed no differences in self-esteem scores by race, nor did the adoptive status of the respondents affect their scores.

We also correlated the self-esteem scores by grades in school and found a significant relationship only for the 22 nonblack transracial adoptees. We also tested for the strength of the association between family integration and self-esteem by correlating the scores of each scale by the four categories of respondents. We found, as shown in Table 6.44, strong and positive relationships for three of the four categories. Only among the white adoptees was the relationship not significant.

Thus among the black and other nonwhite adoptees and among the children born into the family, those who had close ties also experienced high self-esteem.

The Future

Toward the end of the interview we asked all of the adolescents a series of questions about their future. The topics focused on choice of marriage partners, types of communities in which they planned to live, participation in ethnic organizations, and, for the adoptees, any interest or plans they might have to try to locate their birth parents.

On the items pertaining to the types of communities in which the respondents are likely to live when they are "on their own" and whether they are likely to join an ethnic association, the results showed a consistent pattern. The majority of the respondents in each category (the transracial adoptees, the white adoptees, and the birth children) expect to live in mostly white or mixed neighborhoods, and they do not anticipate joining any ethnic organization. The distribution of responses is shown in Table 6.45.

There are several interesting features about the responses in Table 6.45. First, only 2.2 percent of the transracial adoptees said that they plan to live in a mostly black neighborhood. Second, a higher percentage of transracial adoptees, as opposed to birth children, plan to live in a mostly white neighborhood. Third, the large majority of white children born into the families, like their transracially adopted siblings, plan to live in "mixed" racial neighborhoods. These findings are consistent with the other data that showed the desires of the

Table 6.43
Self-Esteem, by Race and Adopted Status

Self-esteem item	TRA	Black	Born	White/ Adopted
			(In Percent)	
1. I take a positive				
attitude toward myself				
Strongly agree	32.4	32.6	44.3	18.8
Agree	64.9	62.9	51.1	81.2
Disagree	2.7	3.4	4.6	--
Strongly disagree	--	--	--	--
No answer	--	1.1	1.1	--
2. I wish I could have				
more respect for myself				
Strongly disagree	9.9	10.1	15.9	12.4
Disagree	55.9	60.7	47.8	43.8
Agree	29.7	24.7	31.8	43.8
Strongly agree	4.5	4.5	4.5	--
No answer	--	--	--	--
3. I am a person of				
worth, at least on an				
equal plane with others				
Strongly agree	45.0	42.7	39.8	31.3
Agree	52.3	56.2	56.8	56.3
Disagree	2.7	1.1	3.4	12.4
Strongly disagree	--	--	--	--
No answer	--	--	--	--

Table 6.43 (continued)

4. I certainly feel
   useless at times

Strongly disagree	12.6	13.5	12.8	--
Disagree	36.0	33.0	31.5	37.5
Agree	43.2	43.8	48.9	56.3
Strongly agree	8.2	9.0	6.8	6.2
No answer	--	--	--	--

5. I feel I have a number
   of good qualities

Strongly agree	33.3	34.8	44.3	43.8
Agree	64.0	64.0	54.5	56.2
Disagree	2.7	1.2	1.2	--
Strongly disagree	--	--	--	--
No answer	--	--	--	--

6. All in all, I am
   inclined to feel that
   I am a failure.

Strongly disagree	55.9	61.8	69.3	56.2
Disagree	40.5	36.0	27.3	43.8
Agree	2.6	2.2	3.4	--
Strongly agree	--	--	--	--
No answer	.9	--	--	--

7. I am able to do
   things as well as
   most other people

Strongly agree	36.9	38.2	29.5	31.3
Agree	59.5	59.6	68.2	56.3
Disagree	3.6	2.2	2.3	12.4
Strongly disagree	--	--	--	--
No answer	--	--	--	--

Table 6.43 (continued)

8. I feel I do not have

    much to be proud of

Strongly disagree	41.4	43.8	46.6	62.5
Disagree	54.1	53.9	46.6	31.3
Agree	3.6	2.3	6.8	6.2
Strongly agree	.9	--	--	--
No answer	--	--	--	--

9. On the whole, I am

    satisfied with myself

Strongly agree	29.7	30.4	35.3	37.5
Agree	64.9	67.4	59.1	62.5
Disagree	4.5	2.2	4.5	--
Strongly disagree	--	--	1.1	--
No answer	.9	--	--	--

10. At times I think

    I'm no good at all

Strongly disagree	23.5	23.6	23.9	25.0
Disagree	45.0	46.1	43.2	56.2
Agree	30.6	30.3	31.8	18.8
Strongly agree	--	--	--	--
No answer	.9	--	1.1	--

transracial adoptees to live their adult lives in an environment and culture similar to the one in which they were reared by their adopted parents. Their white siblings, on the other hand, do not want to live in a white environment. They have been influenced by the presence of their nonwhite siblings and do not see

Table 6.44
Correlations between "Family Integration" and "Self-Esteem"

Blacks	r = .40	p = .000
Other TRAs	r = .24	p = .008
Born	r = .47	p = .000
White/Adoptees	r = .15	p = .29

Table 6.45
Type of Community Respondents Expect to Live in, by Race and Adoptive Status

Type of Community Likely to Live in On Their Own	Respondents by Adoptive Status		
	TRA	Born	White/Adoptee
	(In Percent)		
Mostly white	26.6	10.3	50
Mixed (white and black)	63.8	76.5	50
Mostly black	2.2	--	--
Mostly other combination	--	2.9	--
Don't know	7.4	8.9	--
No answer	--	1.4	--
Total	100	100	100

themselves fitting into a traditional white world.

The distribution of responses to the next item, which concerns the likelihood of their participating in ethnic organizations, is shown in Table 6.46. In each category the large majority do not expect to participate in "ethnic organizations." Again, the pattern is similar among the three categories, and again, the transracial adoptees do not expect to shift their adopted life-style to one that more closely matches their outward appearance.

The responses on the marriage question are somewhat more complicated. As shown by the distribution in Table 6.47, the transracial adoptees are less likely to separate themselves from their ethnic heritage on this issue than they are on the other two.

As the responses show, the white adolescents are more committed than the transracial adoptees to marrying someone of their own background. On the other hand, with one exception, none of the transracial adoptees said that they expect to marry a white person, even though 27 percent expect to live in a mostly white community. The higher percentage of "don't knows" among the transracial adoptees is probably also a function of the age spread among the three categories of respondents.

The responses to the three items about important aspects of their future behavior characterize quite accurately the transracial adoptees' perception of their world as essentially pluralistic and multicolored and that they expect to find a place in that world. Their white siblings share that view. They too perceive the world to be more pluralistic than do white adolescents who have not grown up in a special environment. McRoy and Zurcher's transracial adoptees seem to share a similar view. They report that "twenty-three (77%) expressed acceptance of and interest in interracial marriage." But the black adoptees into black

Table 6.46
Expected Participation in Ethnic Organizations, by Race and Adoptive Status

Participation in Ethnic Organization	Respondents by Adoptive Status		
	TRA	Born	White/Adoptee
	(In Percent)		
Yes, black organization	8.1	1.1	--
Yes, other ethnic organization	8.1	12.0	--
Maybe, probably not	14.4	7.7	12.5
Will not participate	48.6	49.5	68.8
Don't know/no answer	20.8	29.7	18.7
Total	100	100	100

families seemed more definite in their choice of a mate of the same race (90 percent said they expect to marry a black person) than did our white adoptees and white birth adolescents.

We shift now to another aspect of the respondents' future, one that affects only the adopted children. We asked them, "Would you like to be able to

Table 6.47
Choice of Marriage Partners, by Race and Adoptive Status

Racial Characteristics of Likely Mate	Respondents by Adoptive Status		
	TRA	Born	White/Adoptee
	(In Percent)		
White	1.1	65.4	78.6
Black	23.3	1.3	--
Asian	3.3	--	--
Native American	7.7	6.4	7.1
Mixed	2.1	--	--
Don't know, but probably not someone of same racial background	23.3	5.1	--
Other	9.2	3.9	--
Don't know	30.0	17.9	14.3
Total	100	100	100

locate your birth parents? Have you tried to locate them?'' The distribution of responses looked like this:

Want to or Have Tried to Locate Birth Parents*

Yes, and have tried	22.5
Yes, but have not tried thus far	15.3
Not sure, maybe in future	25.2
No	37.0

* The responses are given only for the transracial adoptees. The Ns are too small for the white adoptees, six of whom know who their birth parents are.

About thirty-eight percent of the transracial adoptees have already tried or have some interest in locating their birth parents. When we asked why, most answered, "Curiosity. I'd like to see what I'm going to look like when I'm older." A few said "to find out why they gave me up" or "because I'll feel incomplete until I do."

None of the respondents said that they were looking for their "real" parents or that they hoped to be reunited with their birth parents or family. The adolescents were expressing a sense of incompleteness about their origins and a need for more information about their personal histories. They were not, we believe, declaring their ambivalence about their adopted parents or uncertainty about their feelings of belonging to their adoptive families. Indeed, all the issues discussed in this chapter confirm the adopted adolescents' commitment to their families and their involvement with their adoptive parents, siblings, and other relatives.

NOTES

1. Judith D. R. Porter, *Black Child, White Child: The Development of Racial Attitudes* (Cambridge, MA: Harvard University Press, 1971), p. 22.

2. Ibid., p. 23, citing Bruno Lasker, *Race Attitudes in Children* (New York: Henry Holt, 1929).

3. Ruth Horowitz, "Racial Aspects of Self-Identification in Nursery School Children," *Journal of Psychology* 7 (January 1939):91–99.

4. Kenneth B. Clark and Mamie P. Clark," Racial Identification and Preference in Negro Children," in E. Maccoby, T. Newcomb, and E. Hartley, eds., *Readings in Social Psychology* (New York: Henry Holt, 1958).

5. H. J. Greenwald and D. B. Oppenheim, "Reported Magnitude of Self-Misidentification among Negro Children—Artifact?," *Journal of Personality and Social Psychology* 8 (1968):49–52.

6. Ibid., p. 51.

7. Mary Ellen Goodman, *Race Awareness in Young Children* (New York: Collier, 1964), p. 256.

8. Ibid., p. 257.

9. J. Kenneth Morland, *Racial Attitudes in School Children: from Kindergarten through High School* (Final Report, Project No. 2-c-009) (Washington, DC: U.S. Dept. of Health, Education, and Welfare, National Center for Educational Research and Development, 1972).

10. Ibid., p. 24.

11. J. Kenneth Morland, "Race Awareness among American and Hong Kong Chinese Children," *American Journal of Sociology* 75, no. 3 (November 1969):300–374.

12. Ibid., p. 371.

13. Porter, *Black Child, White Child*, p. 371.

14. J. E. Williams and J. K. Roberson, "A Method for Assessing Racial Attitudes in Preschool Children," *Education and Psychological Measurement* 27 (1967):671–89.

15. Charles E. Osgood, George J. Suci, and Percy H. Tannenbaum, *The Measurement of Meaning* (Urbana: University of Illinois Press, 1957).

16. Joseph Hraba and Geoffrey Grant, "Black Is Beautiful," *Journal of Personality and Social Psychology* 16, no. 30 (1970):398–408.

17. Morris Rosenberg and Roberta G. Simmons, *Black and White Self-Esteem: The Urban School Child*, Arnold M. Rose and Caroline Rose Monograph Series (Washington, DC: American Sociological Association, 1971), p. 9.

18. Ruth G. McRoy and Louis A. Zurcher, *Transracial and Inracial Adoptees* (Springfield, IL: Charles C. Thomas, 1983), p. 127.

19. Owen Gill and Barbara Jackson, *Adoption and Race* (New York: St. Martin's Press, 1983).

20. Ibid., p. 39.

21. Rosenberg and Simmons, *Black and White Self-Esteem*, p. 9.

22. Morris Rosenberg, *Society and the Adolescent Self-Image* (Princeton, NJ: Princeton University Press, 1965), p. 5.

23. Rosenberg and Simmons, *Black and White Self-Esteem*, p. 9.

24. Ibid., p. 5.

25. Ibid., p. 144.

7

How the Parents' and Children's Accounts Match Up

In the 1984 study, we compared responses to questions that were asked of both the parents and the adolescents in their separate interviews. The topics concerned the racial characteristics of friends and dates, grades in school, favorite activities, consensus or lack of it about the adolescent's future regarding schooling and work. We also compared the parents' and the adolescents' perceptions of how close they are likely to be to each other when the adolescent leaves the family home, as well as their expectations about the racial characteristics of the community in which the adolescent is likely to live as an adult and the racial background of the adolescent's choice of a marriage partner. Responses about the adolescents' interests in finding their birth parents and the likelihood that they will try to do so were also compared against the adopted parents' support for such efforts.

We found in examining these issues that, on the whole, the parents' and adolescents' responses indicate that the parents understand their children and that the adolescents reflect views and life-styles that are shared by their parents. Our overall impression of these families is supported by their responses on the specific issues noted above. The families are an integrated unit. The adoption has bound them together and has developed and strengthened ties and commitments to each other that racial differences have neither weakened nor broken, nor are they likely to do so. As different as the children may look from their parents and siblings, they are an integral part of the family, and the assumption of independence as a function of adulthood is not likely to cause a breakup of the family unity. The transracial adoptees' children will be, in every sense, the grandchildren of their parents and the nieces and nephews of their brothers and sisters. Their physical departure and separation from the family home are not likely to cut off family ties and commitments between the adopted children and their parents.

We compared the adolescents' reports about the racial characteristics of their friends and the parents' reports about their children's friendships. Among the adolescents, we had shown that 74 percent of the transracial adoptees, 89 percent of the birth children, and 69 percent of the white adoptees named a white person as their first close friend. In describing their oldest (who is still living at home) child's friends, the parents reported that 72 percent of the transracial adoptees, 87 percent of the children born to them, and 77 percent of the white adoptees had only white friends. The second and third close friends described by the adolescents and the close friends reported by the parents for their second and third children produced the same pattern. Namely, the parents' perceptions about the racial characteristics of their children's friends matched quite closely the adolescents' own reports about their close friends.

There was also a close match between reports of whom the adolescents date and the parents' descriptions of their children's choice of dates. For example, 60 percent of the transracial adoptees said that they date only whites, 78 percent of the adolescents born into the families reported that they date only whites, and 86 percent of the white adoptees date only whites. In describing the racial characteristics of their children's dates, the parents stated that among the transracial adoptees 72 percent dated only whites and among the children born to them 84 percent dated only whites. (There are too few parents of white adoptees to be worth reporting.)

Ruth G. McRoy and Louis A. Zurcher summarized their data on friendships and dates as follows:

The transracial adoptees were more likely to have white friends and dates, and the inracial adoptees were more likely to have black friends and dates. Patterns of association due to the racial composition of the community and school was the key factor in determining the race of the adoptees' friends. . . . Most transracial adoptees stated that they would date either blacks or whites but tended to prefer to date members of the racial group with which they were most familiar in their social milieu.[1]

They reported that the percentage of transracial adoptees who said that most of their school and community friends were white was 86 percent and the percentage who indicated that their best friend was white was 83 percent. Among the inracial adoptees, only 10 percent said that the majority of their friends were white and 6 percent reported that their best friends were white.

These responses generally coincide with those reported by the adolescents in our study. The large majority of the transracial adoptees whom we interviewed have white friends, and a large majority of the white children (birth and adopted) have same race friends, which means "white."

But the responses in our study about dating differed from those in McRoy and Zurcher's: our transracial adoptees were more likely to date whites exclusively. While McRoy and Zurcher reported that 71 percent of the transracial adoptees in their survey stated "that either black or white dates were acceptable," only 23 percent said that they preferred to date whites and only 6 percent revealed that they would date blacks. One explanation for the difference might be that more adolescents in the McRoy and Zurcher study sound as if they are describing hypothetical events rather than actual behavior. These transracial adoptees believe that, in theory, dating persons of both races is preferable to limiting one's dates to either whites or blacks.

An examination of the responses by adolescents and parents concerning the former's favorite activities showed the same pattern. For both the parents and the three categories of adolescents, sports was the favorite activity, as well as the activity, according to both parents and adolescents, at which the adolescents were particularly good.

Even on the matter of grades, where one might be more likely to expect discrepancies in reports between parents and children, the similarities were strong. The average grade reported by the transracial adoptee was 2.5. For the parents describing the first, second, and third transracial adoptees at home (or away at college), the average grades reported were 2.5, 2.6, and 2.7, respectively. The children born into the families reported an average grade of 2.0. The parents of such children reported 1.8, 1.8, and 2.1 for the first, second, and third children. Among the white adoptees, the average grade was 2.0. The parents reported 2.7 and 2.0 for the first and second white adoptees. The latter figures may not be reliable because there were fewer than 10 respondents involved.

Comparisons between parents' and children's accounts of the frequency with which they discussed "racial issues" revealed that more parents than transracially adopted children reported such discussions. Concerning the children's responses, we noted that the transracial adoptees were less likely to report that such discussions took place than were their white siblings, but the percentages reported by parents and white children were close (87 and 79 percent). Perhaps what is considered a discussion about "race" by persons in the majority is not perceived as such by those who are often the target of such conversations.

We did find that parents and transracially adopted children were in agreement about the frequency with which the children experienced insults or were the targets of racial slurs. Sixty-one percent of the transracially adopted children reported such incidents, as did 65 percent of the parents. An additional 7 percent of the parents thought that such incidents might have occurred without the children telling them about it. The parents and children also agreed about the nature of the incidents and their actual as well as likely impact. Almost always they involved name calling by other children, and they were not believed to have left a "lasting" impression or scar.

Shifting to the future, we compared parents' and adolescents' expectations about how close they would be to each other. Unfortunately, the scales on the two interview schedules were not the same. On the parents' questionnaire, the choices were (1) close, (2) fairly close, (3) fairly distant, and (4) distant.

Table 7.1
Future Closeness between Parents and Children

Parents' Ratings About Child*

TRAs			Born			White/Adopted		
1st	2nd	3rd	1st	2nd	3rd	1st	2nd	3rd
1.8	1.6	1.6	1.4	1.7	1.6	1.8	--	--

*1 = Close; 2 = Fairly close

Adolescents' Rating About Parents*

TRAs	Born	White/Adopted
2.3	2.2	2.3

*1 = Very close; 2 = Close

On the adolescents' questionnaire, the choices were (1) very close, (2) close, (3) fairly close, and (4) not at all close. In each category, the lower the score, the greater the closeness. Even though the scales are not identical, the findings nevertheless confirmed the lack of difference in the parents' expectations of closeness with the transracial adoptees and birth and white adopted children and also supported the lack of difference among the children's expectations about how close they are likely to be with their parents. The ratings are shown in Table 7.1 as mean scores.

The results also show that even accounting for the differences in the scales, the adolescents expected to be closer to their parents than the parents expected to be to their children.

Comparisons between the parents' and adolescents' expectations about future closeness among siblings revealed a similar pattern. The adolescents expected to be closer to each other, regardless of race or adopted status, than the parents expected their children to be, irrespective of race and adopted status. The means presented below compare the expectations of the parents regarding their children's closeness to each other against those of the children's expectations about how close they are likely to be to each other in the future.

Remembering that "2" signifies "fairly close" in the parents' scale, while "2" represents "close" in the children's scale, we see from Table 7.2 that the adolescents' expectations are still somewhat more positive than those of the parents concerning closeness among siblings.

Still focusing on the future, we compared parents' and adolescents' expectations about the racial characteristics of the latter's choices of marriage partners and the types of communities in which they would choose to live. We found most of the parents were reluctant to speculate about those issues. Among those who were willing to make a prediction, twice as many thought that their black children would marry someone whose racial characteristics matched their own and that their other nonwhite children (for example, Koreans, Native

Table 7.2
Future Closeness among Siblings

Parents' Ratings	Children's Ratings	
First Adopted and First Born	Older Sibling of Same Sex	
2.0*	TRA 2.6*	Born 2.4
First Adopted and Second Born	Older Sibling of Opposite Sex	
2.0	TRA 2.6	Born 2.5
Second Adopted and First Born	Younger Sibling of Same Sex	
2.1	TRA 2.5	Born 2.3
Second Adopted and Second Born	Younger Sibling of Opposite Sex	
1.8	TRA 2.7	Born 2.3
Among Adopted Children		
2.0		
*1 = Close; 2 = Fairly Close	*1 = Very close; 2 = Close	

Americans) would be as likely to marry a white person as they would be to marry a member of their own community, because the opportunities for meeting others of similar racial background are much more limited. We did not ask the parents for their expectations about their birth children.

Among the adolescents, 30 percent of the transracial adoptees said that they did not want to speculate about the racial characteristics of the person they were likely to marry, but among those who did, almost twice as many replied "a black or a member of another ethnic community." Among the white adolescents willing to speculate (and 85 percent were willing to do so), about one in five expected to marry a nonwhite. On the issue of marriage partners, except for the greater reluctance of the parents to speculate about this issue, the projections of those parents who were willing to respond did not differ in any significant manner from the expectations of their adopted children.

Concerning their expectations about the racial characteristics of the community in which their transracial adoptees are likely to live, among those willing to guess (72 percent), half of the parents thought that they would live in the same type of community in which they had been reared, that is, primarily white middle and upper middle class. About one-quarter thought that they would live in a mixed racial community, and the remaining 12 percent believed that they would live in a black community. The transracial adoptees were more likely than their parents to feel that they would live in racially mixed or nonwhite communities. Sixty-four percent expected to live in mixed communities, 2 percent in mostly black communities, and 27 percent in mostly white communities. The remaining 7 percent said that they did not know. Interestingly, only

10 percent of the white children expected to live in predominantly white communities such as the one in which they were reared.

We conclude from these responses that the experience of multiracial living seems to have been internalized by the children more successfully than the parents anticipated, as demonstrated by the responses of the white children who said that they would seek out mixed communities and the 20 percent or so who would also marry across racial lines. But rather than view their responses as representing a separation from or rejection of their parents' values, the children's responses may be interpreted as meaning they have adapted to and accepted those values beyond the parents' expectations.

The last topic on which we compared the adolescents' and parents' responses was the delicate issue of birth parents—the adopted adolescents' desire to find them and the parents' willingness to cooperate. Forty-seven percent of the parents said that their transracially adopted children have thus far shown no interest in learning about or in learning *more* about their birth parents or in locating them. Seven percent said that they had already given their children whatever information they had about their parents and some were already in contact with them. The parents reported that the others expressed varying degrees of interest ranging from "they have asked but have shown no desire to locate or contact them" (29 percent) to discussing plans "to try and find them" (12 percent). The adolescents' responses were markedly similar. Thirty-seven percent said that they had no interest in locating their birth parents. Thirty-eight percent have tried to locate them or have expressed interest in locating them. Twenty-five percent told us that they had not yet tried to find their birth parents. They might do so later on, when they were adults.

Of all the issues discussed, the matter of birth parents is likely to be the most divisive and the one about which adoptees are least likely to be candid in their discussions with their adopted parents. It is also an issue about which the adopted parents are more likely to allow their wishes and hopes to cloud their perceptions of their children's behavior. Yet even on this topic, the parents seem to be reading their children's interests and plans quite accurately. The majority of the children do not seem to be overcome with curiosity, desire, or need to find their birth parents.

NOTE

1. Ruth G. McRoy and Louis A. Zurcher, *Transracial and Inracial Adoptees* (Springfield, IL: Charles C. Thomas, 1983), pp. 81–82.

8

Problem Families

In an analysis of adoption studies conducted between 1924 and 1968 by 15 different researchers, clinical psychologist Alfred Kadushin reported that 74 percent of the adoptions could be characterized as "unequivocally successful," 11 percent were "questionable," and 15 percent were "unsatisfactory," "unsuccessful," "poor," or "problematic." Success was measured by the level of satisfaction with the experience expressed by the parents.[1] The studies involved 2,236 families. None of the families had adopted transracially.

In the study reported in Chapter 1, conducted for the CWLA by Lucille J. Grow and Deborah Shapiro, of black children in white families who were at least six years of age and who had been in their adoptive homes for at least three years, 77 percent were judged to represent successful adoptions. Grow and Shapiro claimed:

The findings in this study . . . indicate a level of success approximately the same as those obtained in other studies . . . both for traditional white infant adoptions and nontraditional adoptions involving racial mixture and other children.[2]

They described the problem families in their study as follows:

In 13 of the families in trouble, there was little or no evidence that the child's racial identity was a contributing factor to the problem, which might just as easily have developed in the case of a white adoptee or a biological child. In the other 16, however, there was evidence that problems concerning race were at least part of the total problem and, in some instances, the central problems. In two of these families, the parents had apparently been extremely naive about the racial aspects of the adoption. In both instances, the study child had been placed for foster care in infancy. The foster parents had decided to adopt rather than risk giving up the child, apparently without anticipating the impact the racial difference would have as he grew older. In nine cases, there was evidence that the child was in some conflict about his racial identity and his parents were having difficulty in dealing with it. In the remaining five cases, the parents showed a strong tendency to deny the child's racial background by minimizing its importance or passively ignoring it. This was sometimes justified by the child's fair appearance or by lack of specific information about his background. In a few extreme cases, children with a clearly Negroid appearance had not been told of their adoption or their black biological parentage.[3]

This chapter describes the problems that the parents in our study reported they were experiencing with their children over the years of the study. For some families the problems were reported during only one phase of the study, for others they persisted over the entire time span from 1972 to 1984, and for still others they began in early adolescence and continued through to young adulthood. We begin our account of the parents' reports when the children were between three and seven years of age.

In 1972, 62 percent of the parents said that they were not experiencing difficulties or having problems with their adopted child. Initially, for the first few weeks, a large proportion of those who had become parents for the first time claimed that they had had some difficulties adjusting to their new roles. But they felt that they would have had to make the same adjustments if the child had been born to them and/or if the child had been white.

But there was a relationship between the race of the adopted child and the proportion of parents who reported difficulties. For example, 18 percent of the parents who had adopted a white child as their first adopted child said that they had had problems with him or her, in contrast to 39 and 47 percent of the parents who had adopted black and Native American or Asian children. But among all categories (white, black, Native American, and Asian), the explanation most often given for the difficulties was that there were problems that had developed as a result of the foster care the child received prior to the adoption and not because of the child's race.

One of the families had an extraordinary story to tell about their experiences with a seven-year-old Native American black child they had adopted five years prior to the interview. It is the only family in our sample who had a tragic or near tragic experience resulting from their decision to adopt.

Both parents have graduate degrees. They had one child prior to the adoption, who was a year older than ''C,'' the adopted girl. They had tried to adopt a child before their first child was born. Their only requirement was that the child be healthy; the child's age, sex, and race were relatively unimportant. The agency with which they were dealing put them off, urging them to wait until they had been married longer and until, if possible, they had borne a child. The couple went back after their first child was born and indicated that they still wished to adopt a child. By this time they were quite sure they wanted a nonwhite child. A two-year-old American Indian girl was available. The parents were delighted, and the child was placed in their home. After they had adopted ''C,'' the mother gave birth to two other children.

At the time of the adoption the parents did not know, and it is not clear from their story whether the social worker knew, that ''C'' was suffering from PKU. The parents described the following events, which occurred shortly after ''C'' came into their home:

For the first day and night she just did not cry. She did not show any remorse at all for her foster parents. We were expecting a week of crying and were braced for it, but she was so angry that she couldn't be broken up. She didn't seem to know how to play with children. She followed ''G'' (her three-and-a-half-year-old brother) around bugging him. We protected her from ''G'' bashing her, but instead began bashing her ourselves. She had had a hard time. She started screaming out of nowhere. We put the lid on that. Then she started wetting her pants; we could stop one, but the other would erupt in a scene. She started nursery school at the age of three, but she was disruptive. She demanded that the ''mother'' hold her. She screamed, pushed, would not play with other children, and would not sit and listen.

She very early learned how to con adults. She had the habit of sitting in the hospital and pressing the button and having someone come running. She tends to play that game with adults in terms of disruptive behavior. Fortunately, the teachers at the nursery school keyed into that, as we did. You can't ignore it. She was there two years disrupting the place; then she went into kindergarten and they were calling us to come and get her. They said she was screaming and wandering around the class, disrupting everything. We finally had her examined and referred to the Children's Psychiatric Clinic. She's been an outpatient at the clinic now for two years. They also put her on medication when she was in kindergarten, which helps, a little. She also had a real good way of dividing us. We were ready for a divorce. We were all screaming and fighting with each other and would wind up beating up on her. It's really amazing how you can start out with good intentions and end up with such a mess.

None of the girls in the neighborhood, well, with the exception of one, will play with her. She's had trouble competing with ''G.'' He's very bright and very likable and has lots of friends, and she's terribly jealous of him. Then the baby (''D'') came along six months after we adopted her. I guess she's terribly jealous of ''D.'' According to her psychiatrist, it was to the point of slashing pictures and tearing up clothing. She had a period a year ago where she just wrecked up everything ''D'' had. Anything ''D'' got, if she didn't have the same thing, she wrecked it. She's gotten over some of it. ''D,'' of course, came into the house with her here, and as a small baby. She's very active and very silly, and it is really easy to relate to her, so that ''D'' still has a pretty good relationship with her. But she has been asking more and more questions about her. ''D'' tends to put most of the blame on adoption; the kids all make comments like, ''I came from my mommy's tummy, and you didn't,'' which does not help. I suppose it's normal in a situation like this where there are so few adopted children. She has a lot of strikes against her, because she's at a point where, emotionally, she can't keep up with the four-year-olds. She's really had to push herself the past year to stay ahead of ''D.''

I think there's basically a good deal of loyalty between ''D'' and ''G'' and they are both getting more and more tired of her. He is finding himself harrassed by her. She's going through a stage right now where she's just obsessed with swear words—''screw me,'' ''fuck you,'' ''all that shit,'' and all that stuff. He eggs her on, but then he gets it back. ''G'' keys in to the fact that she makes us angry, so he tries to make us happy about him, then he makes her make us angry. It's really complicated.

''G'' blames the PKU rather than the adoption. He says she acts bad because she has PKU. ''G'' has had some really severe times when he's wanted her to go back. ''G'' gets really upset. Also, we've tried to maintain the same standards for her as with ''G.'' And we've been very strict with ''G'' and we felt we had to be strict with her. We did feel that we had to let up on her because she's not functioning as a seven-year-old, she's functioning as a four-year-old, or even a two-year-old, and it's difficult for him to accept this, and some of this is due to the adoption. It's all so complicated.

The question is, if she had been a natural child would this have happened? We have no basis of knowing whether if she'd been born into the family, even if she had come in as an infant and been exactly as she is, how ''G'' would have regarded her. ''C'' has been the scapegoat almost since the beginning. ''G'' plays palsy-walsy with ''D.'' He says, ''We're pals because we're the same color, because we both came out of Mommy's tummy, and we're not adopted.'' He may not say it in exactly those words, but it has the same meaning. You can almost hear him say it.

On family relations, friends, and neighbors they provided the following account:

At first, my family [the mother's] supported it. Then in the past several years we've had quite a bit of trouble with the kids and my parents have gotten more and more discouraged. Last summer they indicated quite strongly that they felt we should take ''C'' back. There was some feeling on the part of the social worker that we might be able to make other arrangements. We had gone through a period of feeling that it was not working out. Then this summer we went to visit his mother and she hadn't seen us since ''D'' was a year old. We had indicated that we didn't want to stay with her because we'd been having trouble with the family. But she finagled around and we ended up staying with her and then we did have quite a scene. So then she told us she's never supported it and we should give her back. She had sort of waited to see how it was working out, and now that it was not working out she's against it. His [the father's] brothers are quite supportive. My sister lives in Japan, and we only see her overnight about once every four years. She's sorry we're not getting along.

We moved here after we had had ''C'' about a year. The neighbors have been quite supportive and very nice to her, and most of them accepting. They have occasionally set limits; one neighbor wouldn't let her on her porch because she screamed so much. Another finally wouldn't let her anywhere in the house except in the basement because she peed in the bed so much, but they still were quite supportive. No one invites her to their home; I think the neighbors got tired of the screaming. They don't invite her to go anywhere.

If she had turned out to be a normal child . . . we told the social worker that we have three children who turned out to be pretty much normal, so we don't think it's us. We don't think we created a monster. [Mother] I think I've become much more angry; I feel I'm angry all the time. [Father] We certainly are more jumpy. [Mother] I think we're very pessimistic. We find it very difficult to go to COAC meetings because we're so pessimistic about adoption. I talked to a couple of girls at church last night, and I warned them about getting older children. They're looking for Vietnamese children. We told the social worker at the very beginning we didn't think we could cope with a child with emotional problems or one who was dull or hard to teach or hard to learn. That was one condition we put down. It turns out that that's what we got, what we didn't want. We don't suffer the guilt problems, necessarily, but we are feeling very sad about the whole business and finding it hard to be in public.

When we encountered the family for the second time, in 1979, "C" was 14 years old. As of 1977 she had been committed to a state hospital and allowed to come home for weekends and for short vacations. The parents reported that relations between "C" and her parents and between "C" and her siblings had deteriorated drastically. Her temper tantrums and her anger got worse. She stole money from her younger sisters. The other children were shunned by the neighborhood because of "C's" bizarre and aggressive behavior. The mother went on:

"C" is not very cooperative and our personalities do not work well together. We antagonize each other. She is very emotionally immature, and she still provokes people. She hangs onto me, but hates me and her own dependence. Everything we ask her to do is a war. She doesn't want to please anyone at all.

"C" steals from the younger girls and the family's money. Anything she wants, she just takes. She has no friends and hangs onto her sisters and cannot play with anyone. She is emotionally still three to four years behind.

"C's" little sister [seven years old] thinks I am too hard on her, that I blame her for everything and am not nice to "C." Some of this is probably true. Her eleven-year-old sister, who has been picked on by "C" for years, is suspicious of her and gets angry at her and wishes she could act more grown up. Her older brother [he is 16] tolerates her, but doesn't care to be with her.

I have had problems in public, living with and explaining her behavior. Because I became too involved in "C's" problems, I had to try to go back to school and work part-time as a librarian, to have something that was mine. "C's" behavior has caused serious disagreement between us [her and her husband]. Much time has been spent arguing and blaming. We have had counselling since she was five and I have had two years of psychiatric help.

The father was more positive and optimistic. He did not mention "C's" stealing. He commented that the other children have come to understand personality problems as a result of having lived with "C". Toward the end of the interview, he said:

Of late it appears that our family has begun to mean more to her ["C"]. She is more loving and demonstrates this love by hugging. She is more interesting to talk to because she initiates conversation.

The mother concluded with the following observations:

I do not have the same feelings for "C" that I do for my biological kids. I was not aware of the pressure that would be placed on us when we adopted. Perhaps we were too optimistic. We thought we could cope . . . I would not do it again—raising a medically handicapped Indian-black child.

The parents also reported that doctors were not optimistic that "C" would be able to live independently and manage her own life as an adult. They predicted that she would have to live in a halfway house or in a supervised apartment.

By 1984, both parents said the family was in much better shape than it was five years ago. "C" was living in a group home, and she was able to come home for brief visits without causing turmoil. The three children born into the family had more positive feelings toward her and their parents than they did in 1979. The parents said they were hopeful that "C" might eventually be able to earn a living and look after herself, a plan they gave little credence to five years ago.

"C's" family is the most extraordinary we encountered in the study. The more typical problems parents related about their initial interactions with the adopted child appear in excerpts such as the following:

He had been in a foster home in Florida in a black home in a ghetto situation. He could only count to three when we got him at age four and a half, so one immediate problem we had was getting him ready for kindergarten next fall. And we put most of our efforts into preparing him because he's a very sharp little boy. He catches on very fast. But, for example, he had never put a puzzle together, never colored with crayons. The average child automatically does this with no questions asked. He's never experienced any of these things so that was one big problem, preparing him to face a school situation, to be on top of the situation. He'll be the top of his class; I'll guarantee it. We're still working on discipline. We'll probably be for a long, long while. In his foster home he was the favorite of three foster children. All the same age, all boys. He was favored because he was the light-skinned child out of three Negro children in a Negro home. There was no father in the home. Just a mother in her sixties and "P" was spoiled rotten. Anything other than monetary things, he had. Until she could not tolerate it anymore, then she beat him. And to him this means love. And so this is the only type of discipline he's known, complete unruliness until wham the lid comes down and you spank him. And so we've had trouble with him, adjusting to our form of discipline. We've been using Rudolf Driekur's form of discipline, and it's hard for him to cope with. He'll push to the point of spanking him. Little by little we are withdrawing the physical punishment, but this is very necessary for him. He will admit it. He wants me to spank him because, he will tell me, it means I love him and I care for him. We've had a problem of bed-wetting. He's been wet a whole year. He'll tell you if you ask, yes, he wets the bed to get even with us for taking him away from his foster home. He's a smart child and he knows why his behavior is as it is. But he is unable to correct it.

"M" has one panic point, and you saw it just now. When a stranger comes, she thinks she's going to be moved. And she hasn't been moved since she was two when we saw her standing there. Especially if she goes into another room that has other children standing around, she thinks, "Oh boy, here I go." She was moved four times before we got her. And so when she sees a bunch of authority-looking figures with briefcases come into the room and look her over she panics. That's one thing. Another thing was it took her a little while to break into the rules of the house. Every now and then she would go right ahead and do something and we'd bring it to her attention. And then she would do something and be surprised no one would say anything—something about the rules of the house where she was before. So it took her a little while.

"P" came at the age of one. And I don't know how to describe it. She was something like a vegetable. She was not a normal type of child. She was extremely anemic, frequently had bronchitis, and did not respond. She just sat on the floor and pounded her head against the wall or against her bed. I had thought that part of it was her adjustment to us. But when we got her, her forehead was all scabbed from banging her head against the wall. So she didn't start this when she came to us. Our doctor told us this child had not been fed right. She was so anemic it was no wonder she was sick all the time. So these weren't adjustment problems—there were no adjustment problems to our family. But she was not a normal child for her age. It took us six months to work her into a responsive sort of child. She couldn't figure out how to get a Cheerio from her high chair tray to her mouth. She would just sit and cry and want me to put it into her mouth. I talked to a pediatrician about this and he said it was typical of a foster child who was spoon-fed because the foster mother didn't want the child to make a mess. And you don't give the child a bunch of Cheerios because they would fall on the floor and get stepped on. So "P" seemed to have been bottle-fed, not given the right kind of food, and she must have been locked up in a crib or playpen because she was not mobile. Not like a normal one-year-old who zips around the house. Things began improving after about six months. But it was awfully difficult to understand her. We would play with her and tickle the bottom of her foot or put our mouths on her tummy and blow and whatever we did she would be frightened. She just couldn't understand why somebody would do something like this to her. "J" [older sister] was the one who pulled her out of it. Not [the father] or me, but "J." "J" is five years older than "P." "J" and "P" slept in the same room, and "J" pulled "P's" crib next to hers. I'd get up in the morning and "P" would be in "J's" bed, and they'd be hugging each other. She was right there, tenderly pulling "P" out. And "P" began crawling within a week and a half, and she was up walking within two and one-half weeks. She went from just sitting. We had to teach her how to crawl at the age of one.

"L" did nothing but sit and shake. He couldn't eat with a spoon. He had nightmares for many weeks. He needs lots of care and babying.

One family was critical of their child's prior foster placement, but not on grounds of neglect or indifference, indeed, quite the opposite. The parents explained that "S" (their adopted son, who was the fifth child in the family but the only one who had been adopted) was raised with a woman who felt that although her own son was six weeks younger, since "S" did not have a mother, all the attention should go to him.

So when he came, I was thinking, and I think we all felt, that to make him secure we would hold him and give him his bottles in the middle of the night. There was also this whole list of things that she [the foster mother] had sent: "He will not eat this," "He will not take medicine." So we were trying to make his adjustment easier. Instead, what we had was a child who had been overly cared for, had had so much attention. In fact, the night before he came, he'd been rocked for two and a half hours. We just reinforced all of that for several months afterwards. Everybody who came in sat and held him for an hour. So we just fed it, more and more and more. The foster mother was killed three or four months later and a friend of hers who was a mutual friend of ours relayed this information to us which we didn't know and possibly the caseworker wasn't familiar with it. It concerned the friend enough that she thought she had to tell us what had been going on because she realized that the child was placed with us and that she thought it was important for us to know—and I think it was.

About half of the parents perceived problems or difficulties involving their adopted child and his or her siblings, but the large majority attributed those difficulties solely to normal sibling rivalry. The proportion did not vary with the race of the adopted child. Only 11 and 15 percent of the parents who adopted black and American Indian or Asian children, respectively, attributed difficulties involving the adopted child and his or her siblings to race. The others did not perceive any problems.

For example, one family who had had a son born to them and then had adopted an older boy described the following first encounter:

The two boys were extremely close, they couldn't be closer if they were natural brothers. They fight and they bicker, and "B" picks on "N," but at the same time is very protective of him. There has never been a problem as far as adoption. In fact, they accepted each other faster than "B" accepted me. He accepted "N" upon their first meeting and "N" did the same. "N" was sixteen months old and was in the stage when he just didn't want to go to strangers for any reason at all. "B" sat down in front of the television and "N" climbed up into his lap and it's been that way ever since. "N" had never seen him before in his life. He just said, "You're my brother," and climbed up into his lap and that settled it.

Another family that had had two children and adopted their third told us:

They [the two birth children] were very anxious to have her [the expected adopted child]. They called the social worker the "new baby lady." Every time she would come, they would run up to her and yell, "Have you got her, have you got her?" So they were very ready. I think this is partly because of our attitude. She was not an intruder, but somebody we were waiting for.

Many of the parents that adopted after they had had children used the phrase "adoption is a family affair." By that they meant that their children were participants in their discussions and in their decision to adopt, especially when the discussion focused on the age, sex, and race of the child.

When asked if their own relations to the children who were born to them had undergone any strain as a result of the adoption, more than 75 percent felt that it had not. Again, the race of the child adopted did not differentiate parents' responses to this question.

In the 1979 and 1984 phases of our study, we broached the topic of "problems" with their adopted children this way.

Now we'd like to ask about the children we met seven years ago. How would you characterize your present relationship with your adopted child(ren)? If more than one child is involved, please answer for each child separately. Would you say it was basically good, happy, positive, etc.? Are there more positive or more negative elements in the relationship? Please check the appropriate category on the scale below.

1. Basically positive and good.
2. There are problems, but the positive elements outweigh the negative ones.
3. The problems are such that the negative elements outweigh the positive ones.
4. Basically negative and bad.

Altogether, out of 133 families, 25 sets of parents, or 19 percent of our respondents, checked either the third or fourth alternative and described problems related to the adoption and/or to the racial difference between themselves and their adopted children. The 19 percent we found matched closely the 15 percent reported by Kadushin and the 23 percent reported by Grow and Shapiro.

In 1979, the most common type of problem described by the families was that the adopted child was stealing from his parents and siblings. Most of these parents reported that siblings had locks put on their bedroom doors to prevent their sibling from stealing money, clothing, and bikes. When confronted by the parents, the child typically lied, denied that he had taken the missing items, and was abusive toward his parents or siblings. In almost all of these families, the problem child was a male. His race, ordinal position in the family, or the number of siblings he had did not seem to matter.

One parent reported that older black boys bribed their 12-year-old adopted black son to steal from them (for example, his sister's bicycle, money out of his mother's purse) and from other families who lived in his affluent neighborhood. One adopted boy was caught breaking and entering into his coach's house. Another family reported that one of their black adopted sons denied that he had stolen from his sibling or neighbors even when he was caught with the goods in hand.

Another mother described problems they were having with one of their adopted sons:

He acts as if he has no conscience. He is totally dishonest. He steals constantly. He gets along with no one. The other children have had to lock their bedroom doors even if they are just going to the bathroom. I'm amazed at how well they get along in spite of his stealing. It's hard to love your 12-year-old brother who will steal your new bike and sell it for a dollar and swear he didn't touch it.

He is very difficult to live with, but race has nothing to do with it. His race has augmented the problems, because as a dishonest person with no morals, blacks bribe him to steal from us and neighbors in our professional neighborhood. He'll do anything for a candy bar. He came to us unable to leave the table as long as any food was left on the table and has been food crazy his whole life.

I keep hoping and expecting he'll eventually grow out of this, given enough love and permanency. He reads a grade above his level. I have worked hard on supplying him with good books, hoping his ability will get him through. He's also a good athlete and we've gotten him into ice hockey leagues, etc., to help him feel capable and a member of teams, Boy Scouts, too. He has really presented a challenge.

The parents' commitment in each of these cases was interesting and reassuring. Almost all of them remained optimistic about their future relations with the child who was stealing and lying. For example, one mother said of her 13-year-old adopted American Indian son who stole from his 18-year-old sister:

Adoption has made me know that I have a universal love of all children regardless of origin. It has made me stretch to understand and help my own particular child.

At the end, she commented:

Our adopted child is loving and enthusiastic toward his family. He is a piece of sunshine most days, but he needs lots of guidance from both his parents, which "tries us" a lot! He is a dear boy and my determination is to help him find his place in the world.

Another mother of 15 children, 12 of whom were adopted, said:

Our newest son came with problems of lying, stealing, bed-wetting, unable to learn, but he's going to be O.K. We still believe in adoption and thank God for each of our 15 children. Yes, there have been tears and trials, but through them we've all grown and become better people. There's been a lot of joys and triumphs too, and we're proud of this family of ours.

Also common among the problem children were physical and/or mental or emotional disabilities. The parents believed these to be either genetic or the result of indifferent or abusive treatment in foster homes. The parents expressed bitterness and resentment toward the adoption agency and the social workers, believing that they withheld information that might have influenced the parents' decision to adopt that particular child. One father said:

Our 12-year-old son has serious emotional and behavioral problems that are affecting school, sibling, and marital relationships. We now know that the agency was dishonest with us about the child's origins, birth circumstances, early care, etc. We are more and more convinced that agencies took horrible advantage of families in several ways: (1) gave false, intentionally incomplete information or withheld information needed when parents did not push, and (2) moved children at inappropriate times and too frequently.

. . . Far too much divorce and pain is occurring because of the failure of skilled ser-vices to be available for families in these circumstances.

The mother added:

The hardest thing in our adoption was the absence of information on our third adopted child and the lack of help in working him into the family. He'd been badly abused and still expects us to send him away. He begs for it. We have *never* threatened it, and we always reply, "You are a member of our family, no matter *what* you do, we still love you."

A similar situation prevailed in a family that adopted a black child who was 20 months old. By the age of 12 he was described as "egocentric" and lacking friends. He caused problems between the parents and the other children and appeared "spaced out." The parents blamed the welfare department and the foster parents for not having told them about his problems. Knowing what they do now, the mother believes the child was badly treated in the foster home in which he was living prior to the adoption. She believes that the welfare agency did not do enough screening of the child before the placement. She said of her 12-year-old son; "He disregards even the most elementary social conventions, such as traffic lights; he will leave a mess, and the other family members have to clean up after him." At the time of the interview, the parents were planning to send the boy to a private, in-residence school. "Maybe he will appreciate home when he is away," the mother concluded.

Another family had one child born to them and then adopted a black boy when he was three and a half years old. The parents discovered that he was diabetic and had some brain damage and severe learning disabilities. The mother said that she needed ten times the energy she had to look after him. She felt that the time that she devoted to him was resented by their older son, who was 14, and their 6-year-old daughter. The situation resulted in marital strain. The parents did not know if the learning disability was genetic or if it was caused by the care he received in the foster home. They were bitter at the failure of the social worker to provide them with more information. The father's parents severed contact with the family for three and a half years when they adopted transracially. Even after some reconciliation, the grandparents were embar-rassed by their black grandson and tried to avoid his visiting them in their small community. In the parents' interview, they emphasize that there are "really great problems in adopting an older child."

In 1974, one of the families adopted their second black daughter. They had adopted a black girl in 1969 and had two sons born to them. Prior to her adoption, "B" had lived in five different foster homes and had been adopted previously by a white family. She was removed from that home when the adoptive mother's condition was diagnosed as "borderline schizophrenic." The parents described "B" as having no conscience. They claimed that her experiences in five foster homes "taught her how to survive." During the first year after her adoption, she used to wake up screaming in the middle of the night. She also had seizures, which the parents attributed to past abuse. The two brothers pleaded with their parents to send her back. The worst problem, however, existed between the first adopted daughter, "K," who was 10 years old, and "B," who was 8. According to the mother,

"K" has troubles competing with "B" for attention. "B" knew all the tricks by the time she came to our family and infuriated "K" constantly. After five years, there is still jealousy and irritation on the part of "K" toward "B."

At the end of the interview the mother commented:

I used to believe that environment was the dominant force in a person's life. Now I think you are born with a certain genetic character and that this remains pure and strong throughout life. Any changes that occur in a basic personality are really very minor. In other words, I think "B" could very well become a juvenile delinquent in spite of the influence living with us might have.

Some parents expressed guilt at having inflicted harm on their birth child(ren) through their decision to adopt transracially. They feared that the birth child(ren) suffered neglect as a result of the time, energy, and attention that the adopted child required due to some emotional or physical scars or handicaps. They also noted that the family changed its life-style in order to participate in the adopted child's culture. Examples included families' moving into largely black neighborhoods, joining a black church, trying to build a social life around black friends, and observing and celebrating events in black history.

In one such family, the father commented that their oldest daughter had learned to repress her hostility toward her two younger adopted black siblings: "She has been taught that only bad people hate blacks or adopted children." This resulted in guilt and confusion. Their younger son, who was born to them, went through a period "of wanting to be black and adopted." The mother added that when the boy was five or six years old he felt he was of "less value—because our social life revolved around the adoption and around a group of adoptive parents." Shortly after they adopted the two children, the parents moved into a racially mixed neighborhood in order to help their adjustment.

In another family, both parents reported that their adopted white daughter was jealous of her adopted brother's American Indian heritage. The mother said that the daughter "refuses to accept family or school rules, is generally negative, and resorts to name calling and tantrums." The family participated in the activities of the local Native American Culture School. Their son danced at powwows.

In the 1984 survey, we asked the parents to check the same rating scale included in the 1979 interviews. Nine of the 96 families checked Category 3,

Table 8.1
Parents' Ratings of Their Relations with Their Children

Child's Status	Mean Score
First TRA	1.57
Second TRA	1.44
Third TRA	1.57
First child born	1.30
Second child born	1.30
Third child born	1.28
First white adopted	1.40
Second white adopted*	1.66

*Frequencies are too small for the third white adopted.

"the problems are such that the negative elements outweigh the positive ones," or Category 4, "the relationship is basically negative and bad." None of these 9 families had checked Category 3 or Category 4 in 1979. In addition, 11 of the 22 families who had checked "3" or "4" in 1979 participated in the 1984 survey, and of those 11, 7 were still having serious problems and 4 families had apparently resolved the problems they had confronted in 1979.

By way of summary, the parents' mean scores for children in the birth and adopted categories are shown in Table 8.1.

Note that the scores varied more according to the adoptive status of the children than they did by their ordinal position in the family. Thus the ratings for the oldest, second oldest, and third oldest transracially adopted children were closer to each other than were the ratings for the transracially adopted children and children born into the family within each ordinal position. Second, the parents evaluated their relationships with the children born to them more positively than they did those with the children adopted, be they white or non-white.

The problems mentioned by the parents who checked Categories 3 and 4 are described in detail in the following pages. But first we report on the four families who resolved their problems, then we describe the seven families whose problems were unresolved in 1984, and finally we consider the relatively new "problem families."

For the first family, consisting of two parents and six children ranging in age from 25 to 10, the focus of the problem in 1979 was their 12-year-old black son. Five of the children had been born to the parents. In characterizing the quality of the relationship with their transracially adopted son, the mother reported that the problems were such that "the negative elements outweighed the positive ones." They had adopted their son when he was 20 months old. Prior to the adoption, he had been in a foster home. The parents reported that the boy had no friends and that he was "spaced out."

Five years later, in 1984, the parents said that if they had an opportunity to begin again, they would do nothing differently. All things being equal, they believed that it was better to place children with families who shared their racial backgrounds or culture, but "the fact is there are more black children available for adoption than there are black families willing or able to adopt." The 12-year-old transracially adopted son was a junior in high school, with average grades between C− and D. He planned to go to college and major in physical education and play sports. The parents reported that he was a "good mixer" and got along well with his 20-year-old and 15-year-old sisters, who were still living at home. The parents now evaluated their relationship with him as "having problems but the positive elements outweigh the negative ones." They continued to view him as self-centered and wished that he was "more tuned in to other people's existence." The parents reported that their son considered himself black, but a "suburban black," like his brother-in-law.

The second family was composed of seven people: the mother and father, three daughters aged 21, 19, and 16, one son born to them who was 18, and one transracially adopted son who was 17. In 1979, the parents had dwelled on the behavior of their adopted son; he was stealing from both his parents and siblings and destroying family property. He did not work in school but disrupted classes and demanded to be the center of attention. The parents said of their relationship with him, "The problems are such that the negative elements outweigh the positive ones." But they went on to describe themselves as "working as a team in trying to solve our problems."

Sometime between 1979 and 1984, the adopted son, his brother, and the youngest daughter ended up in an alcohol treatment center. The sons spent two years away from home living at the center, undergoing a highly disciplined reform program. The parents did not refer to this episode, but both sons discussed their experiences at the center and expressed pride in the fact that they and their sister "graduated" from it and were now on the "right path."

The parents made no mention of the alcohol problem in their interview. Given their willingness to allow their sons to be interviewed (and their acceptance of the conditions of privacy), they must have assumed that their sons would talk about their experiences. The parents reported that they expected to be close to their sons.

The third family's problems in 1979 centered around the jealousy and insecurity felt by one of the children born into the family toward her Korean adopted brother and especially toward her Korean sister. Both of the children were adopted when they were six years old. The two birth children were nine (the oldest son) and eight (the daughter who had the problems) when the adoptions took place. The daughter had left home and moved to the west coast for a few years but had recently returned. In her interview she talked about getting her life together, going back to school, not drinking, and coming to terms with feelings about her sister.

The adopted sister described anger at her Korean mother for giving her up for adoption and a desire to look like the other people in her adopted family. She was jealous of her sister's blond hair. She experienced lots of name calling—"Pearl Harbor," "chink," "gook"—and some children used to spit at her. She went through a period of dependency on drugs (alcohol, pot, LSD) and was sent to a residential treatment center. The parents traced their adopted daughter's problem to her anger at her biological mother for giving her up and for earning a living by prostitution. What came through most clearly in the 1984 interviews was the closeness, the mutual dependency that both sisters felt toward each other, and the hopefulness on the part of the parents that the worst was over for both daughters and for them.

In the fourth family, both parents had died (the father in 1966 and the mother in 1975). There were five children; three were born to the parents, and two were transracially adopted. In 1979, one of the birth daughters answered the questionnaire as a parent surrogate. In 1984, she and the two transracially adopted daughters were living in the family home. The oldest daughter still played a maternal role to her two transracially adopted siblings, viewing herself as their mother. The brothers in the family play tangential roles. By 1983, the oldest daughter had completed four years of college and was planning to go on for her master's degree. She was hopeful that both of her sisters would also finish college and be self-sufficient, although she reported that the 19-year-old had a learning disability. The 19-year-old transracial adoptee had an especially close relationship with the 21-year-old sister, whom she described as her second mother. The two sisters who participated in the survey expected to hold the family together.

We turn next to the seven families in the 1984 survey who reported problems in 1979 and who continued to report serious problems. In six of the seven families, the major problem reported in the 1979 survey was stealing by the transracially adopted child from other family members. The seventh family was the one that we described as "tragic" in both the 1972 and 1979 studies because the daughter had PKU.

In all but one of these families, the children who had had problems in 1979 were no longer living at home. In five of the families, the parents had placed the child in a drug rehabilitation center or a psychiatric hospital or were under court order to send their child to a juvenile facility. In the sixth family, the son had left the area when he was 17 and moved to the Southwest, where he was working and married (to a white woman).

In six of the seven families, the problems with the transracially adopted child had repercussions for the other children in the family. They felt neglected by their parents because of the energy and time it took to relate to the "problem child." Later they felt deceived because their parents made decisions and took actions involving their sibling without discussing it with them or informing them ahead of time. For example, the parents placed their brother or sister in a drug therapy center or a hospital. One of the children born into the family developed a serious eating disorder (anorexia nervosa), which she attributed to lack of parental attention.

All of the transracially adopted children in the six families who had stolen from other family members had been adopted when they were between four and seven years old. Two were American black; the others were Native Americans and Korean. All had been in foster homes or institutionalized before the adoption; all had mental or physical handicaps. In all but one family, the parents and the siblings emphasized that the racial differences were *not* the cause or source of the problem. In their view, the child's early history and the physical/mental disabilities were the important factors.

The one family who did consider race important lived in a "village" outside the larger community where most of the interviews were conducted, and the parents felt that their son was "too different. He needed to go somewhere where he did not stand out, where he could get lost in the crowd." He is the child mentioned above who moved to the Southwest and married a white woman.

The three families who had adopted an American Indian used to attend powwows, prepared ethnic food, and had Indian books and artifacts in their home, but the children showed no interest in their ethnic heritage. In one of those families, a transracially adopted son who was 14 in 1984 was still stealing from his parents and lying to them.

With one exception, the seven sets of parents expected and hoped that "things would get better" and that the children would feel positively toward each other and toward them. There were indications in five of the families that the parents and the transracially adopted child with the difficulties were indeed working through their problems. But the children born into those families did not trust their parents and did not expect to have a close relationship with them. They were bitter and angry. Another transracially adopted son (the one who was still living at home) built walls between himself and his parents and siblings that may be difficult or impossible to penetrate. In the one family where the parents (primarily the father) were negative, the transracially adopted son believed that adopting children after they were two or three years old made "bonding" difficult and unlikely and the problems only got worse.

Although we placed the family with the daughter who has PKU in the "problems in 1979 and 1984" category, the family perceived itself as being in much better shape in 1984 than it was in 1979. The daughter was living in a group home, but she was able to return to the parental home for brief visits without causing turmoil. The three birth children had more positive feelings toward her and their parents than they had five years ago. The parents were now hopeful that "C" might eventually be able to earn a living and look after herself. Five years ago, they were doubtful of that possibility. Each of the children described scars resulting from "C's" adoption, but they were nevertheless more positive toward their parents than were children in the other "problem" families. They did not blame their parents for "C."

In the last category are the nine families who were having serious problems when we interviewed them in 1984 but had not reported difficulties in 1979. In addition, we included two "problem" families whom we could not locate in 1979 but found in 1984.

In 3 of the 11 families, the parents were divorced. That is a much higher rate than the five divorces and three separations reported in the remaining 85 families. Among the 3, the mother had custody of all six children in one family, the father had custody of all four children in the second family, and the mother had custody of three of the four children in the third family. The father had custody of the transracially adopted son.

The parents in the family where the mother had custody of all six children were divorced in 1976. The two youngest children, 15- and 14-year-old sons, were transracially adopted. The oldest of the birth children was 14. The 14-year-old transracial adoptee has a severe learning disability; he cannot read or write and attends a special school. He also had a drug problem, and the family had a history of alcoholism. According to the mother, she, the father, who is a physician, and the second child born to them, who was then 20 years old, were all alcoholics. The mother is a lesbian whose lover lived with her and the children. The older of the two transracial adoptees was very self-conscious about being black. He described experiences in which people stared at the family when they were in restaurants, stores, and other public places. He believed that he would fit in better in his family, his neighborhood, and his school if he were white. Most of his friends are white. He commented, "I don't act like I'm black . . . Yes, I would prefer to be white, so I wouldn't be stared at and because I act like I am white."

The youngest son also noted that "people look at you funny when we are out as a family," but seemed unconcerned about his blackness or about his difference from the family because of race. He talked more about having been "shuffled back and forth" between his mother's and father's homes when he was younger and about his learning disability. He could not remember any incident when someone was nasty to him because of his racial background. For all of the unusual arrangements in this family, the mother and children referred to each other warmly and generously and all the children expected to be close to their mother, though not to each other.

In the second divorced family, the mother had had custody of all four children (the oldest daughter, 17, and the youngest son, 13, who were born to the parents, and the two middle sons, 15 and 14, who were transracially adopted) until a few months prior to the interview, when the father gained custody of the 15-year-old black son, who had a learning disability and problems in school.

His average grade was a D. The mother expressed resentment of the boy. She thought that she might have found it easier to remarry if she did not have him. He produced great strains on her and stress in the family because of his immature, loud, attention-seeking, demanding behavior. The mother also reported poor relations between the child and his siblings. In addition to his learning disability, the boy was small for his age, and the mother felt that his size caused him more problems than his color. His adopted black brother, who was one year younger, was tall and expected to play college and professional basketball. She believed that the divorce also affected the transracial adoptee with the disability more than the other children. Both of the adopted sons considered themselves black and planned to live in black or mixed communities. At the end of the interview, in reflecting on the family and the decision to adopt black children, the mother said she felt that the adoption had been good for "Y" and "L" (the two children born to her). It had "allowed them to reach beyond stereotypes and judge people as people, not on the basis of race. As adults, they will have gotten a complex and enriching experience."

The father was also interviewed, and the responses reflect his closeness to the son who was living with him. When asked how he felt about the position of the NABSW, the father said, "I told them right back what I thought. That what blacks do to prepare kids for a hostile system is wrong. They make a lot out of nothing." The father saw whatever problems "O" had as stemming from the conflict between himself and his ex-wife. He anticipates a warm/close relationship with "O" as "O" continues to live with him and after he leaves his home.

In the third divorced family, the father had custody of all four children since the divorce in 1973. The mother no longer lived in the state. Of the four children, the two oldest (daughters, 19 and 17) were born into the family and the two youngest (sons, 15 and 14) were transracially adopted. The 15-year-old had a learning disability; "he was kicked out of high school last year." The father described him as "very self-centered. The whole world revolves around him. He does not get along with his siblings." The father rated his own relationship with the boy as a "3." ("The problems are such that the negative elements outweigh the positive ones.") The heart of the problem stemmed from the boy's mother (the ex-wife), who, according to the father, suffered a "severe depression" when "C," the 15-year-old black adopted son, was between two and five years old. Again according to the father, "during her depression, she would say directly to C, 'I hate you,' and tell the other children how she felt about him." The mother's rejection continued to the present and was evidenced in the absence of any relationship between her and "C." For example, on the day of the interview, the mother was in town and took her daughters and youngest transracially adopted son out for the afternoon, but "C" was not invited. He receives no birthday or Christmas presents from her as the others do. "C" was in therapy. The father believed that he was maturing very slowly and that "it may take 20 or 30 years before he is independent."

Among the remaining eight families, all of whom were intact, there were four in which the parents described some problems with one or more of their children. But the children, while they admitted that there were some difficulties, generally drew a positive family profile and reported that they anticipated close and positive ties to their parents and siblings in the future. For example, in one family with a 17-year-old transracially adopted daughter as the only child, the parents were "desperate about her drinking at parties and her poor performance in school." In 1979, this was a family who talked about their daughter in glowing terms. She was a gifted student, musician, and skater. The parents traced their daughter's subsequent problems to her feelings of abandonment by her birth mother. They would no longer recommend transracial adoption to anyone. In contrast, interviewing their daughter was like talking about another family. She described close and strong relationships with her parents, acknowledged that her behavior did not meet their standards, but viewed this as a "bad period" that they were all going through. Their relationship would improve, she predicted. They were her parents; she expected to be close to them always.

A similar theme emerged in three of the other "problem" families. The parents made negative, harsh assessments about the quality of their relationships with their children and expressed the feeling that the adoption had been a mistake. Although the children reported problems, they described positive, warm, upbeat feelings toward their parents and toward each other.

In the fourth such family, one of the transracially adopted sons, who was 20 years old, had run away from home and had become involved with a family who trained children to carry out robberies. He was a child with a severe learning disability who could not read or write. He had two transracially adopted siblings and one brother who was born to the parents. In this family as well, the children all had positive feelings toward each other, toward their parents, and toward the family as a unit. The parents sounded exhausted.

In the remaining four problem families, a different pattern emerged: One or two transracially adopted children, out of many others in the family, were angry, hostile, bitter, and anxious to separate themselves from the family. In one family of 14 children, of whom 3 were transracially adopted, the 2 youngest transracially adopted daughters, who were 17 and 15 years old, described a lack of trust in the family, a belief that their parents would not stick by them, and anger at the rude behavior exhibited by their parents toward their friends. The two children born to the parents who were still at home shared none of their siblings' perspectives.

The same pattern appeared in a family of four children, three of whom were transracial adoptees, but only the 18-year-old daughter, who dropped out of school when she was 14 and has been arrested for prostitution, assault, and shoplifting, was angry and wanted out. In another family, one of the transracially adopted daughters was in a correctional facility for shoplifting and prostitution. The daughter, who was 15, started running away from home periodically when she was in the eighth grade. According to the parents, the other children, who included transracial adoptees and those born into the family, did not engage in antisocial behavior and seemed to have positive, close ties to their parents and siblings.

In the last of the 1984 problem families, the oldest of two Vietnamese adopted daughters left home and was living with her boyfriend, whose family took care of their expenses. She was 17 years old and was attending high school. The parents had not spoken to her in several months. They described her as having a "borderline personality." The clinical psychologist to whom they had taken her several years ago told them, "Her self-concept is poor; she becomes confused easily, is subject to emotional outbursts, and is unable to properly label her emotions." The parents described positive experiences with their 15-year-old Vietnamese adopted daughter and with their two older sons, who were born to them. The sons shared their parents' feelings, but the 15-year-old daughter did not. She had closed herself off from her parents, but not from her brothers and her sister, whom she used to see without her parents' knowledge. The younger daughter does not believe that her parents understand her or her sister, to whom she is sympathetic. About her parents, she hoped that "perhaps, in the future, I will find it easier to talk with them."

In sum, we have found that 18 of the 96 families were experiencing serious problems. Among 7 of them, the problems were long-standing, going back at least five years. They manifested themselves initially when the transracially adopted child began to steal from parents and siblings. None of those children were living at home. They had been placed in drug rehabilitation centers, psychiatric hospitals, or juvenile facilities. In one family, the son left on his own when he was 17. The children were all adopted when they were at least four years old and had serious mental and/or physical handicaps at the time. They had lived in foster homes or public institutions prior to their adoption. The parents, with one exception, emphasized that in their view race was not the source of the child's difficulties. They focused instead on the child's experiences in the institution and on the child's disabilities. The parents were still hopeful that the child would overcome his/her problems and that they would have a positive relationship with him/her.

Three of the 11 families whose problems were reported to us for the first time in the 1984 interviews were divorced. Some of the children's problems stemmed from the parents' relationship, but learning disabilities and other developmental problems were also reported for the children in these families.

There were two patterns in the eight other problem families. In one group, the parents portrayed their problems and their sense of estrangement from their transracially adopted child in harsher, more negative terms than those used by the child or the siblings to describe the relationship. Some of these parents attributed their problems with the child to racial differences. They were hurt, disappointed, and pessimistic. The children, on the other hand, characterized much of what they were experiencing as a phase or bad period. In the long run, the adopted children believed the relationship with their parents would be a good one.

In the second group, most of the children, those adopted and those born into the family, and the parents felt positively toward each other. One child had engaged in delinquent behavior or had rejected the family's rules and left. These parents, like many of the others, did not trace the source of the problems to the child's racial background. Instead, they emphasized developmental and personality characteristics. They also pointed out that their other transracially adopted child did not engage in antisocial behavior.

NOTES

1. Alfred Kadushin, *Adopting Older Children* (New York: Columbia University Press, 1970), p. 63.

2. Lucille J. Grow and Deborah Shapiro, *Black Children, White Parents: A Study of Transracial Adoption* (New York: Child Welfare League of America, 1974), p. 102.

3. Ibid., p. 103.

9

Ordinary Families: A Collective Portrait

The previous chapter described and examined all of the bruises, warts, and ugliness we discovered in the families who were experiencing problems. Some of the vignettes portrayed deceit, ignorance, and lack of trust between parents and children, between the adopted and birth children, and among adopted siblings. We reported anger, disgust, lack of communication, and indifference by persons in each of these categories. We have to assume that the reader has been affected by those accounts and wonders about the wisdom and practicality of transracial adoption. The collective portrait that we draw in this chapter is not meant to disavow the facts described by the "problem families," but it is intended to depict the dominant themes, the life patterns, the emotions, and the interactions among the majority—indeed, among at least four out of five of all the families in the study. This picture was developed after reading all of the parents' and children's interviews and examining the tables derived from the descriptive statistics.

In journalism, it is "bad news"—catastrophes, tragedies, both human and naturally induced—that sells newspapers, makes headlines, keeps listeners glued to their radios and TV sets. But in science, we are more interested in the major trends, in the larger patterns, in what seem to be the dominant themes, without of course discarding the deviant cases. Thus what we did in the previous chapter was to provide the reader with all the information we could glean from our data about the difficulties our families were confronting and the ways in which they were responding to their problems.

This chapter looks at the "ordinary families." We believe that the portrait that emerges is a positive, warm, integrated picture that shows parents and children who feel good about themselves and about their relationships with each other. On the issue of whether to adopt a child of a different race, almost all of the parents would do it again and would recommend it to other families. They believe that they and their birth children have benefited from the experiences. Their birth children have developed insight, sensitivity, and tolerance that they could not have acquired in the ordinary course of life. Their transracial adoptees may have been spared years in foster homes or institutions. They have had the comfort and security of loving parents and siblings who have provided them with a good home, educational and cultural opportunities, friendship, and the belief that they are wanted.

We found that almost all of the families made some changes in their lives as a result of their decision to adopt. Most of the time, however, the changes were not made because of their decision to adopt a child of a different race, but because they decided to add another child to the family. Thus the parents talked about buying a bigger house, adding more bedroom space, having less money for vacations and entertainment, and allowing less time for themselves. Most of the parents did not dwell on what they wished they had done but did not do; nor did they berate themselves for things they did and wished they had not done. Most of them feel that they did their best. They worked hard at being parents and at being parents of children of a different race.

In the early years, many of them were enthusiastic about introducing the culture of the transracial adoptees' backgrounds into the family's day-to-day life. This was especially true of the families who adopted Native American and Korean children. They experimented with new recipes, sought out books, music, and artifacts, joined churches and social organizations, traveled to the Southwest for ceremonies, and participated in local ethnic events. The parents of black children primarily introduced books into their homes about black history and black heroes, joined black churches, sought out black playmates for their children, and celebrated Martin Luther King's birthday. In a few families, a black friend is the godparent to the transracially adopted child. One mother told us: "Black parents regard us as black parents."

But as the years wore on, as the children became teenagers and pursued their own activities and social life, the parents' enthusiasm and interest for "ethnic variety" waned. An increasing number of families lived as their middle- and upper-middle-class white neighbors did. Had the children shown more interest, more desire to maintain ethnic contacts and ties, most of the parents would have been willing to do so, but in the absence of signals that the activities were wanted by and meaningful to their children, the parents decided that the one-culture family was an easier route. Almost all of the parents said that they were affected by the stance of the NABSW and that of the Native American Councils in the 1970s concerning the adoption of black and American Indian children by white families. Almost all of the parents thought that the position taken by those groups was contrary to the best interests of the child and smacked of racism. They were angered by the accusations of the NABSW that white parents could not rear black children, and they felt betrayed by groups whose respect they expected they would have. "Race," they believed, was not and should not be an important criterion for deciding a child's placement. In their willingness to adopt they were acting in the best interest of a homeless, neglected, unwanted child. One parent said, "Our children are the ones no one wanted. Now they are saying you are the wrong family."

Some parents (a handful) felt guilty as a result of the attacks on them, and that guilt resulted in their decision not to adopt a second or, in some instances, a third nonwhite child. "Perhaps," some of them said, "the position of the NABSW is right." They had ventured into a far more complicated social world than the one for which they were prepared. Goodwill and the desire to have and love a child (or another child) were not sufficient reasons for adopting a child for whom they could not provide the desired or necessary racial or ethnic heritage. Among this handful, some said that they could understand "their [the NABSW's] position because our kids have white values." Others among this small group said, "We are not, and cannot be, appropriate black role models. We've learned that is important." It is important to emphasize that only a handful of parents made those observations.

While almost all of the parents felt that they had been affected one way or another by the NABSW's position, practically none of them believed that it had any effect on their children, primarily because the children were too young to hear about and understand the issues.

While we have said this earlier, we think the observation bears repeating: namely, our sense of the respondents' (both the parents' and the children's) candor and honesty in describing their feelings, their hopes, their disappointments, and their regrets. At no time during the interviews did this come through more clearly than in the families' evaluations of the quality of their relationships with each other and in their assessments of the relationships among other members of the family. In their responses to our request to characterize their relationship with each child on a scale of 1 to 4—"basically positive and good" to "basically negative and bad"—the mothers and fathers talked out their feelings, evaluated the pros and cons in their relationships, compared the past few years to the present, and then came up with an answer. In most instances, when the mother and father were participating in the interview together, they provided a joint evaluation, but not always. There were families in which the mothers and fathers disagreed. There was no consistent pattern that would limit more negative evaluations to one parent rather than the other. When the parents disagreed, however it was never by more than one position on the scale.

The parents went through the same detailed, historical analyses when they were asked to evaluate the quality of the relationships among their children. The majority were willing to explore their children's personalities, strength, and weaknesses in great detail.

On the whole, as the data reported in Chapter 5 show, the evaluations were positive, but there were more 2's (that is, "there are problems, but the positive elements outweigh the negative ones") than 1's ("the relationship is basically positive and good"). There was no consistent pattern in their evaluation of the birth children as opposed to those whom they adopted, nor in their judgments about the relationships between siblings born into the family and those adopted. The parents emphasized "interests," "tastes," "age differences," "jealousy," and "competitiveness." The adoptive status of the child was not a primary determinant of those qualities or feelings, according to the parents.

The children answered the questions posed to them about their relationships with family members with the same frankness and honesty that was apparent among the parents. We noted earlier that somewhat to our surprise, in many families the children made more positive evaluations of the quality of their family relationships than did the parents. The parents, in some instances, seemed willing to step back and disengage themselves from the situation; the children—and here we have to take special note of the transracial adoptees—continually said, "They are my parents. Yeah, we've had our differences, but I know I can count on them, and I want to be close." That is not meant to indicate that many of the older ones (those in their late teens) were not anxious and ready to move out of the parental home; they were. But the transracial adoptees unequivocally did not perceive their relationships with their parents as temporary or transitional. Practically none of them, even those who expressed anger and bitterness about their current relations, said that they were likely to cut off ties completely or walk out of the family.

We did not find the same type of commitment among the siblings. But here again, it is important to stress that negative or indifferent feelings were not restricted to the relationships between adopted and birth children. As in the case of the parents' judgments, the siblings' evaluations were based on personality characteristics, interests, tastes, age differences, sex, talents, and prior history, not adoptive status.

One topic that seemed to have been exhausted by the third phase of our study was the quality of the transracial adoptees' relationships with other relatives—grandparents, aunts, uncles, and cousins. No parent reported that their transracially adopted children had been rejected or that ties had been severed by the grandparents or other relatives. In many families, one or more of the grandparents had died or grandparents and other relatives lived too far away to make frequent contact feasible, but there were also numerous families in which the children talked warmly about their vacations at grandparents' homes, their visits with aunts, uncles, and cousins, and their sense of strong family ties. We rarely heard transracial adoptees describe situations in which they felt rejected by their extended family members. Large family gatherings, however, were most likely to provoke awareness by the transracial adoptees of the differences in appearance between them and the rest of their relatives. It was on these occasions that they were most likely to wish that the differences did not exist. For the most part, adoption meant membership in the extended family unit, according to both parents and children.

Much of what we have portrayed thus far has been gleaned from the perceptions and opinions of the parents. And there is still more to be said from that vantage point, especially about the future. But let us briefly turn from the parents and begin drawing the children's collective portrait. There are two major thrusts to our comments about the children. First, we demonstrate that the children born into the families and the transracial adoptees resemble each other far more than they differ in their tastes and interests, educational aspirations, choice of friends, and feeling about their parents. Second, we characterize what is distinctive about being black or American Indian or Korean in a white family, in a largely white neighborhood, and assess whether that distinctiveness has made a difference for better or worse.

We wrote earlier at some length about the uses of the Self-Esteem Scale and the scores achieved by black and white adolescents in the Baltimore school system and other areas. The Rosenberg and Simmons study reported consistently higher self-esteem (meaning lower scores) for black than for white children in the same grade and school system. It also reported that the crucial factor in determining self-esteem was the role of "significant others." That is, the respondents' views of the assessments made by their friends, classmates, teachers, and mothers heavily influenced their own self-esteem.

We applied the same scale to the adolescents in our study and found no differences by race or adoptive status. Because we wanted to make the best possible comparison between our respondents and those included in the Rosenberg and Simmons study, we examined the scores of our black transracial adoptees separately from those of the other transracial adoptees and from those of the white born and white adopted children. The scores for all four groups were virtually the same. No one category manifested higher or lower self-esteem than the others.

The lack of difference among our respondents on the Self-Esteem Scale reminds us of the lack of difference we reported for these children in the first study when we asked them to choose dolls of different races. A child received one point each time he or she selected the white doll in response to: "Which doll would you: (a) like to play with the best? (b) think is a nice doll? (c) think is a nice color?" and did not select the white doll as the doll that (d) looks bad. The scores obtained demonstrated that none of the children manifested a white racial preference. Out of a possible score of 4, which would have meant that the white doll was selected in response to items (a) through (c), the average score was 1.7, thus showing that none of the children selected the white dolls even half the time.

On the basis of all the responses to the items in which dolls were used to measure racial attitudes, racial awareness, and racial identity, we found no consistent differences between the adopted and nonadopted children and among the black and other transracially adopted children. We wrote in our first volume:

There was no consistent preference for the white doll among the black, white, and Indian or Oriental children. There was no indication that the black children had acquired racial awareness earlier than the white children, and there was no evidence that the white children were able to identify themselves more accurately than the nonwhite children.

Our 1972 study was the first to report that there were no white racial preferences among American black and white children. The responses suggested that the unusual family environment in which these children were being reared might have caused their deviant racial attitudes and resulted in their not sharing with other American children a sense that white is preferable to other races. We noted that the children's responses also demonstrated that their deviant racial attitudes did not affect their ability to identify themselves accurately.

Both sets of responses, those obtained in 1972 and in 1984, consistently portray a lack of difference between black and white children in these special, multiracial families, when differences have been and continue to be present between black and white children reared in the usual single race family. It seems accurate to conclude that something special happens to both black and white children when they are reared together as siblings in the same family.

The lack of differences among our adolescent responses is also again dramatically exemplified in our findings on the Family Integration Scale. The hypothesis was that adopted children would feel less integrated than children born into the families. But the scores reported by our four groups of respondents (black transracial adoptees, other transracial adoptees, white birth, and white adoptees) showed no significant differences and, indeed, among the three largest categories (not including the white adoptees) the mean scores measuring family integration were practically identical: 15.4, 15.2, and 15.4.

Looking for additional indicators of the extent to which the adopted as opposed to the nonadopted respondents felt that they were integrated into the family, we examined responses to items asking to whom they would go if they were happy about something, worried about something, wrongly accused of stealing, and whom they thought really knew best what they were like as a person. On these items as well, we found no difference by adoptive status. But one pattern did emerge that warrants comment: the differences in responses between daughters and sons.

In their study of transracial adoption in England, Owen Gill and Barbara Jackson found that girls scored better than boys on the Family Integration Scale (that is, their responses showed that they felt more integrated into their family than did the boys).[1] Our item-by-item examination revealed a small but consistent tendency for the transracially adopted daughters to feel *less* integrated than the transracially adopted sons. There was no such pattern among the sons and daughters born into the families. Similarly, on the items asking "whom would you tell," the transracially adopted daughters were consistently *less* likely to select a parent than were the transracially adopted sons or the sons and daughters born into the family. The differences were even smaller on the "expected closeness" to parents and siblings in the future, but on these items as well, the transracially adopted daughters signaled that they did not anticipate seeking out either their parents or their siblings to the extent indicated by the children in the other categories. One explanation for these differences is that the girls feel the rejection by their birth mothers more keenly than the boys do and as a result are less trusting of their adoptive parents.

Turning to the matter of perceptions about race and racial identities, we reported that 71 percent of the transracial adoptees said that they had no problem with the fact that they were the only black or Korean or American Indian person in the family. They simply took it for granted. And the same percentages of transracial adoptees as white children answered "No" to the item that asked: "Have there been times in your life when you wished you were another color?" We did find, however, that when we asked them to identify themselves so that someone whom they had never met would recognize them at a meeting place, many more of the transracial adoptees than the white children mentioned race. Such a choice, though, may have more to do with the practicalities of the situation than with any sense of "affect" or evaluation. If one is black or Korean or American Indian in a largely white area, recognition is much easier.

Eleven percent of the transracial adoptees told us directly that they would prefer to be white, and 27 percent of the parents believe that their transracial adoptees identify themselves as white. According to the parents, all of those children are of mixed backgrounds. Since the parents' responses on such matters as their children's choice of friends, dates, interests, aspirations, and so on, demonstrate that they are knowledgeable about and understand their children's thoughts, activities, and tastes, the above mentioned discrepancy between the children and the parents concerning the former's racial identity should not be assumed to represent the parents' lack of insight or recognition regarding their children's beliefs and desires. But some part of those 27 percent of parents who believe that their transracial adoptees identify themselves as white could reflect wish fulfillment by the parents. Most of those children look as if they are white; the parents might like to believe that the children also consider themselves to be white, like the rest of the family. Some evidence for this hypothesis may be seen in the parents' and adolescents' estimates about the adolescents' future. For example, a greater number of transracial adoptees said that they would opt to live in a racially mixed community than did the parents, more of whom thought the transracial adoptees would choose to live in a community like the one in which they were reared (predominantly white). Interestingly, about 25 percent of both the parents and children thought the children would marry exogamously. Thus the evidence we have for parental ambivalence about having a child of a different race is the 16 percent difference between the parents' and adolescents' responses on the item about racial identity, together with the expectations on the part of more transracial adoptees than parents that the former would live in racially mixed rather than predominantly white communities. Neither of these issues, however, is directly tied to the sense of integration or cohesion felt by the parents and children regarding their own relationships.

We found that parents and children saw eye to eye on two other "race"-related issues. First, we reported that 60 percent of the parents and 65 percent of the adolescents told us that they talked about race, including racial differences, racial attitudes, and racial discrimination, in their homes. Both parents and adolescents also agreed that the context for most of the discussions involved the families' and children's friends, activities at school, and community events. The next most often cited context concerned political figures, with Jesse Jackson most frequently mentioned. (Remember that many of the interviews were conducted during the 1984 presidential primary campaign.) The third most popular context involved stories on TV and in the newspapers. The birth children were more likely to report discussions of race than were the transracial adoptees.

A second topic on which there was strong agreement between parents and children concerned the extent to which the transracial adoptees encountered nasty or unpleasant experiences because of their race. Sixty-five percent of the parents and 67 percent of the transracial adoptees reported at least one such incident. Both the parents and their children agreed that most of these occurrences involved name calling—"nigger," "jungle bunny," "chink," "gook," and so forth. About 10 percent in both groups described incidents in which, in the opinion of the children and the parents, a teacher or a parent of a friend made insulting, racist remarks. The majority of the adolescents did not seem to be deeply affected by these encounters; temporary anger, more than hurt, was their main reaction. The parents reported talking to the child about the experience and in some instances going to the school or talking with the parent of the child involved. The parents typically used the experience to make the point that "this is the way of the world" and that the children were likely to encounter even worse situations as they grew older and moved out on their own.

We believe that one of the important measures of the parents' unselfish love and concern about their adopted children may be found in their responses to the question about the birth parents. Approximately 40 percent of the parents told us that their children expressed interest in learning about their birth parents. Of those, 7 percent also wanted to locate and meet one or both of their birth parents. An additional 10 percent of the parents had provided their adopted children with whatever information they had, even prior to or in the absence of the children's request. Only three out of the 40 percent of the parents whose children asked about their birth parents were sufficiently threatened by the child's interest to refuse to provide the information they had.

On the question of "principle," 84 percent of the parents told us that they believe adoptees should have all the information available on their birth records when they are adults. The types of information that some of the parents would withhold included the child having been born out of wedlock, one or both parents having served time in prison, or the mother having been a prostitute. Three percent of the parents believed that adoption records should remain closed. An additional 8 percent would place some conditions on opening such records, such as medical needs. But as we have shown earlier, the large majority of the parents believe that their adopted child should have access to as much information about his or her birth parents as they can provide, and they do not feel that it is a sign of disloyalty or lack of commitment to them if the child wants that information.

Looking at the issue from the adoptees' perspective, we found that 38 percent of the transracial adoptees had already tried or plan to try to locate their birth parents. The others said that they had not decided or did not plan to try to find them. The most typical response was: "I am happy with my family. My other parents gave me up." Most of the adoptees did not have deeply rooted feelings about their reasons for wanting to locate their birth parents; curiosity seemed to characterize most of their feelings. Many said, "I would like to see what I will look like when I'm older." Those for whom the issue was more traumatic were children who were adopted when they were three or more years of age, had some memory of a mother, and felt a sense of abandonment or betrayal. They expressed their feelings in the rather muted phrase: "I'll feel incomplete until I do."

At the conclusion to our earlier studies, we emphasized that it was too soon to draw any conclusions on two matters. One concerned the parents' evaluations of how "good," how "meaningful," how "positive" an experience their decision to adopt transracially had been, and the other pertained to our evaluation of the families' experiences, whether they had lived together in a positive, loving, committed relationship. The bases for our eventual conclusions on the latter issue would be a study of the families themselves over the 12-year period, including the parents' as well as the children's responses, and our observations of the family's interactions.

We would also take into account our comparison of these families with other studies of families who have adopted transracially, as well as with our knowledge of middle-class families in the United States. For example, in the concluding chapter of their book Ruth G. McRoy and Louis A. Zurcher wrote:

The transracial and inracial adoptees in the authors' study were physically healthy and exhibited typical adolescent relationships with their parents, siblings, teachers, and peers. Similarly, regardless of the race of their adoptive parents, they reflected positive feelings of self-regard. Throughout the book, the authors have shown that the quality of parenting is more important than whether the black child has been inracially or transracially adopted. Most certainly, transracial adoptive parents experience some challenges different from inracial adoptive parents, but in this study, all of the parents successfully met the challenges.[2]

Gill and Jackson, in summarizing the results of their study, wrote:

We found no general evidence of the children being isolated within their families. Close and intimate family relations had developed for the large majority of the children. The children saw themselves as "belonging to this family." . . . [I]n spite of their often having very little contact with other children of the same racial background, we found that the large majority of children were able to relate effectively to peers and adults outside the family. Also, there is no evidence of the children doing worse academically than their age-mates; if anything, the study children seemed to be doing better.[3]

We turn finally to the judgments made by the parents in our study about their experiences. We think the best indicator is the parents' responses to this item: "Would you advise a family like your own to adopt a nonwhite child?" We reported in the first study, when the children were between three and eight years old, that all but 3 percent of the parents said that they would urge the family to adopt. (Seven percent answered that as a matter of principle they would not advise anyone on such a personal, complicated issue.) In the present study, conducted when the transracial adoptees were adolescents and young adults, 6 percent said that they would advise against such a decision, 1 percent were uncertain about the advice that they would give, and 8 percent would not offer advice as a matter of principle. Eighty-five percent would urge the family to adopt transracially.

Is 85 a high percentage? Compared to what—to families who have adopted inracially or to families who have only had birth children? Would more than 85 percent of the latter advise other couples to bear children? Would there not be some small percentage who would believe as a matter of principle that they should not advise people on such a personal issue, and would there not be a small category of, say, 7 percent who would feel, for different reasons, that having children had been a mistake for them and who would be willing to generalize their experiences to others? In the end, whether 85 percent is a large or small proportion of families, whether it is an indicator that families believe transracial adoption was a success or failure, is up to the reader to decide.

We urge the reader to take note of the direct responses by the parents to the question posed to them. They emphasized love and the desire for a child as the major reasons why anyone should want to adopt transracially. One family said, "It is the best thing that has happened to us." They warned that the families should be prepared for complications and problems—but is any child rearing free of anxiety and difficulties? Just as in 1972, the parents warned: do not adopt for political motives; do not do it as part of a crusade or to wave a banner or out of white liberal guilt. They also cautioned prospective adoptive parents that the race issue could prove more complicated than they anticipated and urged learning as much as possible about the child's racial heritage. The major and strongest messages were: "Be sure you are committed to adoption." "Adopt if you love and want children." "Pray about it, keep your motives straight; adopt because you need and love a child."

In essence, these were the messages the parents sent in 1972, in 1979, and in 1984, when, for many of them, their transracial adoptees had graduated from childhood into young adulthood.

NOTES

1. Owen Gill and Barbara Jackson, *Adoption and Race* (New York: St. Martin's Press, 1983), p. 39.

2. Ruth G. McRoy and Louis A. Zurcher, *Transracial and Inracial Adoptees: The Adolescent Years* (Springfield, IL: Charles C. Thomas, 1983), p. 138.

3. Gill and Jackson, *Adoption and Race,* p. 130.

Postscript

As this book goes into production, we are beginning the fourth and probably last phase of our study of transracial adoptees and their families. We were able to locate 88 of the 96 families who participated in the 1984 study. Of those 88 families, 80 (91 percent) provided us with the names and addresses of their adult transracially adopted and birth children. We are now in the process of contacting those children and arranging for personal interviews with them. This last phase focuses almost exclusively on the adult children. Brief telephone interviews will be conducted with their parents, mostly to ask them whether, with the knowledge of hindsight, they would have adopted across racial lines and whether they would advise families like themselves to adopt a child of a different race. But the long, in-depth personal interviews will be conducted only with the children. We shall ask them to talk about their experiences growing up in an unusual family environment, in order to assess how their family situation affected their social and racial identity, their racial attitudes, and their sense of awareness about racial issues. Many of these themes were explored in the earlier phases of the study. But now the children have become young adults, and we shall ask them to reflect and comment on their experiences.

We shall ask them, for example, to describe how they felt about being the only black (Korean, and so forth) person in their family. How did it affect their overall personality, their sense of security, and their identity? What would they have wanted their parents to do differently? Would they have wanted them, for example, to move into mixed racial neighborhoods rather than continue to live in the predominantly white neighborhoods in which most of the families resided? Were there other aspects of their family life (for example, the churches they attended, the friends the family had, the relations they maintained with grandparents, aunts, and uncles, the groups and organizations with which they were involved) that they would have wanted their parents to change? Would they have wanted their parents and siblings to interact differently with them?

Coming up to their present circumstances, we shall ask them about the years of schooling they have had, the work they are doing, the amount of money they are earning, and whether they are married and have a family. We shall also ask them to describe their close friends and the type of community in which they are living. When did they leave their parents' home and what were the circumstances? Do they perceive themselves as integral members of their family? For example, we shall ask: How much time do they spend with their parents and siblings? How much of their lives do they share with them? What efforts, if any, have they expended on locating their birth parents? If they did seek out one or both parents, what motivated them to do so and how successful were they in locating one or both of them?

The results of this fourth phase of our work should be ready for publication in the fall of 1992, 20 years after the initial contacts and interviews were conducted.

Selected Bibliography

Altstein, Howard, and Rita James Simon. *Intercountry Adoption: A Multinational Perspective*. New York: Praeger, 1991.

Anderson, David C. *Children of Special Value: Interracial Adoption in America*. New York: St. Martin's Press, 1971.

Bagley, Christopher, and L. Young. "The Identity, Adjustment and Achievement of Transracially Adopted Children." In Gajedra Verma and Christopher Bagley, eds., *Race, Education and Identity* (pp. 192–219). London: Macmillan, 1979.

Benet, Mary K. *The Politics of Adoption*. New York: Free Press, 1976.

Billingsley, Andrew, and Jeanne M. Giovanonni. *Children of the Storm: Black Children and American Child Welfare*. New York: Harcourt Brace Jovanovich, 1972.

Clark, Kenneth B., and Mamie P. Clark. "Racial Identification and Preference in Negro Children." In E. Maccoby, T. Newcomb, and E. Hartley, eds., *Readings in Social Psychology*. New York: Henry Holt, 1958.

Day, Dawn. *The Adoption of Black Children*. Lexington, MA: Lexington Books, 1979.

Fanshel, David. *Far from the Reservation: The Transracial Adoption of American Indian Children*. Metuchen, NJ: Scarecrow Press, 1972.

Feigelman, William, and Arnold Silverman. *Chosen Children: New Patterns of Adoptive Relationships*. New York: Praeger, 1983.

Grow, Lucille J., and Deborah Shapiro. *Black Children, White Parents: A Study of Transracial Adoption*. New York: Child Welfare League of America, 1974.

Jaffee, Benson, and David Fanshel. *How They Fared in Adoption: A Follow-Up Study*. New York: Columbia University Press, 1970.

Kadushin, Alfred, and Judith A. Martin. *Child Welfare Services*, 4th ed. New York: Macmillan, 1980.

Kirk, David H. *Adoptive Kinship: A Modern Institution in Need of Reform*. Washington, DC: Ben Simon, 1985.

———. *Shared Fate*. New York: Free Press, 1964.

Ladner, Joyce. *Mixed Families*. New York: Anchor Press, Doubleday, 1977.

McRoy, Ruth G., and Louis A. Zurcher. *Transracial and Inracial Adoptees: The Adolescent Years*. Springfield, IL: Charles C. Thomas, 1983.

Nutt, Thomas E., and John A. Snyder. *Transracial Adoption*. Cambridge, MA: Massachusetts Institute of Technology Press, 1973.

Porter, Judith D. R. *Black Child, White Child: The Development of Racial Attitudes*. Cambridge, MA: Harvard University Press, 1971.

Rosenberg, Morris. *Society and the Adolescent Self Image*. Princeton, NJ: Princeton University Press, 1965.

Sachdev, Paul. *Adoption: Current Issues and Trends*. Toronto: Butterworths, 1984.

Simon, Rita James, and Howard Altstein. *Transracial Adoptees and Their Families*. New York: Praeger, 1987.

——. *Transracial Adoption*. New York: Wiley, 1977.

——. *Transracial Adoption: A Follow-up*. Lexington, MA: Lexington Books, 1981.

Young, L., and Christopher Bagley. "Self-esteem, Self-concept and the Development of Black Identity: A Theoretical Overview." In G. Verma and C. Bagley, eds., *Self-concept, Achievement and Multicultural Education* (pp. 41–59). London: Macmillan, 1982.

Zastrow, Charles H. *Outcome of Black Children–White Parents Transracial Adoptions*. San Francisco: R. & E. Research Associates, 1977.

Index

ABOUT THE AUTHORS

RITA J. SIMON is a sociologist and university professor in the School of Public Affairs and the Washington College of Law at the American University in Washington, D.C. She has recently authored *The Crimes That Women Commit and the Punishments They Receive* (1990) and *Women's Movements in America* (Praeger, 1991) and has co-edited with Howard Altstein *Intercountry Adoption: A Multinational Perspective* (1991).

HOWARD ALTSTEIN, a professor in the School of Social Work at the University of Maryland, is the co-editor of *Intercountry Adoption: A Multinational Perspective*. He has also collaborated with Rita Simon on their 20-year study of transracial adoption.